William Jennings Bryan campaigning in 1896. Library of Congress, RN: LCUSZC2-6259.

WILLIAM JENNINGS BRYAN

AMERICAN PROFILES

Norman K. Risjord, Series Editor

Thomas Jefferson
    By Norman K. Risjord

Mary Boykin Chesnut: A Confederate Woman's Life
    By Mary A. DeCredico

John Quincy Adams
    By Lynn Hudson Parsons

He Shall Go Out Free: The Lives of Denmark Vesey
    By Douglas R. Egerton

Samuel Adams: America's Revolutionary Politician
    By John K. Alexander

Jefferson's America, 1760–1815: Second Edition
    By Norman K. Risjord

Martin Van Buren and the Emergence of American Popular Politics
    By Joel H. Silbey

He Shall Go Out Free: The Lives of Denmark Vesey, Revised and Updated Edition
    By Douglas R. Egerton

Stephan A. Douglas and the Dilemmas of Democratic Equality
    By James L. Huston

William Jennings Bryan: An Uncertain Trumpet
    By Gerald Leinwand

WILLIAM JENNINGS BRYAN

An Uncertain Trumpet

GERALD LEINWAND

ROWMAN & LITTLEFIELD PUBLISHERS, INC.
Lanham • Boulder • New York • Toronto • Plymouth, UK

ROWMAN & LITTLEFIELD PUBLISHERS, INC.

Published in the United States of America
by Rowman & Littlefield Publishers, Inc.
A wholly owned subsidiary of The Rowman & Littlefield Publishing Group, Inc.
4501 Forbes Boulevard, Suite 200, Lanham, Maryland 20706
www.rowmanlittlefield.com

Estover Road
Plymouth PL6 7PY
United Kingdom

British Library Cataloging in Publication Information Available

Library of Congress Cataloging-in-Publication Data

Leinwand, Gerald.
  William Jennings Bryan : an uncertain trumpet / Gerald Leinwand.
    p. cm.
  Includes bibliographical references and index.
  ISBN-13: 978-0-7425-5158-9 (cloth : alk. paper)
  ISBN-10: 0-7425-5158-X (cloth : alk. paper)
   1. Bryan, William Jennings, 1860–1925. 2. Statesmen—United States—
Biography. 3. Legislators—United States—Biography. 4. Presidential
candidates—United States—Biography. 5. United States—Politics and
government—1865-1933. I. Title.

E664.B87L39 2006
973.91092—dc22   2006017947

Printed in the United States of America

∞™ The paper used in this publication meets the minimum requirements of
American National Standard for Information Sciences—Permanence of Paper for
Printed Library Materials, ANSI/NISO Z39.48-1992.

For my grandson Mark Andrew Opper, who put me on the scent of the possible connection between Baum's *The Wizard of Oz* and William Jennings Bryan; and to my great-grandsons Devan Maxwell Opper and Levi Bresler Opper.

You may dispute over whether I have fought a good fight, you may dispute over whether I have finished my course, but you cannot deny that I have kept the faith.

Bryan to fellow Democrats in 1904

If you would be entirely accurate you should represent me as using a double-barreled shotgun, firing one barrel at the elephant as he tries to enter the treasury and another at Darwinism—the monkey—as he tries to enter the schoolroom.

Bryan's response when asked how he wished his life's work to be captured in a cartoon

CONTENTS

List of Illustrations   xi

Acknowledgments   xiii

Prologue   xv

1   The Boy Orator   1

2   Young Man in a Hurry   17

3   "Cross of Gold"   41

4   "I Have Kept the Faith"   71

5   Hero of Lost Causes   97

6   "I Didn't Raise My Boy to Be a Soldier"   115

7   The Waning Years   127

8   The War on Science   139

9   Bryan: Joshua of American Fundamentalism   159

Epilogue   167

Suggestions for Further Reading   173

Index   175

About the Author   183

LIST OF ILLUSTRATIONS

	William Jennings Bryan campaigning in 1896.	frontispiece
Figure 1.1.	Cartoon comparison of Abraham Lincoln and William Jennings Bryan.	2
Figure 1.2.	Intercollegiate debaters. Bryan fourth from the left, standing. Jane Addams, seated.	10
Figure 3.1.	William Jennings Bryan and Arthur Sewall, Democratic nominees for president and vice president, 1896.	57
Figure 3.2.	Cartoon showing William Jennings Bryan touting 16 to 1 from the back of his campaign train.	63
Figure 3.3.	Literal stump speech.	64
Figure 4.1.	Depicting Bryan chipping away at imperialism while McKinley raises the flag of imperialism.	75
Figure 4.2.	Political cartoon showing William Jennings Bryan as a Populist Party python swallowing the Democratic donkey.	79
Figure 4.3.	William Jennings Bryan, a portrait, 1907.	87
Figure 4.4.	William Jennings Bryan addressing the 1908 convention of the Democratic Party.	90
Figure 4.5.	Fairview, Bryan's home on D Street in Lincoln, Nebraska.	92

Figure 5.1.   President Woodrow Wilson and his new
secretary of state, William Jennings
Bryan, 1913.   103

Figure 5.2.   William Jennings Bryan speaking to a
crowd at a state fair in Sante Fe, 1913.   104

Figure 8.1.   William Jennings Bryan and Clarence
Darrow in the courtroom during the
Scopes trial in Dayton, Tennessee, 1925.   142

Figure 8.2.   William Jennings Bryan yawning in the
courtroom at the Scopes trial, 1925.   151

ACKNOWLEDGMENTS

I wish to acknowledge expert research assistance from Dan Prosterman, outstanding doctoral student in American history at New York University.

PROLOGUE

"His face was pale and lined. He had lost weight."[1] But William Jennings Bryan was elated with the jury's verdict five days earlier that John Scopes had been guilty of violating Tennessee's law against the teaching of evolution in the public schools of that state. While he knew the victory for which he had worked so hard was but a Pyrrhic one, he was ebullient and in good spirits, convinced that God had called him to wage the good fight for his strongly held religious convictions. It was a fight he would be unable to carry any further.

On Sunday, July 26, 1925, William Jennings Bryan died while taking a nap at the home of a friend, Richard Rogers, in Dayton, Tennessee. The cause of death was never precisely determined. No doctor was present when he died and no autopsy was performed. He was sixty-five. Although his death was sudden and unexpected, he had not been in good health. He suffered from diabetes and was overweight; much of his diet consisted of heavy, fattening foods. Toward the end of the Scopes trial he had collapsed from overexertion, but he had quickly recovered. After attending services and offering a prayer in church that Sunday, he returned to the Rogers home and ate a heavy lunch, which made him yearn for that afternoon nap from which he never woke.

William Jennings Bryan did not fade away, but remained the focus of the national attention on the so-called "monkey" trial in Dayton, Tennessee, which wide publicity had elevated to the level of a melodramatic spectacular, with elements similar to those of a three-ring Barnum and Bailey circus. Although the trial was over, Bryan was just catching his second wind. Less than twenty-four hours before his death Bryan was still delivering stirring speeches from the rear platform of a railroad car that had carried him across two hundred miles of southeastern Tennessee in a manner reminiscent of his three campaigns for the presidency. This time, however, this man of great causes, the cause of world peace, of free silver, of the direct election of senators, of prohibition, and of women's suffrage, had undertaken what he believed to be the greatest cause of them all, namely, the story of the creation of heaven and earth as literally described in the Bible. In this crusade—he was convinced that it was nothing less—he felt he represented the forces of light running full tilt against the forces of darkness.

Banner newspaper headlines announced his death, and generous space was given to summaries of his career and burial plans. That he died on the Sabbath was not lost on the humble Christian faithful of Dayton, Tennessee, who quit their work in field, mill, mine, and store, to file past the coffin. A large American flag hung at half-staff from a pole at the village center. Smaller flags were hung from every lamppost of the four blocks that made up Dayton's business section. Stores, banks, city and county offices, even the local post office, were all closed in his honor, so people could pay their respects to a visitor who had come to defend their Bible, values, and lifestyle, and who had died there among them. Brief religious services were held on the lawn of the Rogers' home in Dayton, the Ku Klux Klan burned crosses in his memory, and plans were made to move the body to Washington, D.C.

Clarence Darrow, his erstwhile opponent at the infamous "Monkey Trial"[2] at Dayton, Tennessee, was among the first to pay tribute to an adversary he had mercilessly mocked. "I differed with him on many questions but always respected his sincerity and devotion."[3] President Calvin Coolidge, "Silent Cal," on vacation in Swampscott, Massachusetts, requested only that the orchestra at the Ocean House Hotel where he was a guest play "Nearer, My God, to Thee." The following morning the White House released a copy of President Coolidge's letter of condolence to Mrs. Bryan. The president paid tribute to the Commoner's "sincerity" and "conviction," and his "leadership" for moral and political reform. The president ordered that all national flags be lowered to half-staff.

Vice President Dawes likewise paid tribute to Bryan by once again remarking upon the deceased's "high purposes" and "sincerity." Secretary of State Frank B. Kellogg made a formal announcement of Bryan's death, and in Santa Barbara, California, former Treasury Secretary William McAdoo expressed the opinion that Bryan had no equal in American history, "the most conspicuous of our public men."[4] Senator Hiram Johnson, from his home in Southern California, asserted that Bryan's death was "the Nation's loss" and that death "had silenced a voice of sympathy and a champion of humanity."[5] Governor Alfred E. Smith of New York was more restrained and expressed only that "he had heard of the death of Mr. Bryan with a great deal of regret."[6] Yet to The *London Times* no one but Abraham Lincoln could compete with him as to "quality of mind and character."[7] The *Washington Post* asserted that Bryan was "true to his sense of duty."[8]

But even before he was interred in Arlington Cemetery there were those who, perhaps with unseemly haste, began to question the legacy of William Jennings Bryan. In an editorial, the *San Francisco Chronicle* observed that Bryan lacked the "intellectual depth" of Lincoln but that the "plain people" sensed his "innate goodness of heart."[9] To the *Chicago Daily News* he was "brilliantly superficial . . . [and] clung to impressions and prejudices that were outworn."[10] The *Los Angeles Times* described him as a "faddist, a seeker of the limelight, and expert in the spectacular."[11]

Eugene Debs, American labor leader and frequent presidential candidate, believed William Jennings Bryan had betrayed the progressivism with which he had started his political activities: "In the early years of Mr. Bryan's career his views, political or otherwise, were centered around progressivism, but since his first campaign he grew more and more conservative until he finally stood before the country, a champion of everything reactionary in our political and social life. To speak with perfect frankness, the cause of human progress sustains no loss in the death of Mr. Bryan."[12]

The *New Republic*, a journal of political commentary, likewise demeaned Bryan's contribution to American life. The magazine described his views as "uncritical," "undisciplined," and in the end, his efforts were "futile." According to the journal's editors he had a "deplorably defective" education and a "second-rate intelligence." Moreover, he seemed to them to be chronically ill prepared, "inflexible," and incapable of grasping the larger picture; he had become a progressive by accident rather than by conviction. As such, he seemed to them, to be "disqualified" for leadership in the world in which he lived, let alone in the post–World War I world that was emerging.[13]

Although confined to a wheelchair and despite sometimes severe pain, Mrs. Bryan took charge of her husband's funeral in a manner not unlike that of Jacqueline Kennedy, using the occasion of her husband's death to enhance his memory in the public consciousness while establishing a platform upon which a positive historical legacy might be built. Thus, Mary Bryan let it be known that, as a pacifist Bryan had not wanted a military funeral, but as a prominent man in public life and as a Spanish-American War veteran, her husband had expressed a desire to be buried in Arlington National Cemetery and was entitled to such interment.

As Bryan's funeral train made its way from Dayton, Tennessee, past Chattanooga, Cleveland, Athens, Sweetwater, Knoxville, and Greenville to Johnson City, across the state line to western Virginia, through Bristol, Roanoke, and Lynchburg, there were spontaneous outpourings of ordinary people who sought to express their grief at the death of a man they believed had fought the good fight in their behalf. "Every where [*sic*] at every station, men in shirt-sleeves and overalls, women in gingham and barefoot children, have come to see the train pass and to gaze with bared, bowed heads and sorrowful faces at the last car on the train which contains the mortal remains of the great Commoner they loved and which bears his mourning invalid widow."[14]

In the nation's capital, services were held at the New York Avenue Presbyterian Church, "the church of the presidents." Here Abraham Lincoln once worshipped, as did Presidents Andrew Jackson, Franklin Pierce, James K. Polk, James Buchanan, and Andrew Johnson, among numerous others eminent in the life of the nation. As he lay in state, some twenty thousand people filed past his coffin. Radio stations WCAP in Washington, D.C., and WEAF in New York prepared to carry the church services as far west as Minneapolis. Among the numerous floral tributes was a huge cross of bright red roses, a gift of the Ohio Ku Klux Klan.

At 4:00 p.m., on a cool and rainy July 31, 1925, the funeral cortege made its way past streetlamps, turned on to cut through the fog and heavy rain, to Bryan's interment in Arlington National Cemetery. At a preferred location known as "Dewey Knoll," named after the granite mausoleum of Admiral Dewey who was first buried there, a spot in full view of Washington's spires, monuments, and public buildings, Bryan was buried. As troops stood at attention, a bugler sounded taps, but there was no gunfire salute. On his tomb is inscribed:

Bryan
He Kept the Faith

At the time of his death no man in public life had more devoted followers and none had more political enemies than William Jennings Bryan. Yet, his political record is one of failure. His only elective office was two terms in the House of Representatives. He lost his bid to serve in the Senate and three times lost the presidency. In later years his primitive fundamentalism made him an easy target of ridicule for the emerging forces of modernity and progress.

Yet how does one explain the four-column headlines announcing his death, or the reverence in which he was held by ordinary Americans of his day? How could a man who was wrong so many times, on so many issues, who alienated so many people, dominate American life for nearly thirty years? The short answer is, according to the historian Henry Steele Commager, that he was "the most representative American of his time."[15]

As if sensing the emerging controversy governing her husband's place in history, Mary Bryan announced that she would complete her husband's memoirs. In a letter to Francis (Fannie) Baird, Mary's older sister, she declared that her only purpose in doing so was to "correct the many misunderstandings people had about him and to give him his proper place in history." She expected that the memoirs would be "the best thing for his future."[16]

William Jennings Bryan had been a prominent but unlucky political player in American life for nearly forty years. As historical myth, Bryan has been equally unlucky. To be remembered as a "cowardly lion," as some interpret L. Frank Baum's *The Wonderful Wizard of Oz* (see p. 167), can hardly be comforting, but to be portrayed as a buffoon, as in the 1955 play *Inherit the Wind*, based on the Scopes Trial (see p. 169), is to make one squirm in one's grave. Indeed, popular literature has tended to diminish rather than enlarge the memory and stature of William Jennings Bryan. Historical fact and myth conspire to erode his reputation as a political player in the nation's history.

NOTES

1. *New York Times*, July 27, 1925.
2. See pp. 139–57.
3. *New York Times*, July 27, 1925.
4. Ibid.
5. *San Francisco Chronicle*, July 27, 1925.
6. *New York Times*, July 27, 1925.
7. Quoted in the *New York Times*, July 28, 1925.
8. Quoted in the *New York Times*, July 27, 1925.
9. *San Francisco Chronicle*, July 27, 1925.
10. *New York Herald*, July 28, 1925.
11. *Los Angeles Times*, July 27, 1925.
12. *San Francisco Chronicle*, July 27, 1925.
13. "William Jennings Bryan," *New Republic* (August 12, 1925): 304–6.

14. *New York Times*, July 29, 1925.

15. Henry Steele Commager, *The American Mind* (New Haven: Yale University Press, 1950), p. 346.

16. Mary Bryan to Fannie Baird, October 1925, Mary Bryan Papers. Quoted in Lawrence G. Buckley, *William Jennings Bryan in American Memory* (PhD diss., University of Hawaii, 1998), p. 30.

1

THE BOY ORATOR

"Mary, I have had a strange experience. Last night I found that
I had power over the audience. I could move them as I chose.
I have more than usual power as a speaker. I know it. God
grant I may use it wisely." [Then] he prayed.

The Memoirs of William Jennings Bryan[1]

Two months before William Jennings Bryan was born on March 19,
1860, the tumultuous Republican convention turned to a westerner
as their candidate for president of the United States. Abraham Lincoln, the
son of a Southern mountaineer, made his home in the new lands of the
Middle West. He studied law but preferred politics. His whole political approach was Jeffersonian, individualistic, and hostile to vast combinations of
wealth. He sought a federal job but was refused. He was a soldier during
wartime but saw no fighting. He was elected to the House of Representatives, where he served ably. He debated with important political figures
and tried unsuccessfully to be elected to the U.S. Senate but, stunningly,
was nominated by the Republican Party and elected by the people to be
president.

Bryan was likewise the son of a Southern mountaineer who made his
home in the newer lands of the Midwest. He, too, studied law, made political speeches, and preferred the excitement of politics to a pedestrian legal
practice. His political approach was likewise Jeffersonian, individualistic, and
hostile to vast industrial concentrations of wealth. He sought a federal job
and was refused. He served ably in the House of Representatives, lost in his
attempt to be elected United States senator, debated political issues with the
leading political figures of his day. He, too, was a soldier in a war in which

he did no fighting. And, in Chicago, he was nominated enthusiastically by the Democratic Party for the presidency of the United States.

Here the parallelism ends, as Lincoln narrowly won the presidency and Bryan narrowly lost it. Both Lincoln and Bryan were "representative Americans," but why did one succeed and the other fail? Surely men less able than Bryan became president. Why did he fail in his quest? Was he "out of sync" with the times during which he lived? Was there something lacking in his political or intellectual skills that caused success to elude him?

To former President Harry S. Truman, "Old Bill Bryan was a great one. One of the greatest." Asked why Bryan never got elected, Truman replied:

> I don't know. I don't know. I've given it a great deal of thought but I've never figured it out. I think . . . the best I've come up with is that he was just too far ahead of his time, and the people in the East, the big-money people, were against him and did everything they could to defeat him. Three different times they did it. . . . If it hadn't been for Bill Bryan there wouldn't be any liberal outfit in the country at all now. At least that's what I think. Old Bryan kept liberalism alive, kept it going.[2]

Figure 1.1.   Cartoon comparison of Abraham Lincoln and William Jennings Bryan. *Puck,* October 28, 1896. Library of Congress, RN: LCUSCZ4-4361.

THE STORY OF MY GOOD FORTUNE

With all the pomp that a republic can muster, the Prince of Wales made a state visit to America in 1860. The prince ate his way through public dinners and danced the nights away at extravagant balls. On his itinerary were Detroit, Chicago, St. Louis, Cincinnati, Washington, Philadelphia, New York City, Boston, and Portland, Maine. The prince shook hands with two Irish farmhands in Illinois and traded autographs with the only survivor of Bunker Hill. But, it is doubtful that Silas and Mariah Jennings Bryan paid much attention. For one thing, the prince's visit could not have been more untimely inasmuch as in 1860 the nation was wondering if the union, so laboriously assembled, would hold together. For another, the Bryan family was anticipating the birth of the child whom they would name William Jennings and whom the people and press would later describe as the Great Commoner.

The village of Salem, where William Jennings Bryan spent his youth, was a community on the great prairie of south central Illinois. The thirty-one counties of Illinois, dubbed "Egypt," began at the 39th parallel and extended southward to the 37th parallel. The origins of this nickname are uncertain. According to legend, when there was drought in the northern counties, rains fell in southern Illinois and people from the north came in search of corn and wheat as did the peoples of ancient Egypt. The city of Cairo, pronounced "Kerro," at the southernmost tip of Illinois, lay between the Mississippi and Ohio Rivers. Salem, about the same latitude as Norfolk, Virginia, lay in a triangular section surrounded on two sides by the slave states of Missouri and Kentucky.

Of the two thousand people who lived in Salem in 1860, the seat of Marion County, most owned their own farms, and a few owned small retail businesses or one of the small mills that produced flour and lumber. Only a few worked for wages. More than a quarter of Salem's adults had been born in slave states, and many of the people of "Egypt" generally sympathized with the Confederacy.

In his *Memoirs*, William Jennings Bryan set out to, as he put it, "tell the story of my good fortune. I was born in the greatest of all ages. . . . I was born a member of the greatest of all races—the Caucasian, and had mingled in my veins the blood of English, Irish, and Scotch. . . . I was born a citizen of the greatest of all lands."[3] As Bryan asserted, "ancestry counts."[4]

When Virginia and John, the first two children of Silas and Mariah Jennings Bryan, died around Christmas and within a week of one another of whooping cough, the bereaved parents were certain that they would never be able to accept the deaths of their children and wondered whether the Lord would ever bless them with other offspring. But Frances and William Jennings were born in 1858 and on March 19, 1860, respectively, and both children were warmly welcomed by their parents, who looked to them to make up for the earlier deaths.

As Bryan explained in his *Memoirs*, his father favored the name William and his mother, Jennings. They compromised and decided upon William Jennings. In his youth, William Jennings Bryan's friends and family called him by an assortment of first names:

> In my youth my name went through all the forms of which it was capable; like the boy of whom James Whitcomb Riley writes,
> "Father calls me William,
> And mother calls me Will;
> Sister calls me Billy,
> But fellers call me Bill."
> Possibly Willy was more frequently used by my mother and brothers and sisters during the early years, while Will became my settled name as I advanced from boyhood into young manhood.[5]

Silas Bryan, born in Virginia of Scotch-Irish descent, was a devout Baptist and a staunch Democrat. Following others in his family, he trekked westward and lived for a time on his brother's farm in Missouri, where he went to school. After graduating from McKendree College in Illinois, he taught school, read law, and moved to Salem, where two of his sisters lived. He was admitted to the bar at age twenty-nine and made a youthful foray into politics by campaigning for the position of county superintendent of schools. He won the election.

Mariah Jennings, his devoted wife, was but eighteen and one of his pupils when she married thirty-year-old Silas Bryan in 1852. "He was tall, thin, prematurely bald. . . . She was tall, straight, with brown hair and gray eyes, a prominent nose, and high cheekbones."[6] She was musically talented and loved to sing and play the piano. Although a devout Methodist, she was less fundamentalist in outlook than her Baptist husband. Not long after the wedding, Silas was elected to the state senate.

In all, Mariah Bryan, William's mother, gave birth to nine children, three of whom died before the age of five, a common circumstance in those days. Young Will grew up with an older sister, two younger brothers (one of whom died at seventeen), and two younger sisters. Also in the Bryan household was Mollie Smith, an orphaned niece of father Silas and ten years older than the oldest Bryan child. In time, Mariah's mother also lived with the Bryans. Also living in Marion County were a host of uncles, aunts, and cousins. Will grew up in the warmth of a closely knit family, which tended to shield him from the turmoil of the Civil War and its aftermath.

When Will was six, his family moved from the house in which he was born to a new and larger one, a farm just outside Salem. Together with his brothers and sisters, Will obediently but grudgingly shared in what he called the drudgery of farm work. But he came to appreciate the effort farmers had to make to wrest a living from an often resistant soil, erratic weather, and the vagaries of the marketplace. Silas Bryan was more lawyer than farmer and freely hired laborers to do the heavy chores that needed to be done on the farm. By 1870 Will's father, one of the most important men in Salem, owned eighteen thousand dollars worth of real and personal property, a sum that put him sixth in the township. A history published in 1881 described him as one of five Salem residents who had achieved state or national reputations.[7]

Silas Bryan, a Democrat, made vigorous speeches in support of Stephen A. Douglas in the 1858 election for senator from Illinois and plotted strategy that contributed to Douglas's victory. But the euphoria of the senatorial triumph was short-lived when, in the presidential election of 1860, Douglas, the "Little Giant," lost to "Honest Abe" Lincoln. The Republicans also captured the Illinois legislature, and Silas was defeated for reelection, but later that year he was elected a judge in the state courts.

Silas was considered fair-minded, thoughtful, reserved, and a man of upright character and good judgment. As a devout Christian, he prayed three times a day and used the scriptures as a guide for the kind of behavior he expected from those who came before his court. He was no bigot, but when his mind was made up he rarely changed it. "No use pounding on the log," he would snap at the lawyers pleading their cases before him on the circuit bench. "The coon's out."[8] What he meant was that he had reached a decision, and further argument was useless.

Silas did not smoke, drink liquor, dance, gamble, or swear. His son followed willingly his father's stern example. Before he was twelve William signed pledges to refrain from tobacco and alcohol and adhered to this youthful pledge all his life. Wistfully, perhaps, Will envied some of the other boys, whose upbringing was seemingly less proscribed. But between young William Jennings and his parents there was little in the way of rebelliousness—no generation gap and little challenging of adult authority.

When William was twelve he made the only independent decision of his youth, namely, to join the Presbyterian Church rather than the Methodist one in which his mother was brought up or the Baptist one, which his father would have preferred. But in the Bryan household, differences in theology among Protestant faiths were unimportant. When Silas was on his deathbed, he did confess that he was disappointed that his son had not become a Baptist, but when young William made his decision Silas did not object. It must be said that the choice of Protestant denomination did not alter either the son's or the parents' family rituals. Thus, Will grew up a Democrat in politics, Christian in his beliefs, and Victorian in his values.

Among William Jennings Bryan's lasting memories was the big meal that the family took at noon. If his father was present, the meal did not end until there was biblical reading and discussion. To the accompaniment of Mariah at the piano, the family would sing hymns and uplifting popular selections. On Sundays it was church, hymns, and Bible readings.

The war years were not good ones for Silas Bryan. Transplanted Virginian that he was, he opposed the Civil War and did not volunteer to serve in the military. And when Lincoln issued the Emancipation Proclamation in 1863, Silas, with a good deal of vehemence, urged its revocation. Since he felt that Lincoln had betrayed the war's aims by shifting its goals from the preservation of the Union to the abolition of slavery, Silas likewise urged the war's immediate end. As an outspoken opponent of the Civil War, he was viewed by Unionists as a traitor and branded a "Copperhead," a proslavery, Southern sympathizer. Silas was arrested and held without trial on more than one occasion. In 1864, when Lincoln ran for reelection, Silas again voted against him, as did most of the people of Salem.

In 1872, when his father was nominated by the Democratic Party to run for a seat in the House of Representatives from a district with an overwhelming Democratic constituency, William Jennings Bryan was twelve years old. He was old enough to accompany his father on the campaign trail and listen to his father's not inconsiderable oratorical skills. Silas should have won handily, but he lost by 240 votes to John Martin, a former Union Army general and backsliding Democrat, who was carried into office on a wave of patriotic zeal and as a reward for heroic efforts in defense of the Union. Silas took his defeat with equanimity; the people had spoken. By so doing he set an example for his son, for whom the will of the people would become a prominent lodestar of his political life. For William, the taste of politics was on his tongue. It was a taste he would never lose.

From the end of the Civil War to Silas's death in 1880 from a stroke, patriotic zeal was expressed in traditional Independence Day orations and in the newly created Memorial Day observances to honor the Union soldiers who died in the Civil War. Judge Silas Bryan was often a speaker at these devotions and a proud son listened intently as his father declaimed. From his father's gifted tongue, William Jennings became first a witness to political rhetoric and then its master.

THE LURE OF THE PRIZE

In 1953, in a poll of 277 professors of American history or government, "The Cross of Gold" speech that William Jennings Bryan made at the Democratic Convention in Chicago on a hot and humid July 9, 1896, (see pp. 52–53) was voted among the fifty most significant documents in American history.[9] The speech would help catapult a relatively obscure politician onto the stage of national politics. The "Cross of Gold" speech was no impromptu address. Instead, Bryan wrote and practiced it for many months, and he thoroughly prepared for his great opportunity. Perhaps he did so even from the cradle.

Bryan was born with a silver tongue in his head. Young William's mother taught him to read and encouraged him to declaim excerpts from the McGuffey Readers. During the first decade of his life, under his mother's disciplined guidance he learned his earliest lessons and honed his skills as a public speaker. Perched precariously on a table, his mother listening intently, he would recite:

> *You'd scarce expect one of my age,*
> *To speak in public on the stage.*
> *If I should chance to fall below*
> *Demosthenes or Cicero*
> *Don't view me with a critic's eye,*
> *But pass my imperfections by.*[10]

From his father he inherited his oratorical skills and had the benefit of a fine example. Silas Bryan loved to hear his son recite William Cullen Bryant's "To a Waterfoul," and Will often and willingly obliged:

> *He who, from zone to zone,*
> *Guides through the boundless sky thy certain flight,*
> *In the long way that I must tread alone,*
> *Will lead my steps aright.*[11]

When Will was ten he was sent to the "Old College," a former school for girls that became a common elementary school, some distance from his home. The curriculum was dominated by McGuffey Readers and Webster Spellers and the Horatio Alger stories of the rise of poor but virtuous boys to wealth and prominence. Will adapted well to his school environment. His mother continued to watch his school progress carefully, as she had done when she taught him at home, and required that he continue to recite his lessons to her.

In 1875, at the age of fifteen, William left his father's house to attend Whipple Academy, a preparatory school for Illinois College at Jacksonville, Illinois. He spent two years at the Academy and four at the college. Silas had hoped to send his son to an Eastern college and then perhaps to Oxford. But the depression of 1873 intervened, and, with depleted family fortunes, William had to be content with a college education at a less distinguished institution.

Nevertheless, Illinois College was a good choice. Jacksonville itself was a more heterogeneous community than youthful William Jennings Bryan had heretofore experienced. Not only was there a substantial community of African-Americans but large numbers of German, Irish, and Portuguese. Despite this admixture of people from a variety of migrant and immigrant backgrounds, the white Anglo-Saxon population dominated in numbers. Illinois College was its intellectual center, and Bryan remained cloistered in its embrace.

During his college years Bryan lived with Dr. Hiram K. Jones, who was a distant relative, a practicing physician, and a part-time teacher at the college. Dr. Jones eased the transition for his young pupil from living at home to living a less sheltered life away from the strict supervision of his parents. The doctor also served as his intellectual mentor, as guests such as Ralph Waldo Emerson, Bronson Alcott, Wendell Phillips, Henry Ward Beecher, and the philosopher William T. Harris often gave public lectures in Jacksonville and were guests in the Jones's home. Although intellectual controversies including evolution, among other dynamic topics of the day, were frequently and often assertively disputed, the exposure apparently had little impact on the young student. In a speech in Jacksonville, on June 3, 1925, shortly before his death, Bryan told of meeting his former geology teacher, Dr. Henry E. Storrs, who asserted that it was not he who taught Bryan that man descended from a monkey.[12] Bryan remained serene in his religious fundamentalism and traditional values.

Illinois College, founded in 1829, was a New England educational outpost, a child of Yale. Under its first president Reverend Edward Beecher, it had been a hotbed of radical abolitionism and William's father could not have been altogether happy about sending his son to an institution with abolitionist traditions. For thirty-two years Julian Monson Sturtevant, its influential president, sought to make the college in the image of his more distinguished alma mater. In Bryan's day he was no longer president but stayed on as a professor. Sturtevant was the author of an economics textbook that discussed free trade and bimetallism, subjects later at the core of Bryan's political career. Bryan would later mistakenly assert that Sturtevant had advocated bimetallism.

Wendell Phillips, who likewise had a great influence on young Bryan, spoke on the subject "The Lost Arts" and motivated Bryan to read his other speeches. Bryan agreed with Phillips on the dangers of corporate wealth fostering special privileges and eroding the principle of equal rights for all. It may have been that Phillips piqued the interest of young Bryan in social betterment, prohibition, woman suffrage, and currency reform. An orator as formidable as Daniel Webster, Phillips also contributed to the development of Bryan's skills as a speaker even if only by example rather than by direct tutelage.

There were seventy-eight students at Whipple Academy and sixty more enrolled in the college. Most came from the "Egypt" area of Illinois and fifteen-year-old Will Bryan, according to Professor Storrs, arrived as a "typical farmer lad with all the crudities that are characteristic of the species." But "he grew up into a tall, graceful man and became a real asset to the college."[13] As is typical for that age, he had yet to decide upon a career, but he narrowed his choices to minister or lawyer, the latter probably a prelude to a political life.

At college Bryan took a rigorous classical curriculum in Latin, Greek, rhetoric, and mathematics. The curriculum offered no subject at an advanced level save for mathematics and the classics. The method of instruction was recitation; the method of study was memorization. The limited library, which often had a "No Trespassing" sign in front of it and was open for but one hour a day, discouraged the development of original research or even independent thinking. Instead, students and their professors took comfort in the certainties of a single textbook for each course. Tradition not innovation, conventionality not originality, certainty not questioning, were the guidelines of higher education in America and were closely mirrored in the methods and educational philosophy of Illinois College. As a product of Illinois College and perhaps the school's most famous student, Bryan the pupil was not viewed as an original or innovative thinker.

Bryan's academic record justified the conclusion that he was a "grind" rather than a brilliant student. According to one historian, "He did not acquire knowledge with facility, but he was conscientious and industrious in painstaking study. He did not take naturally to books and probably did not love learning for its own sake. He loved men rather than scholarship, learning from observation more than from reading."[14]

In following the development of Will Bryan from child to adolescent to young adulthood, it is better to follow the growth of his oratorical skills rather than his academic progress. His academic progress was good, his oratorical progress brilliant. As rhetorician Edgar Dewitt Jones commented, "One might say that he majored in oratory not only at college but throughout his life."[15]

One columnist, with tongue in cheek wrote, "Beware of the college orator, he's always loaded."[16] Bryan was, indeed, a college orator and in some sense remained so all his life. Year by year, with the encouragement first of parents and later through coaching by teachers of elocution, William Jennings Bryan honed his speaking abilities. From the beginning he showed some talent for oratory, and in time his speaking skills were described as brilliant, even breathtaking. "I felt the lure of [the speaking or debating] prizes from the start and took part in every contest for which I was eligible," Bryan wrote in his *Memoirs*.[17]

Figure 1.2.   Intercollegiate debaters. Bryan fourth from the left, standing. Jane Addams, seated. Nebraska State Historical Society.

Developing young Bryan's oratorical skills was an important value his parents shared, and it was an element highly thought of in American higher education during Bryan's undergraduate years. As a popular handbook on public speaking in 1896 declared, "Oratory is the parent of liberty."[18] Because he had won the Junior Contest in oratory in May 1880, he was chosen to represent the college in the state oratorical contest the following October in Galesburg. A local newspaper described Bryan's performance as "magnetic." "His full voice, his clear articulation, good and not affected modulation, his natural style of gesturing and delivery made him from the first a favorite with the audience."[19] His performance was judged good enough only for the second prize.

Disappointed that he had not won the first prize, young Bryan continued to practice at every opportunity. For example, yearning for the elusive first prize, he describes in his *Memoirs* how in 1880 with the help of Mary Baird, his wife-to-be, he practiced his oratorical skills for yet another contest. The occasion, Mrs. Bryan recalls, was in May and Dr. Jones, the physician with whom Bryan lived during his college years, gave a party on a woodsy pasture he owned, which adjoined the grounds of an insane asylum. Bryan contrived to reach the site an hour early so that he could try out his new speech. By chance a farmer who had been cultivating a nearby field heard Bryan orate to the stones, rocks, and trees that made up the audience. When the farmer saw the ladies approach the site of the party, he surely thought he was behaving heroically when he frantically intercepted the group of advancing women lest they confront the man who was shouting and waving his hands. "I think," the farmer exclaimed, "he must have escaped from the [insane] asylum." It was a story Mary Baird loved to tell and retell.

In his college career, he was active politically and was a "big man on campus," sort of—but he never achieved the goal he sought, namely, the presidency of one of the two literary societies at the college. At various times he served as chaplain, sergeant at arms, treasurer, and even vice president. Was this a forerunner perhaps of the fate that would follow him throughout his political career, that he would never capture the first prize of the presidency?

Bryan's academic achievements combined with his speaking ability were enough so that he was designated the valedictory speaker at his graduation. With his mother, brother Russell, and his fiancée Mary Baird, in the audience, Bryan spoke on the subject of character. He was twenty-one years old, and the speech summed up the values he held. Character, he believed, was "a priceless gem," ever developing as forces of good and evil fight for control over one's soul. Men like Washington and Lincoln, he said, were beloved and successful presidents more because of their character than their intellectual or political talents. In the end virtue was more important than genius. The "Perfect Model" was Jesus and was the measure by which the development of human character should be measured.

As he graciously thanked his college for the years spent in its halls of learning and spoke of the awe with which he viewed the big step of moving into the wider world, his mentors may have been struck by the anti-intellectualism of his remarks, the oversimplicity of his message, and may have wondered how successful they had been with this young man during his six years of study with them. Neither his views nor his speeches were to change very much. But armed with a magnificent voice and clad in the armor of righteous causes, he enthralled his audiences as he expressed in their behalf the indignation at injustices he knew they felt. Composed in a vocabulary middle-Americans could readily understand and refraining from detailed analysis, his speeches catered to the emotions rather than the intellect of his listeners. To his audience, Bryan became the "Great Commoner."

Perhaps only Daniel Webster owes as much to oratorical ability and verbal powers of persuasion for his progress in politics as William Jennings Bryan. But it was Bryan's bad luck that the florid oratory of which he was a master was, even in his own day, rapidly falling out of favor. No longer would a good heart, a glib tongue, or even a righteous cause carry the day for the speaker's view. But Bryan could not see that change in political speech was in the air. As Richard Hofstadter insists, "It was never success he demanded but an audience."[20] This quality may have been enough for Bryan as a boy orator; it may not have been enough for a politician aspiring for the presidency.

William Jennings Bryan, even as a young orator, entered the lists of those who would urge reform and speak in behalf of middle-America, the farmer, the small town, the virtues of rural communities. But his radicalism went no farther than the speakers' platform. What kept Bryan before the American public was the entertainment value of his speeches, not their content; nor did he call upon his listeners to "rise up" and slay the dragons that were violating them. With superb oratorical skills, Bryan became a political evangelist rather than a social activist. If a man can be "born again," might not a nation, he queried his audience. "[I]f the ideals of the people can be changed," he thought, they could surmount the forces that betrayed them. Bryan's oratory rarely soared to the level of Daniel Webster, Henry Clay, John C. Calhoun, Stephen A. Douglas, or Abraham Lincoln because these men, in addition to skilled orators, were likewise analytical masters of the issues they addressed. Theirs was mostly a call to arms; Bryan's was a call to conscience and to God.

That Bryan approached oratory as a profession was both a strength and a weakness. It was a strength because in the absence of elective or appointive office, without the lecture circuit to keep him before the public, he would have remained in the political shadows, perhaps forever. It was a weakness, however, because those who came to hear him came to be entertained, to be energized, to be inspired, rather than to be informed. There were no radios during Bryan's early years, to carry his voice to the American people. Thus, he spoke face-to-face for thirty-five years to more people than any other man in history. But he spoke so often that the intellectual component of his speeches was often thin. While he could move a crowd, reflection the morning after revealed that his remedies were mere nostrums that would not hold up in the cold light of economic or political analysis. As a result, he alienated the more intellectually oriented. In his book *Prophets True and False* (1928) journalist Oswald Garrison Villard vehemently asserted, "Of all the men I have seen at close range in thirty-one years of newspaper service, Mr. Bryan seems to me to be the most ignorant."[21] The people listened to Bryan and loved what they heard, but in the end, most voted for others.

Bryan's was the technique of a preacher, and as such, he did not believe in tiring his audiences with factual detail or critical analysis. He believed that the great issues of his lifetime were, at their root, moral issues, and so he drew on the Bible for support of the course he urged upon his listeners. "Eloquence," he wrote, "is heart speaking to heart. . . . The orator must have faith—faith in God, faith in the righteousness of his cause, and faith in the ultimate triumph of truth."[22] But if God is in the details, it was in the intellectual mastery of those details that Bryan faltered.

He was endowed by nature with a magnificent voice. Without the aid of a microphone, he could be heard by thirty thousand people in the open air. And, while speaking to the mass, Bryan could make each listener think he was speaking to each and every one of them. During the winter of 1898–1899, William Jennings Bryan had a speaking engagement in Corpus Christi, Texas. Mary Bryan was too tired to attend. "I was reading in my upstairs room," she wrote in the *Memoirs*, "when I heard someone speak. I went to the open window and found that Mr. Bryan was talking. I listened for several minutes, hearing every word quite clearly. Next morning I asked how far the meeting had been from the house and found that it was three blocks distant." His adoring wife continued: "The skill with which he used his voice was natural, no force or straining. . . . His words flowed along like the steady current of a stream and always fitted the subject."[23]

Every summer he spoke at Chautauqua, a lake in upstate New York and the site of a Methodist Sunday School and teacher-training institute. Chautauqua at its peak attracted millions of American families who came to be entertained and inspired in a wholesome, Christian environment. Thus, they came from many miles to marvel at firework displays, howl at the antics of clowns, meet those with political ambitions, listen to orchestras, glee clubs and operas, or watch magic lantern slides of the Holy Land or, later, of the building of the Panama Canal. Many states and localities sponsored "chautauquas," which became a catchall term for a combination of activities incorporating entertainment, education, and inspiration.

Among the activities, however, which seemed to be most popular were the lectures that were held in circus-sized tents and, in later years, in enclosed wooden structures. Of the many inspirational lecturers who participated in the chautauquas none was more popular than William Jennings Bryan. He would deliver more chautauqua lectures than any other popular political figure. Sometimes he delivered two to three hundred speeches a summer. Those who came to hear him paid no more than between twenty-five and fifty cents, but, although the admission fee was small, so numerous were those who came to hear him that the Bryan family sustained themselves by his virtuosity on the lecture circuit. But lecturing several times a day, traveling mostly by train for hours on end, is not an easy way to earn a livelihood.

Charles F. Horner, who from 1909 until Bryan's death was his agent for these engagements, never ceased to be amazed with Bryan's popularity and stamina. Here's how he described a Bryan performance:

> [A]t exactly the appointed moment, we would escort him quietly into the tent from the rear so that only a few people could see him enter. . . . When Mr. Bryan was introduced the audience would clap their hands, some would shout, . . . Bryan would stand with a smile on his face and a fan in his hand. . . . In a moment or two he would raise his arm, the palm of his hand turned to the people, and a quiet would come like the fall of a rose leaf on the grass.[24]

The palm leaf fan was never still; his other hand rested on a block of ice in a basin on the table, and with his cool hand he would wipe his face so that cold water would stream down it. The sun beat mercilessly down on his balding pate, but, Bryan never seemed aware of either fatigue or heat. Like a fish in water he could not live without the speaker's platform. Bryan relied on the hypnotic quality of his voice, the simplicity of his language, the salience of his message, to attract his listeners. Fearful that he would be viewed only as an entertainer rather than as a speaker delivering an important political message, he tended to shun humor. Although, in private, he could be witty and even humorous, "In public he was always as solemn as a sexton."[25]

According to historian George R. Poage, "William Jennings Bryan had come to Illinois College an unformed boy of fifteen . . . he left a self-confident man of twenty-one."[26] Many of the ideas he would advocate in his political career germinated during his college years and would remain essentially unchanged during a quarter of a century during which the momentum of change in the nation at large would accelerate with frightening rapidity.

NOTES

1. William Jennings Bryan and Mary Baird Bryan, *The Memoirs of William Jennings Bryan*, vol. 2 (Port Washington, NY: Kennikat Press, 1925), pp. 248–49.

2. Quoted in Merle Miller, *Plain Speaking: An Oral Biography of Harry S. Truman* (New York: G.P. Putnam's Sons, 1974), p. 116.

3. Bryan, *Memoirs*, p. 10.

4. Ibid., p. 18.

5. Ibid., p. 32.

6. Paolo E. Coletta, *William Jennings Bryan*, vol. 1, *Political Evangelist, 1860–1908* (Lincoln: University of Nebraska Press, 1964), p. 3.

7. Robert W. Cherny, *A Righteous Cause: The Life of William Jennings Bryan* (Boston: Little, Brown and Company), pp. 3–5.

8. Quoted in Paxton Hibben, *The Peerless Leader: William Jennings Bryan* (New York: Russell and Russell, 1929), p. 6.

9. Cherny, *A Righteous Cause*, p. 61.

10. Quoted in Louis W. Koenig, *Bryan: A Political Biography of William Jennings Bryan*, (New York: G.P. Putnam's Sons, 1971), p. 20.

11. Quoted in ibid., p. 21.

12. Coletta, *William Jennings Bryan*, vol. 1, p. 9.

13. Quoted in George R. Poage, "College Career of William Jennings Bryan," *The Mississippi Valley Historical Review* 15 (September 1928): 173.

14. Ibid., p. 172.

15. Edgar Dewitt Jones, *Lords of Speech: Portraits of Fifteen American Orators* (Freeport, NY: Books for Libraries Press, 1937), p. 216.

16. Quoted in ibid., p. 220.

17. Bryan, p. 85.

18. Quoted in Daniel J. Boorstin, *The Americans: The Democratic Experience* (New York: Random House, 1973), p. 462.

19. Quoted in Poage, "College Career of William Jennings Bryan," p. 177.

20. Richard Hofstadter, *The American Political Tradition* (New York: Vintage Books, 1957), p. 199.

21. Oswald Garrison Villard, *Prophets True and False* (New York: Alfred A. Knopf, 1928), p. 210.

22. Bryan, pp. 259–61.

23. Ibid., p. 253.

24. Charles F. Horner, "Strike the Tents," in *The Credo of the Commoner*, ed. Franklin Modisett (Los Angeles: Occidental College, 1968), p. 123.

25. Quoted in Myron G. Phillips, "William Jennings Bryan," in *A History and Criticism of American Public Address*, ed. William Norwood Brigance (New York: Russell and Russell, 1960), p. 909.

26. Poage, p. 165.

2

YOUNG MAN IN A HURRY

He was tall enough, but his face was pale and thin; a pair of keen, dark eyes look out from beneath heavy brows; his nose was prominent—too large to look well, I thought; a broad, thin lipped mouth and a square chin, completed the contour of his face. He was neat, though not fastidious in dress, and stood firmly and with dignity. I noted particularly his hair and smile. The former black in color, fine in quality, and parted with distressing straightness. . . . It was not love at first sight.

Mary Baird Bryan[1]

It was in the fall of 1879, when he was nineteen, that he saw her, Mary Elizabeth Baird, an eighteen-year-old student at the "Jail for Angels," as the locals called the Jacksonville Female Academy. "Her features were clear-cut but gently molded into an oval-shaped face. She had full, curved lips, large gray-brown eyes, curly brown hair, lightness of movement, and a ready laugh, but a searching expression revealed that there was an intellect behind her attractive appearance."[2]

It was not easy in those days to "make a date" with the woman who was the object of one's attention. One needed to conform to the conventions of the time, to observe the proprieties as well as the rules of Illinois College and the Jacksonville Female Academy. But William, although a rather conventional man, contrived imaginative ways of meeting her. For example, when the girls of the academy took their daily walks around the campus by way of exercise, Bryan managed to make his way to the edge of the campus to wave and smile at her, and before long she anticipated his presence. When Mary's mother was in a sanitarium in Jacksonville during the winter of 1879–1880, William called upon her mother the same time

Mary did. Contrary to college rules, he rented a buggy and took Mary for rides. He urged the wife of the president of the college to invite Mary to her home during an evening so that he too might call.

While the courtship did not go smoothly, Mary and William knew that their relationship was maturing and that they would overcome whatever obstacles to marriage they encountered. E. F. Bullard, the principal of the Jacksonville Female Academy, was one such obstacle. When their clandestine meetings were discovered as the academic year was drawing to a close in May 1880, Bullard ordered Mary to return home before the term ended. To make sure she left, he personally escorted her to the train. As the train pulled out of the station, Bryan, who had been hiding in the baggage car, entered her carriage. He proposed marriage, they exchanged rings, and he offered to go home with her and ask for her hand in marriage. Mary was not yet ready for a confrontation with her parents and insisted that he get off at the next stop. This he reluctantly did.

In the fall of 1880, in a typical Bryanesque approach, he fell back on the Bible to ask Mr. Baird for permission to marry his daughter:

"Mr. Baird, I have been reading *Proverbs* a good deal lately and find that Solomon says that 'Who findeth a wife findeth a good thing and obtaineth favor of the Lord.'"

"Yes, I believe Solomon did say that," replied Mr. Baird, "yet Paul suggests that '"he that giveth her in marriage doeth well; but he that giveth her not in marriage doeth better.'"

Bryan was stumped but pushed on. "Solomon would be the best authority upon this point because Paul was never married while Solomon had a number of wives."[3]

Bryan, the young debater, had made his point, and John Baird happily agreed to the marriage. The college newspaper, the *Rambler*, noted the engagement by wryly reporting that, Bryan was, "Another man whose destiny was sealed during his college days."[4] After securing permission from Bryan's mother, his father having died that year from a stroke while visiting his son in Jacksonville, the engagement was formalized. But it would be a four-year engagement, as the couple would not marry until 1884.

Mary Baird and Will Bryan were well matched. She would become the most supportive figure in his life, and their devotion to one another would be complete, without rancor or reservation. Paxton Hibben, one of Bryan's early biographers, notes that Mary Baird had her share of ambition as well. She had even dreamed of a career, but in a fashion typical of the day willingly gave "her man's" career priority over her own. "[U]nseen in the pilot house she charted the course of their ship."[5]

Although critical biographers would later say that he was something of an "old fogy," whose views never changed with changing times, in their youth William and Mary were ambitious—a couple on the move. Upon his graduation from Illinois College, it would seem that some of his fellow students remarked on the ambition of this "cute youth," whose prissy ways turned off some of his classmates. They noted, with some malice that while in his speeches he had admonished his classmates to "fling away ambition!" his entire "college life has been one continuous endeavor to secure place and power."[6]

Mary delivered the valedictory address to the graduates and their guests of the Jacksonville Female Academy while William delivered the valedictory address to the eleven graduates and their guests of the Illinois College. Seemingly, this was a couple that bore some watching.

BECOMING A LAWYER

Among the most difficult years of Bryan's life were those he spent at the Union College of Law in Chicago. The streets might have been paved with urban gold, but Chicago could not possibly look good to a man who had eyes only for his Mary, and to make matters worse, Chicago's hurly-burly was off-putting to a moral man from small-town America. To make a leap from towns like Salem and Jacksonville to Chicago, with its population of over half a million, its seventy-two miles of stone sidewalks and eleven miles of concrete ones, its two hundred miles of improved streets, and its Art Institute and Athenaeum, was a formidable undertaking to a country boy.

Moreover, his father dead and his financial resources limited, how could a great city look good to a man whose dingy room lacked a window and whose nearly empty pockets made it difficult for him to participate in the cultural life of the city? It is not surprising that Bryan's letters to Mary reflect the heart of a lonely man and portray the dissonance he found in living in a big city. For all her ambition, while William was pursuing his study of the law, Mary was taking a practical course in the domestic arts, with her parents as her teachers. She wrote to her husband-to-be, "I am practical enough to see that repeated avowals of affection would not hold your affection as effectually as a neat, tidy house and well cooked food." She took her apprenticeship in good humor, as when she reported in a letter to William, "You would laugh to see me tugging away," she wrote. "I now milk indiscriminately—sometimes the stream hits Pa, sometimes the cow's legs goes [*sic*] in the bucket. Pa says my object is to remove the milk."[7]

In Chicago, Bryan began to see something of the problems of American industrial labor. He never got used to seeing boys hawking newspapers while trying to keep warm during Chicago's cold winters or to escape the excessive heat of summer. He was appalled at the conditions under which men worked while building Pullman railroad cars so that the rich could travel in comfort. He deplored the fact that trusts and monopolies were growing and because they were, stockholders were enriching themselves at the expense of workers. But he noted a bit smugly that most of the malefactors of great wealth were Republicans, not Democrats. He anticipated violent confrontations between labor and management, and his fears were realized some years later when violence broke out at Pullman, Illinois, and in Chicago's Haymarket Square. Bryan was likewise appalled at the political corruption he found in Chicago, and he was embarrassed by it too, inasmuch as Chicago was a town controlled by the Democrats. His partisanship nevertheless was such that he assumed that matters could be much worse under Republicans. While dismayed by what he saw, "He shrank from [industrial] America as a woman might, never seeking to understand it, always a little fearsome of the complexity of its problems."[8]

Union Law School, in Bryan's day, was associated with the University of Chicago and later became the law school of Northwestern University. It offered a respectable two-year legal program scheduled so that its law students could at least partially support themselves by finding work in a law office. This the young William Jennings proceeded to do. For five dollars a week Bryan performed clerical and custodial services in the office of Judge Lyman Trumbull, Chicago's most distinguished attorney. A memorial in the Chicago Bar Association described Trumbull as "a quiet, sincere, frank, honest American gentleman . . . one of the very great men of the nation."[9] Judge Trumbull was to have a decisive influence on Bryan's career.

Lyman Trumbull was a distinguished Democrat who had broken with his party on the subject of slavery and had supported Abraham Lincoln and the quest to rid the country of slavery. He had been a confidant of Lincoln, and as a United States senator he had been the chief writer of Amendment Thirteen, which freed the slaves and thereby cast into law the principles of the Emancipation Proclamation. As senator, he again stood by his principles and as one of the "seven traitors" voted against the impeachment of President Andrew Johnson. This decision cost Trumbull his Senate seat and cast him into near political oblivion. In 1882, however, he was aging but still the most distinguished lawyer in Chicago. While his own career was winding down, he took a personal interest in the career of a young intern whose father had been a political associate, both a rival and an ally. Trumbull schooled young Bryan in the injustices growing out of the increasing concentration of industrial wealth. His son Henry was a classmate of Bryan's, and the elder Trumbull was hopeful that Bryan's moral code would influence his son for the better. Another of Bryan's classmates noted the influence Trumbull had on Bryan: "Will," he wrote, "was eagerly impressed with the idea that the people were being unjustly burdened by monopolies. He maintained even then that the menace of the country was the encroachment of wealth on the commonwealth, and he thought there was serious trouble ahead for the country."[10] Trumbull appeared to recognize that in Bryan there was the promise of an extraordinary political if not legal career.

In 1883, Bryan completed his study of the law and made haste to begin its practice in precincts other than Chicago. In his search for a community in which to make his start Bryan sought the smaller America, as it became evident that Chicago and the brawling cities of America were not for him. He undoubtedly was much relieved to find a place in a prominent law firm in Jacksonville, the beloved city of his college years. At twenty-three he was distinctly the junior associate of the locally important firm of Kirby, Brown, and Russell. His distinguished appearance, complete with a full, black beard, however, did little to attract clients willing to pay for his services. Instead, he had to content himself with the leavings of more senior attorneys with cases too insignificant to warrant their attention. Although his tiny income threatened his marriage plans, he received financial help from his mother to build a house in Jacksonville, and on October 1, 1884, Mary and he were married. When their house was finished, Mary's parents moved in with the young couple and lived with them, happily, for nearly all of their lives. In 1885, a daughter, Ruth, was born to Mary and William Bryan.

It soon became clear that Jacksonville was not the right community for Bryan's ambitions. His law practice was merely a means to an end, that end being elective office, and Bryan, with deep ties to the Democratic Party, saw little future for his political aspirations in so heavily a Republican community. And so the couple began to look around. Where could they live so that they could make a living through the law while making a life in politics? A detour to Lincoln, Nebraska, while on a business trip to Kansas, enabled Bryan to visit his friend Adolphus Talbot, who was practicing law in that city. In 1887 "Dolph" Talbot and Bill Bryan formed a law partnership in the fourth largest city west of the Missouri River. At the time, Lincoln was a city on the make. Historian Robert W. Cherny describes the town when the Bryans moved there as follows:

> As late as 1880, Lincoln had no paved streets, no water system, no sewers, no streetcars; by 1890 the city was to boast seventeen miles of paving, street lights along major thoroughfares, sewer connections to one house in five, a city water system, horse-drawn street cars, and forty-six daily passenger trains that stopped in the city. A handsome new capitol building loomed over the southeast section of the city.[11]

LAW AND POLITICS IN LINCOLN

The Talbot-Bryan partnership had the potential for developing a respectable law practice. Talbot was a Republican and Bryan a Democrat, and the opportunities for legal work in a new and growing community in what was still on the western frontier were many. As Bryan made the return journey to Illinois, with Nebraska fever coursing through his blood, he reviewed in his mind how best to infect Mary with his enthusiasm for Lincoln. In fact, Mary required little persuasion. If her husband thought it best that the family move to Lincoln, that was enough for her. The plan was for him to go to Lincoln and arrange for temporary housing until a fitting abode could be built.

William Jennings Bryan arrived in Lincoln on October 1, 1887, on his third wedding anniversary. Later on, Bryan often used this date as the one that marked not only the beginning of his marriage but as the beginning of his legal and political career. He believed October 1 to be his lucky day and he tried, as often as was feasible, to begin new and chancy undertakings on that day. On his own in Lincoln, a temporary bachelor, he slept on a cot in his office to keep his expenses low. And, indeed, he needed to economize, for between October 1, 1887, and his return to Jacksonville in December, Bryan earned a mere $82.25.[12]

With financial help from his father-in-law, Bryan began to build a new home that was scheduled to be ready to be occupied by June. The law firm of Talbot and Bryan rented a suite of offices that was probably somewhat extravagant for the minor work, mostly of debt collecting, in which they were initially engaged. In June the Bryans, accompanied by Mary's parents, moved into their new home. Mary and William became active in church affairs and took the leadership in establishing discussion groups for men and women on topics of religion, philosophy, and politics. Bryan became active in the Lincoln YMCA, the Chamber of Commerce, Rotary, Elks, Moose,

Odd Fellows, and Knights of Pythias, nearly all of whom called upon him to speak at their meetings. Unfortunately, financial prosperity eluded him.

The problem may have been that Bryan was too interested in politics to succeed at the law. Kansas journalist and Republican confidant William Allen White wrote, "He was a poor practitioner; he neglected to prepare his cases, and gained no reputation at the bar. But he did rise and shine as a political leader because he could talk."[13] Within a year of his arrival in Lincoln, Bryan plunged himself into local politics.

The political climate of Nebraska was made to order for him. Nebraska was, to be sure, solidly and stolidly Republican, and the Democrats were split, comatose, and casting about for a leader. Bryan's self-confidence, his egotism, was such that despite his youth he had the temerity to believe that he could be that leader. The most important Democrat in Nebraska was the wealthy and conservative, J. Sterling Morton, the former publisher of the *Nebraska City News*. He was a prominent agronomist and is widely credited as the founder of Arbor Day. Morton invited Bryan to his opulent home in Nebraska City to observe Arbor Day and to talk politics. They found that while they disagreed on much, their common ground was opposition to the protective tariff. Morton had been the gubernatorial nominee of the Democratic Party in 1880, 1882, and 1884, and it was assumed that he could be nominated to any statewide office he desired.

Bryan made an impression on Morton. Since the young man was handsome, poised, ambitious, and an excellent speaker, Morton welcomed Bryan to the "Slaughter House" wing of the Democratic Party, critical of Cleveland, of which Morton was the leader. George L. Miller was the leader of the "Packing House" Democrats, a group close to President Grover Cleveland and the recipient of the patronage largesse a party in control of the White House could provide. But at the state level, the "Slaughter House" Democrats clearly controlled the Democratic machine in the state. In 1888, Bryan became a delegate to the Lancaster County convention, where he supported Morton's successful maneuvering for control. As a reward, Bryan was elected a delegate to the state convention. His anti-tariff speech was one of the most effective of his career to date, met with Morton's strong approval, and impressed his listeners. The speech, according to one of Bryan's biographers, "may have been more important in determining Bryan's future than the 'Cross of Gold' speech."[14] Even ordinarily cynical journalists were extravagant in their praise. With Morton's backing, Bryan was offered his choice of the nomination for lieutenant governor or for attorney general. He refused both. Bryan would never be a candidate for state office—he saw no opportunity for advancement in a Republican-controlled state. As a Democrat, he was convinced he would lose.

Morton was the nominee for Congress, and at the latter's request Bryan scoured the district, speaking in behalf of Morton and in opposition to protective tariffs. Although Morton was defeated, Bryan was rapidly becoming the best-known Democrat in the state. Bryan's ego, massaged by his widespread popularity, convinced him that although he was still a newcomer to Nebraska and still in his twenties, he could get the nomination of his fellow Democrats for the House of Representatives from the first district in 1890.

After campaigning for Morton, Bryan returned to his long-neglected legal practice and resumed an active social life. Mary Bryan became a lawyer, was admitted to the Nebraska bar, and in 1889 gave birth to a son, William Jennings Bryan Jr. Despite the hold the Republicans had on the politics of Nebraska, Bryan decided to take the plunge and campaign full-time for a seat in the House of Representatives. In February 1890, he was rewarded when the leaders of the Democratic Party offered him the nomination. Clearly, the move to Lincoln, Nebraska, had been a politically shrewd one for the youthful Bryan, for nowhere else was it likely that he could have risen with such lightning speed, leapfrogged over men of greater seniority, and secured the Democratic nomination for national office.

But what did this political meteor believe?

BRYAN AT TWENTY-NINE

At twenty-nine Bryan was a conventional married man with a growing family and a house with a mortgage held by his father-in-law. He had tremendous physical vitality that manifested itself on the political hustings and, as a devout Christian, in his regular attendance and participation in church and communal affairs. He had little interest in athletics or physical fitness; he neither went fishing nor hunting, nor did he play golf. Although he often found himself in difficult, frustrating circumstances, he had an even temperament and remained good humored, unruffled, confident, optimistic, and serene. "There was no pose in Bryan, only a very simple and unaffected democracy," wrote political scientist Charles Merriam. "His genial manner, his broad smile, his ready wit, his democratic simplicity, were entirely genuine, and never wore through to arrogance, impatience, and irritation. If men were impressed by the energy and solidity of Roosevelt, if they were touched by he sadness of Lincoln, if they were dazzled by . . .

Wilson, they were moved to consider Bryan as 'just one of them,' a common man."[15]

In the Bryan *Memoirs*, written by husband and wife, Mary Bryan asserted that two years before her husband was nominated by the Democrats to run for Congress he had predicted that he would in fact be nominated and that he would win. Although his district was heavily Republican, Bryan predicted that in 1890 Republicans would be split by independent voters and a Democrat offering youth, vigor, enthusiasm, and fresh ideas.[16]

In his early political career he seemed to personify the principle, frequently reflected among the politically agile, that to get along one had to go along. Later in his political life he would become rigid and often refuse to "go along." Through a political lifetime his personal contacts and political network were unsurpassed except perhaps by Lincoln.[17] The result was that he became something of a favorite among leadership Democrats. Because his was a fresh face, he appealed to rural America, despite the fact that his views were not yet finely honed. It was enough that he appeared to understand the desperation of farmers and could effectively articulate their woes from the speakers' platform.

During the course of a long political life he would be called a revolutionary, a radical, and a socialist, but politically he was a Democrat and remained so for the rest of his life. Political science professor and occasional Chicago mayoral candidate Charles Merriam notes that Bryan geographically represented the West and the South, sections of the country that in earlier times had been strong enough to bring Jefferson and Jackson to the presidency. But by 1890, with urbanization a growing phenomenon in America, support from a rural South and West would not be enough to catapult Bryan into the White House. At twenty-nine, Bryan did not yet recognize these facts of political life, however, and perhaps he never did. Bryan would remain a man of the frontier and would never accept the fact that the frontier as such was vanishing. Thus, blind to most urban forces, he was guided in his political life by an echo of the American past, while failing to hear the voice of America's future.

The wellsprings of his political philosophy were Jeffersonian as well as Jacksonian. Not given to political introspection, he may not have recognized his philosophical forebears as such. With Jefferson, he stood essentially for an agrarian America. "Those who labor in the earth," Jefferson declared, "are the chosen people of God." In this Bryan would surely agree. With Jackson he made majority rule absolute. As Walter Lippmann put it, to Bryan "the majority is of right sovereign in all things."[18] Thus, he would later support the extension of the suffrage to women, direct election of

United States senators, and the election of federal judges. He would support the direct primary initiative and referendum and would fight for the limitation on the use of the injunction in industrial disputes. As a young man, although he never touched alcohol, he was a moderate on prohibition and did not feel the government ought to regulate social preferences. As we shall see, he later changed his mind and became a leader in the fight for a prohibition amendment to the Constitution (see pp. 120–24). He was opposed to a high protective tariff and favored an income tax. He also favored cheap money, though not yet the principle of sixteen ounces of silver to one of gold.

He was strongly inclined to be a reformer both of individuals and of institutions. Thus, through his piety, he sought to show the way men and women could be made, as the Bible asserted, in the image of God. And if men and women could be made in the image of God, why not the political institutions that served them? His approach to reform was that of a pragmatist and gradualist rather than that of a revolutionary. Moreover, such reforms as he favored could come about only through an expression of the popular will. Although he never became a farmer, he identified with the needs of small farmers and, to a somewhat lesser degree, to industrial laborers. He never really understood corporate America, which drew his barbed criticism for industry's tendency to form monopolies and manage prices. Although he took the time to study the role of the tariff and mastered much of the arcana of currency reform, he never seems to have taken the time to study the role of corporate America in contributing to the economy and prosperity of the nation. Business was always suspect, and trusts were always bad. When, in February 1890, the managers of the Democratic Party informed Bryan that he could be their nominee for the First Congressional District, a district that included that state's two largest cities of Lincoln and Omaha, Bryan hedged his reply. William Jennings Bryan remembered, perhaps, that when in 1872 his father ran for Congress, Silas Bryan was sharp enough to recognize that he had no chance of victory if nominated by the Democrats alone. He sought and achieved the support of what later became the Greenback Party, a group who thought that the end to the farmer's economic plight could be achieved by cheap money. Although Silas Bryan lost his bid for a seat in the House of Representatives, his astute son, eighteen years later, sought the support of a new Independent Party, which consisted of splintered groups of farmers loosely organized as the Farmers' Alliance.

The political, economic, and self-help activities of farm organizations collectively constituted the populist movement of the 1890s. At its best populism sought to make the allegedly creaking machinery of government more responsive to the needs of the people, especially to the needs of the farmer. They fought the trusts, the bankers, and the railroad barons, all of whom, they felt, were contributing to the impoverishment of the farmer. The Populists quickly became the party of revolt and drew on an eclectic group of those who thought they had found solutions to the agrarian ailments in "cheap" money, as in the free and unlimited coinage of silver, greenbacks, lower protective tariffs, railroad rate regulation, or the single tax on land as favored by Henry George or utopian economic schemes as advocated by Edward Bellamy.

The Populists inspired a host of colorful political personalities, each of whom pleaded a special cause and a preferred course of action. Among them was "Pitchfork Ben" Tillman of South Carolina, a lifelong Democrat, who became governor by pursuing pro-farmer policies to thwart the Populist Party's expansion in his state. Tom Watson likewise became governor of Georgia while working on behalf of that state's tenant farmers and mill hands. James Weaver of Iowa represented those who favored greenbacks and became the Populist presidential candidate. In Kansas, Mary Lease, born in Ireland, mother of four, a lawyer, famously urged the farmers to "raise less corn and more Hell." In Kansas, too, "Sockless" Jerry Simpson proposed Henry George's single tax and exposed the alleged sins, high freight rates, and obscene profits of the railroads. And there was "General" Jacob Coxey, whose solution for the farmer was paper money. Indeed, so strongly did he believe that he named his son "Legal Tender." "And from Nebraska came the greatest of all the farmers' leaders, a Democrat of the new dispensation, William Jennings Bryan."[19] While many farmers in their desperation were drawn to populist Pied Pipers with questionable panaceas, some of whom were clowns, fools, bigots, or mountebanks, Bryan was none of these. While he would turn every public issue into a moral question and every campaign into a crusade, he would also be a shrewd politician and a truthful one.

"WHO THE HELL IS BRYAN?"

On July 29, 1890, the Farmers' Alliances of Nebraska organized themselves as the Independent Party and nominated the formidable Charles H. Van Wyck, a former United States senator and a leader of the antimonopoly wing of the Republican Party. It must have taken youthful zeal, political courage, and brashness for Bryan to encourage his supporters to approach

Van Wyck and seek his withdrawal from the congressional campaign in Nebraska's First District. When Van Wyck withdrew, the twenty-nine-year-old Bryan ran mainly against his Republican opponent, pro-tariff but pro-silver incumbent William J. Connell. In the campaign that followed, Bryan wrapped himself in the cloak of populism while remaining, as he would all his life, a stalwart Democrat.

Bryan's platform included opposition to the tariff, subsidies, and bounties to industry. He took aim at trusts by opposing the holding of land by nonresidents. He opposed also the alleged authoritarian rules "Czar" Reed, Speaker of the House, had imposed on that body. Interestingly, he opposed government ownership of railroads and telegraphs, a plank much favored by the Independents (Populists). He railed against Republicans for their "reckless extravagance," and directed his barbs against a Republican Party that was, he believed, in an unholy alliance with Wall Street, the symbolic enemy of the people.

And, surprisingly, he opposed an amendment to the state constitution calling for prohibition. Instead, he was content with a plank that favored local option and high license fees for those establishments selling whiskey. As if to reinforce the general opposition of Democrats to prohibition, the party choice for governor of Nebraska was James E. Boyd, a "wet."

The Democratic Convention adopted Bryan's platform unanimously, and when his opponent for the nomination to the House of Representatives, Charles W. Brown, gave up the challenge, Bryan's nomination became unanimous. Even Dr. George L. Miller, leader of the "Packing House" Democrats, who had once asked, "Who the hell is Bryan?" congratulated the young candidate.

ON THE CAMPAIGN TRAIL

Bryan's was a Don Quixote style of campaigning, as he viewed himself not merely as a political campaigner seeking high political office but also as a moral crusader tilting at the evil opposition. While the Man of La Mancha tilted at imaginary foes, the man of Lincoln, Nebraska, faced very real ones in trying to rescue Midwestern farmers from the deep depression in rural America. And, his proposals for reform, cheap money, free and unlimited coinage of silver as well as gold, and tariff reductions were by no means without merit.

Upon his nomination he received numerous letters of congratulations and many offering advice. One such letter said, "Speak everywhere—kiss all the babies—you can do it—you have mouth enough for both."[20] During the course of his campaign for Congress, Bryan gave more than eighty speeches in opposition to the tariff, and his words were exactly what the hard-pressed farmers of his district wanted to hear. In one speech to a group of farmers, he stood on a manure spreader and jauntily declared, "Friends, this is the first time that I ever spoke from a Republican platform."[21] A Kansas woman described the campaign of 1890 as "a religious revival, a crusade, a Pentecost of politics."[22] One well-wisher hoped that in Bryan "a Moses had been discovered to lead the chosen people out of their bondage to trusts, tariff abuses, and irrational taxation."[23] That voter had no cause for worry. He declared, "I shall go forth to the conflict as David went to meet the giant of the Philistines, not relying upon my own strength, but trusting to the righteousness of my cause."[24] Every political campaign in which Bryan was involved became a holy cause, and although he would win his seat in Congress this time, as a campaign style it would not serve him well during his political life. He was seemingly addicted to it, however, and never backed away from this losing technique.

During the course of the campaign, as it became evident that Bryan was gaining the upper hand over his Republican opposition, conservative newspapers stepped up their criticism. His youth became the butt of newspaper humor and of critical cartoons. The press called him a "calamity howler," and described him as "effervescent as a bottle of soda pop." Republicans criticized him for his lack of a Civil War record and for being a Jekyll and Hyde personality. They noted that he went to church regularly and taught Sunday School but was not above sitting in saloons and bars with the other denizens of the drinking classes. Bryan responded that he often spoke to people who drank liquor but that he never took a drop himself. He also declared that he was opposed to prohibition legislation in that the drinking of alcohol was a moral question, not a political one.

Toward the end of the campaign, Bryan's single-minded devotion to the ills of his farm constituency led him to commit a major political gaffe. On October 18, 1890, he declared, "I am tired of hearing about laws made for the benefit of the men who work in shops." The Republicans were quick to point out that in Bryan's district there were thousands of men who work in shops. The statement was enough to swing the Knights of Labor away from Bryan, and its members were urged to vote, instead, for Connell. Bryan exacerbated the situation by failing to make a prompt correction. When he did so, he declared that what he meant to say was that he was opposed to class legislation of any kind.

Despite this gaffe, Bryan won handily, to become only the second Democrat elected to Congress by Nebraskans. The Republicans retained all statewide offices except that of governor, but they lost control of the state legislature. The Republicans lost all three congressional races, one to an independent, another to a fusion Independent-Democrat, and to Bryan the pure Democrat. The official count gave Bryan 32,376 votes, Connell 25,663, and Root, the Independent candidate who ran when Van Wyck withdrew, but 13,006 votes. Bryan had won a significant victory, and the Democrats now spoke with pride of their "boy congressman" and others hailed him as "the Henry Clay of Nebraska."

A CONGRESSIONAL FRESHMAN

In November 1891, with his family still in Lincoln, William Jennings Bryan took the oath of office as a member of the United States House of Representatives. Between the election and the beginning of the session, Bryan diligently studied the major issues he knew would come before the House. The most notable questions concerned the tariff, currency, and the graduated income tax. In his two terms as congressman, he would give major speeches on each of these issues.

But settling in the nation's capitol was no easy matter for the Bryans. As Mary Bryan reported in their *Memoirs*:

> December 1891 found us en route to Washington, where Mr. Bryan took up his duties as Congressman. Our children then numbered three, the youngest being nine months old. . . . Even at that remote date the hotel and apartment owners of Washington had declared against children, and Mr. Bryan had a long search to find a home for us. At one time we regarded the drowning of our entire family as a necessary prelude to establishing ourselves. We saw race suicide from a new angle, and experienced great relief when we had secured pleasant quarters opposite the National Library on Capitol Hill.[25]

The Bryans occupied a spacious rented apartment on the second floor of a house on B Street that faced the Library of Congress, then under construction. In addition to William and Mary Bryan and their children, the Bryan household included Mary's blind father (Mary's mother had recently died in Lincoln). Cotter Timothy Bride, the owner of the B Street housing complex, and his nephew, Daniel, became close friends. Prone to bouts of illness, which the unhealthy climate of the nation's capitol did little or nothing to alleviate, Daniel found some refuge with the Bryans, with whom he often shared meals and, although a Catholic, shared also morning worship services with the devout Presbyterians.

Little by way of Washington social life could attract the Bryans. Accustomed as they were to rural surroundings, the Bryans initially felt alienated from the more sophisticated modes of thought, speech, dress, and lifestyle in the nation's capital. Mary Bryan was often at a loss as to what to wear at public functions, and her husband could not be helpful. They could have accepted the invitation of Mrs. John Wanamaker, the wife of the postmaster general and a prominent retail merchant, but they did not. They chose not to hear Mrs. Ballington Booth, daughter-in-law of Salvation Army General William Booth, speak on the subject "Rescue Work." They could have attended a meeting of suffragists and listened to Julia Ward Howe at the opera house, but despite the young congressman's advocacy of votes for women, again they did not attend. Surprisingly, even when they were invited by the Countess Esterhazy to a large luncheon at the Carroll Mansion in honor of the president's lady, Mrs. Harrison, with other wives of Washington's mighty present, they did not attend. Less surprisingly, they did not hear Sarah Bernhardt in *Tosca*, nor were they interested in James Henry Moser's watercolor exhibit.[26]

But they were a happily married couple, and if they appeared to shun Washington society and culture they were warm and gregarious, and popular among other young legislators. Moreover, together they formed a mutually supportive political partnership. Mary became familiar with the holdings in the Library of Congress and, being a lawyer, she often did much of the research for her husband's speeches and legislative proposals. From her choice seat in the visitors' gallery, Mary, with a wink or nod, smile, frown, or gesture, offered her husband encouragement and coaching.

While Washington, D.C., may have awed the new congressman, his political sagacity was such that he appeared to master his environment with alacrity. During the course of his first congressional term he met every member of the House of Representatives: 235 Democrats, 14 Alliancemen (Populists), and 86 Republicans. He also met many senators and noted with interest the growing importance of the Populists. He frequently invited colleagues to his apartment to share good political talk and some of Mary's good cooking.

In Congress, he gave strong support to William Springer as Speaker of the House. Springer lost the speakership but he had enough votes to throw to Charles F. Crisp in exchange for making Springer chairman of the Ways and Means Committee. Springer secured Bryan's appointment to this powerful committee.

In mid-March Bryan grabbed the opportunity to deliver a major address on the proposal of the Democrats to reduce the tariff on wool, woolen items, binding twine, and other farm items. As Mary Bryan describes it, "I was exceedingly anxious about this first speech in Congress and sat in the gallery of the House of Representatives with my hand clasping the arm of the seat so tensely that my glove was split across the palm."[27] She and her husband "worked out that celebrated speech together, line by line."[28]

Her husband spoke for three hours and four minutes and, with the practiced skill of a man to whom oratory was as natural as breathing, he berated a policy that "was conceived in greed and fashioned in iniquity."[29] He offered few new arguments in favor of lower tariffs, but his rich baritone voice and elocutionary techniques marked him as a speaker to whom it was worth listening. House members applauded enthusiastically when he was finished. Journalists reported favorably on both the ideas and the eloquence. He was an anonymous congressman no more.

Because of Republican opposition in the United States Senate, however, tariff reform failed once again that year.

Bryan took advantage of his newly earned stature to introduce legislation desired by his constituency. A proposal requiring greater publicity for court orders foreclosing land mortgages was passed by both houses of Congress, signed by the president, and became law. Congress passed his bill to give Nebraska two judicial districts, and he obtained for Lincoln an extra fall term of court. On the other hand, his bill to revoke a patent after its holder had made $100,000 from it, though a gesture against monopoly, was too impractical—and probably unconstitutional—to reach the House floor.

Adding to the Dependent Pension Bill of 1890, Bryan "obtained more pensions for his constituents than all his predecessors put together."[30] He opposed the autocracy of the Reed rules, which still governed the procedures of the House, and he opposed naval expansion. He favored investigation of the role of the Pinkerton detectives in the Homestead Strike of 1892, and he supported aid to Western states for irrigation and stricter regulation of trusts. He favored a graduated income tax, and boldly sought to begin the long constitutional process that would lead to the direct election of United States senators. The time, however, was not yet ripe for this important constitutional democratic reform.

He sought rural free delivery, lower postal rates on educational material, a national bankruptcy law, improved safety devices on railroads, and the removal of the duty on medicines for diphtheria antitoxins. "Thus Bryan tenaciously and consistently pursued what he considered historic Democratic doctrine," wrote Paolo Coletta in his detailed three-volume account of Bryan's life. "No major legislation bears his name, yet the bills he introduced and the speeches he made show that he followed in the spirit of Jefferson and Jackson. With energy, eloquence, and sincerity, he sought laws that would operate equally upon all, give special privilege to none, and make government more responsive to the will of the people."[31]

Through the tariff speech, Bryan became a serious contender in the national political arena. Among the glowing letters he received congratulating him on his forensic virtuosity was one that read, "I don't rightfully know your age, but in case you are old enough [he wasn't] to be president of the United States, I sure favor it."[32] While the quest for the presidency was in the future, reelection to a second term in the House of Representative was by no means assured.

Bryan returned to Nebraska, where he found that in an attempt to unseat him, his own congressional district had been gerrymandered by the Republican-dominated Nebraska legislature "and was more hopelessly Republican than ever."[33] Moreover, he found his party split between the "gold" Democrats, of which his former friend and mentor, J. Sterling Morton, was the leader, and Independents, who sought to go it alone rather than "fuse" with the Democrats. In the state convention, which was held the day before the national convention, the Democrats renominated Bryan for Congress. When his party rejected his platform proposal in favor of the free and unlimited coinage of silver he and his supporters made a dramatic exit. Instead of Cleveland, he would support Governor Horace Boise of Iowa for the presidential nomination.

Bryan knew that winning in his gerrymandered congressional district would be an uphill battle. But with boundless energy, unmatched enthusiasm for the fray, and his customary optimism, he made a point of speaking at every country fair where he found a ready audience. Bryan received support from such prominent Populists as Mary Ellen Lease and the 1892 Populist presidential candidate, General James B. Weaver. Returning the favor, Bryan supported Weaver in the presidential election.

In this second run for Congress, Bryan displayed an uncharacteristic flexibility in his views. For example, he spoke for Weaver but, as a stalwart Democrat, voted for Cleveland. Even on such issues as currency and tariff reform he remained vague and tempered his views to the wishes of the majority of Nebraskans. "I don't know anything about free silver but the people of Nebraska are for free silver and I am for free silver. I will look up the arguments later," he said somewhat disingenuously.[34] Although Bryan claimed that he had spent so much time studying the tariff issue that he had not had time to study about currency, he had been studying currency since his first election to Congress.

How much of a study he really made is not clear. The literature and the people he consulted on the subject were mostly favorable to silver, and it does not appear that he went to any great lengths to study the arguments of those currency experts who were opposed to silver. That he would first heed the people's voice and study the solutions later provided him with a flexibility that prompted J. Sterling Morton, his one-time mentor, jealously to observe, "Bryan is so self-adjusting that—in his fine flexibility—he can agree with a greater number of persons who hold different views on the same question than any pinfeathered economist I have ever met."[35] Nevertheless, in the election, Cleveland won the presidency, Morton was defeated for governor, and Bryan won a second term in the House of Representatives by a scant 140 votes.

Although his margin of victory was narrow, Bryan had once again proven himself a vote getter. Despite the gerrymandered district in which he had been required to run, he was the only Democratic congressman from Nebraska who had won reelection. He had overcome the gold Democrats, hostile speakers such as William McKinley of Ohio, and money—twenty thousand dollars from Eastern bankers and railroad barons who, bent on muting his influence in Congress, promised four times as much.

It is nevertheless interesting to conjecture what Bryan's political career might have become had there been no gerrymandering, if a relatively large, urban, constituency such as provided by Omaha would have remained in his political camp. During his first campaign for Congress he appeared to be more ready to compromise, as he did on prohibition and on issues relating to control and regulation of trusts. The campaign for his second term for Congress depended on his willingness to appeal to the farm belt, the fading frontier, and the traditional values of a Bible-bound, conservative, God-fearing, rural America. Although America was changing, the frontier disappearing, cities growing, farming becoming less important and less attractive, he hitched his political wagon to a fading constituency.

He bonded with the views of rural America as if he could not do otherwise. He was, as Willa Cather observed, a man of the West and his times, reflecting "all its newness and vigor, its magnitude and monotony, its richness and lack of variety, its inflammability and volubility, its strength and its crudeness, its high seriousness and self-confidence, its egotism and nobility."[36] But, in the end, he chased a rainbow of his own rigidity only to find at the rainbow's end he had not only failed, but had even become the object of ridicule.

"THAT YOUNG UPSTART FROM LINCOLN"

Despite his victory, Bryan's return to a lame-duck session of the Fifty-second Congress would be inauspicious. His second term as a member of the House of Representatives would be marked by a David and Goliath confrontation between the young, brash, Democratic two-term congressman from Nebraska, and the twice-elected president of the United States from the same party. Although he was the only elected Democrat in Congress from Nebraska, Bryan was shackled by President Cleveland, who appointed J. Sterling Morton, the defeated gubernatorial candidate, secretary of agriculture without consulting Bryan. As if to rub salt into an open wound, it was Morton, not Bryan, who had access to political patronage in Nebraska. But the real confrontation would not be over patronage but how best to respond to the Panic of 1893, which, only two month's after the inauguration of President Cleveland, threatened the economic foundations of the nation.

Just as he had become the recognized leader in the House of Representatives for low tariffs so, in the lame-duck session of the Fifty-second Congress and in the Fifty-third, Bryan became the acknowledged leader for those who favored the free and unlimited coinage of silver. In his campaign for free silver he took a principled position against President Grover Cleveland, the head of the Democratic Party, and so became a thorn in his side.

During the severe economic downturn of 1893, unemployment reached four million. Many railroads, such as the Union Pacific and the Santa Fe, passed into the hands of receivers, and the Reading failed. A plague of rural bank failures made it difficult for farmers to finance next year's crops and sell this year's harvest profitably. In the financial panic, businesses were rapidly exchanging their silver certificates for gold, therefore draining America's gold reserve and allegedly aggravating the depression. Congressman Bryan found the cause of the depression in the "monied sharks of Wall Street." President Cleveland found the cause in the Sherman Silver Purchase Act of 1890, which required the Treasury to buy an additional 4.5 million ounces of silver bullion each month and coin it into silver dollars. Cleveland's solution was the repeal of the Sherman Silver Purchase Act. Bryan thought otherwise. His conclusion was that the free and unlimited coinage of silver in a ratio of sixteen ounces of silver to one of gold was about right. It would create modest inflation and help farmers pay their debts by getting better prices for their crops.

Silver had become a popular cause among a number of otherwise diverse groups. Because silver mining interests from Western states sought to increase both the price and mining of silver, silver advocates urged their Republican senators and representatives to support them. Populists were behind silver as an inflationary means of relieving the problems of the farmer; some labor unions and many Democrats from the South and West were likewise behind silver. Bryan urged a union of these politicians and organizations to join in a concerted drive in behalf of the free—that is, without a minting charge—and unlimited coinage of silver at a ratio of sixteen ounces of silver to one of gold.

When a Republican Congress put America on a gold standard, "the Crime of '73" it was called, depression followed, with farmers hit especially hard. In 1890, in response to the urban and rural debtors, Congress passed the Sherman Silver Purchase Act, requiring the Treasury to purchase 4.5 million ounces of silver every month. This was a step applauded by the silver crowd. It was not enough, in that it failed to raise farm prices. Silverites sought nothing less than the unlimited coinage of silver. In Bryan, the silverites found a silver tongue to enhance their cause. In urging sixteen ounces of silver to one of gold, the silverites recognized that the intrinsic price of silver was eighty cents, or one-twentieth the price of gold. Bryan's advocacy of silver did not come without a political price. He could no longer count on uniting gold Democrats and silver Democrats. While he remained a lifelong Democrat, he increasingly relied on Populist support.

The summer of 1893 was an especially difficult one for President Cleveland. Shortly before Congress convened, the president underwent an operation for a cancerous growth in the roof of his mouth. The surgery took place in secrecy, aboard a ship anchored in New York harbor. The president was fitted out with an artificial jaw of vulcanized rubber and, steely nerved as he was, went back to work with few aware of what had taken place. In the David and Goliath debate over silver that would unexpectedly be led by William Jennings Bryan, the young congressman from Nebraska, the president would need all the fortitude he demonstrated in his serious illness.

In a special session of Congress called by Cleveland to urge the repeal of the Sherman Silver Purchase Act, Bryan, on August 16, 1893, gave another of his celebrated speeches. The visitors' gallery was filled to overflowing, members of the House of Representatives were in their seats, and many senators stood in the aisles to listen. To Bryan this was a grave moment, not because it would further his political career, but because it would make him "an instrument in the hands of Providence of doing some good for my country."[37] According to biographer Louis W. Koenig, "He stood tall and strong, handsome as a matinee idol, dressed with the simplicity of the people's delegate and yet with a consciousness of the honor of his politician's calling."[38]

With some hoarseness in his voice betraying a smidgeon of stage fright, he shuffled his notes more out of sense of drama than of tension and launched into his remarks. With hyperbole to match his zeal, he portrayed the proposal to repeal the Sherman Silver Purchase Act as no less significant than the successful battle of "the Crescent against the Cross" waged by Charles Martel. Just as Martel saved the West "from the all-destroying grasp of Islam" (in A.D. 732), so today, "a greater Tours is here. In my humble judgement the vote of this House on the subject under consideration may bring to the people of the West and South to the people of the United States, to all mankind, wealth or woe beyond the power of language to describe or imagination to conceive."[39]

Driving a spike between the president's supporters and the "silver" Democrats, Bryan asserted, "I have read with care the message [the president] sent to us last week. . . . If I am able to understand its language it points to the burial of silver, with no promise of resurrection. Its reasoning is in the direction of a single standard. It leads irresistibly to universal gold monometallism—to a realm over whose door is written: 'Abandon hope, all ye who enter here!'"[40]

Bryan went on to describe simply and clearly the dire consequences of a single gold standard. He insisted that a gold standard would contract the global supply of money when a growing world population required an expansion of the money supply. A single gold standard would, as it has in countries around the world, make the price of gold soar and so the "debt of the debtor is increased, to his injury and to the advantage of the creditor."[41] Using a homely illustration, he continued, "If a [person] should loan a Nebraska neighbor a hog weighing 100 pounds and the next spring demand in return a hog weighing 200 pounds he would be called dishonest, even tho [sic] he contended that he was demanding only one hog—just the number he loaned. A poor man who takes property by force is called a thief, but the creditor who by legislation makes a creditor pay a dollar twice as large as he borrowed is lauded as the friend of sound currency. The man who wants the people to destroy the Government is an anarchist, but the man who wants the government to destroy the people is called a patriot."[42]

Bryan demonstrated an impressive grasp of the literature on currency and insisted that a monetary system based on both gold and silver would bring a truly stable economy. He admitted that there was an honest difference among knowledgeable people as to the precise ratio of gold to silver but he believed that the ratio of sixteen to one was probably right in that it would cause the least injustice to the American people. Bryan concluded that bimetallism was in the spirit of Jefferson, Jackson, and the Democratic Party:

> He was called a demagogue and his followers a mob, but the immortal Jefferson dared to follow the best promptings of his heart. He placed man above matter, humanity above property, and, spurning the bribes of wealth and power, pleaded the cause of the common people. It was this devotion to their interest that made his party invincible while he lived and will make his name revered while history endures. And what message comes from the Hermitage? When a crisis like the present arose and the national bank of his day sought to control the politics of the nation, God raised up an Andrew Jackson, who had the courage to grapple with that great enemy, and by overthrowing it, he made himself an idol of the people and reinstated the Democratic Party in the public confidence. What will the decision be to-day? The Democratic Party has won the greatest success in its history. Standing upon this victory-crowned summit, will it turn to face the rising or the setting sun? Will it choose blessings or cursings, life or death—which? Which?[43]

When the Fifty-third Congress adjourned Bryan announced that he was available to speak on invitation on such topics as lower tariffs, prohibition, the graduated income tax, and the free coinage of silver. Of these topics it was the last that most piqued the interest of the nation as it sought to alleviate the worst of the fallout from the Panic of 1893. And who better than William Jennings Bryan to gallop, like Paul Revere, to every hamlet, village, and town urging the free and unlimited coinage of silver at sixteen to one. Cleveland was furious that a member of his party should be so effective in opposition. Little wonder that he would urge Morton to kill off that "young upstart from Lincoln, Nebraska."[44]

Bryan chose not to run for a third term to the House of Representatives. Instead, he decided to make a run for the United States Senate. But when Bryan put himself forth as a senatorial candidate, senators were chosen by the highly charged political climate of the state legislature, and in the Nebraska State Legislature Bryan stood little chance. However, he took advantage of a little-known electoral procedure to have his name listed on the popular ballot as a candidate for Senate. Although this provision carried no requirement that the Nebraska legislature choose him, he thought that his popularity might be such as to sway its members. Although Bryan received the most votes, most voters ignored the opportunity to express a senatorial preference. Moreover, Bryan could not win the support of Nebraska's Populists, who decided to run a candidate of their own. The legislature remained unimpressed, and a Republican won handily.

Mary Bryan used the stalemate in which her husband found himself by making a rash proposal of her own. She suggested that he give up politics, return to a law practice where he could make a good living, travel less, and be home with the family more. Much as he loved Mary, she was asking too much of a man who viewed his political life as an extension of the work God required of him. Although the United States Senate appeared beyond his grasp, a run for the presidency remained a possibility. A letter from Jim Dahlman, an officer of the Free Coinage League, seemed to think so. "I have begun to talk you for president. . . . No gift in the hands of the people is too high for you."[45]

NOTES

1. William Jennings Bryan and Mary Baird Bryan, *The Memoirs of William Jennings Bryan* (Chicago: John C. Winston Company, 1925), p. 222.

2. Paolo E. Coletta, *William Jennings Bryan*, vol. 1, *Political Evangelist, 1860–1908* (Lincoln: University of Nebraska Press, 1964), p. 21.

3. Quoted in ibid., pp. 22–23.

4. Quoted in George R. Poage, "The College Career of William Jennings Bryan," *Mississippi Historical Review* 15 (June 1928 to March 1929): 174–75.

5. Paxton Hibben, *The Peerless Leader: William Jennings Bryan* (New York: Russell and Russell, 1929), p. 88.

6. Quoted in ibid., p. 87.

7. Quoted in Coletta, *William Jennings Bryan*, vol. 1, p. 27.

8. Hibben, *The Peerless Leader*, p. 91.

9. Quoted in ibid.

10. Quoted in Louis W. Koenig, *Bryan: A Political Biography* (New York: G.P. Putnam's Sons, 1971), p. 43.

11. Robert W. Cherny, *A Righteous Cause: The Life of William Jennings Bryan* (Boston: Little, Brown and Company, 1985), pp. 21–22.

12. David Anderson, *William Jennings Bryan* (Boston: Twayne Publishers, 1981), p. 34.

13. William Allen White, *Masks in a Pageant* (New York: Macmillan Company, 1930), p. 240.

14. Anderson, *William Jennings Bryan*, p. 36.

15. Charles Edward Merriam, *Four American Party Leaders* (New York: Macmillan Company, 1926), pp. 74–75.

16. Bryan, *Memoirs*, pp. 299–300.

17. Merriam, *Four American Party Leaders*, p. 74.

18. Walter Lippmann, *Men of Destiny* (New York: Macmillan Company, 1927), p. 48.

19. Samuel Eliot Morison and Henry Steele Commager, *The Growth of the American Republic*, vol. 2 (New York: Oxford University Press, 1937), p. 240.

20. Quoted in ibid.

21. Quoted in Anderson, p. 46.

22. Quoted in Cherny, *A Righteous Cause*, pp. 34–35.

23. Quoted in Coletta, p. 43.

24. Quoted in Anderson, p. 45.

25. Bryan, *Memoirs*, p. 238.

26. Koenig, *Bryan*, p. 96.

27. Ibid.

28. Willa Cather, "The Personal Side of William Jennings Bryan," *Prairie Schooner* 13 (1949): 334.

29. Quoted in Coletta, p. 54.

30. Ibid., p. 50.

31. Ibid., p. 52.

32. Quoted in Anderson, p. 55.

33. Bryan, *Memoirs*, p. 253.

34. Quoted in John N. Garraty, "The Progressives," *American Heritage* 13 (December 1961): 7.

35. Quoted in Anderson, p. 58.

36. Cather, "The Personal Side of William Jennings Bryan," p. 337.

37. Quoted in Coletta, p. 83.

38. Koenig, p. 121.

39. William Jennings Bryan, *Speeches of William Jennings Bryan*, vol. 1 (New York: Funk and Wagnall's Company, 1913), p. 78.

40. Ibid., p. 81.

41. Ibid., p. 85.

42. Ibid., p. 86.

43. Ibid., pp. 144–45.

44. Charles Morrow Wilson, *The Commoner William Jennings Bryan* (Garden City, NY: Doubleday and Co. 1970), p. 186.

45. Quoted in Cherny, p. 47.

3

"CROSS OF GOLD"

> The strength of a nation does not lie in forts nor in navies, nor yet in great standing armies, but in happy and contented citizens. . . . It is for us of this generation so to perform the duties of citizenship that "a government of the people by the people and for the people shall not perish from the earth."
>
> William Jennings Bryan, Memorial Day Address, 1894

In 1894 William Jennings Bryan was called upon to deliver an address at Arlington National Cemetery as part of the Memorial Day observances. Bryan was more than pleased to be invited. With President Grover Cleveland and many of his cabinet in attendance, Bryan proceeded to deliver a jewel of an address: "With flowers in our hands and sadness in our hearts we stand amid the tombs where the nation's dead are sleeping. It is appropriate that the Chief Executive is here, accompanied by his Cabinet; it is appropriate that the soldier's widow is here, and the soldier's son; it is appropriate that here are assembled in numbers growing less each year, the scarred survivors, Federal and Confederate, of our last great war. . . . The essence of patriotism," he continued, "lies in a willingness to sacrifice for one's country, just as true greatness finds expression, not in blessings enjoyed but in good bestowed." Bryan quoted from Lincoln's Gettysburg Address and asserted, "Every generation leaves to its successor an unfinished work."[1]

As the president and his distinguished guests were leaving Arlington National Cemetery, Secretary of State Walter Q. Gresham, riding in the president's carriage back to Washington, shared his opinion of Bryan with President Cleveland, "We can be sure of one thing," declared Gresham, "while he lives he must be reckoned with as a force in American politics."[2]

Inasmuch as Bryan was looming as a formidable opponent of the president's hard money politics, Cleveland could not have been happy with what he heard.

IN THE POLITICAL WILDERNESS, BRIEFLY

On March 4, 1895, Bryan, now no longer a congressman but still politically ambitious, was out of a job and looking for work. The job he sought was nothing less than the presidency of the United States.

Now thirty-five, and constitutionally eligible to serve as president, he felt that the tide in the affairs of his political life was such as to make the job by no means out of his reach. He determined that, despite his youth, relative inexperience, and failure to be elected United States senator from Nebraska, he had a God-mandated command to pursue the highest political post in the land. How best to remain in the public consciousness remained the question. How to walk the high wire without tipping his hand too soon and betraying his ambitions and how to so organize as to have a fighting chance of winning the Democratic nomination? The path to the presidency, he knew, lay through the Democratic presidential nominating convention to be held in Chicago in 1896. In the meantime, how best to make a living so as to support his family?

Three careers were open to him. He was a lawyer, and as a well-known politician, could, quite likely, attract a considerable clientele. But making a living in the law seemed dull and rather tame for a man who loved the struggles of the political hustings. Instead of the law, he pursued a dual career in journalism and in popular lecturing.

The silver question was rapidly becoming a political issue of widespread interest, and who best to make such an arcane topic understandable to mass audiences than William Jennings Bryan? And he did so tirelessly. With the help of several speakers' bureaus he became a paid lecturer and soon was earning the then considerable sum of $50 per lecture and even, in some cases, as much as $100. Before long, even $200 dollars a lecture was not out of his reach.

Bryan usually agreed to make major paid speeches four or five times a week, but he often spoke for no fee at all. In his public appearances he honed his campaign skills. His speeches were often heralded in a circuslike atmosphere, as "advance men" and brass bands prepared the audience for the "featured" speech of the afternoon or evening. There were hawkers to sell refreshments; souvenirs such as "16-1" paper hats; fireworks to amuse adults and children; and sometimes farm animals to pet, sell, or be judged for excellence. As an evangelist for free silver, he sprinkled his speeches with appealing examples from the work-a-day lives of his audiences. His still youthful, vibrant voice carried, seemingly effortlessly, to the last rows. For nearly three hours he could hold his audience during a sultry summer's day or humid summer evening, and keep them awake, aware, and enthusiastic.

Nor were public speeches the only way William Jennings Bryan sought to keep Americans from forgetting about him. Since 1894, while still a congressman, he continued to write editorials for the *Omaha World-Herald*. Gilbert M. Hitchcock, the publisher, offered to list Bryan as editor-in-chief and publish his political ideas but sought first to get Bryan to invest $25,000 in his newspaper. Bryan, with the aid of his father-in-law could raise only $9,000, but Hitchcock did not insist upon the remainder. As a result, the future presidential candidate had a written as well as oratorical platform from which to express his views.

Bryan drew a small salary for his literary efforts, but while his oratorical skills soared, his efforts in print were remarkable for their dullness. Speaking styles change, and Bryan's speeches when read today seem flamboyant, filled with histrionics and hyperbole, but they can still move the reader. Not so his written efforts, as in his *Memoirs* or in his letters, nor in *The First Battle*, which details his fight for the presidential nomination of the Democratic Party at the 1896 convention. These remain soporific for the reader or researcher and are remarkable for how little they reveal about the man's thoughts; conflicts; desires; ambitions; and relationships with family, friends, political allies, or antagonists. By 1896, however, through his efforts in speaking and writing, he made the silver question his own, kept his name before the public, and made a decent living. Thus, between the close of his congressional career on March 4, 1895, and the presidential nominating convention of the Democratic Party in July 1896, "Bryan showed himself to be more than a brilliant orator; he was a masterful political strategist and tactician, who exploited the trend of events."[3]

Henry Steele Commager and Samuel Eliot Morison noted in their *Growth of the American Republic*, "The year 1894, year of the Wilson tariff and the income tax decision, was the darkest Americans had known for thirty years. Everything conspired to convince the people that democracy was a failure."[4] The corn crop failed, cotton had dropped to six cents a pound, and wheat sold for less than fifty cents a bushel. Half a million workers struck against intolerable conditions. Most of the strikes were unsuccessful, including that of Pullman workers that sparked a general railway strike led by Eugene V. Debs of the American Railway Union. The strikers could not win against the federal troops President Cleveland sent against them.

In 1894, in what was generally described as the Cleveland Depression, ragged armies of the unemployed staged demonstrations and marches on Washington, D.C. The most colorful of these was that led by "General" Jacob S. Coxey, a wealthy owner of a quarry in Massillon, Ohio, who, on Easter Sunday, with his wife and infant son named "Legal Tender" Coxey, led a band of demonstrators in a march on Washington. This ragged "army," including, the journalists who followed them, buoyed their spirits by singing as they marched:

> We're coming, Grover Cleveland,
> five hundred thousand strong,
> We're marching on to Washington
> to right the nation's wrong.

Actually, Coxey and his family road in a carriage while perhaps a maximum of five hundred people marched on Washington, D.C., as a "living petition," to urge Congress to address the depression by issuing noninterest-bearing bonds, and make appropriations for good roads and other public improvements. Eligible to work on these projects would be any unemployed man, who would be paid $1.50 for an eight-hour day. These measures, Coxey believed, would inflate the currency, lower interest rates, provide jobs as a form of workfare, and give America a much-needed system of good country roads and other public improvements.

While the ideas of "Coxey's Army" were not very far different from the works program adopted by President Franklin D. Roosevelt and passed by Congress forty years later, in 1894, these proposals were met with derision, as unemployment continued to be viewed by many, in and out of government, as an act of God. And to add to the humiliation, the marchers in "Coxey's Army" were arrested for trespassing on the capitol lawn.

As lobbyists for industry and banking were never similarly charged and had easy access to the leadership in Congress and the administration when Congress passed a law against trusts, it was only labor unions that were seen to have joined "in restraint of trade." The Supreme Court dismissed a suit against the sugar trust although it controlled 98 percent of the country's sugar refining capacity (*U.S. v. E. C. Knight*, 1895.) The income tax, enacted by Congress with help from Bryan, was declared unconstitutional (*Pollock v. Farmer's Loan and Trust Company*, 1895). The federal courts sent Eugene V. Debs to jail for contempt of court in the Pullman strike. "And, the president sold bonds to Wall Street, while silver, the poor man's friend, was disinherited and disgraced!"[5]

Bryan and much of the distressed nation thought the answer to the Cleveland depression was the monetization of silver at sixteen ounces of silver to one of gold. And Bryan had long since established his bona fides as the chief spokesman for silver. When John Peter Altgeld, governor of Illinois, convened a conference on silver in that state for June 5, 1895, the stage was made to order for Bryan to bask in silver's and the people's reflected light. Governor Altgeld, a formidable politico, a man of presidential potential and superior mental abilities, might have won the presidential nomination of the Democratic Party but was not eligible to run for the presidency because of his German birth. Moreover, because he pardoned those implicated in the Haymarket bomb explosion of 1886, he was viewed by some as an anarchist. He was a formidable adversary also of Grover Cleveland, who sent federal troops to Chicago during the railway strike without prior discussion with him. Altgeld was not initially magnetized by Bryan but was won over in due course.

But as the way was being paved for his ascendancy, Bryan, on June 27, 1895, attended the funeral of Lyman Trumbull, his mentor and role model. And in the fall of 1895, he visited his ailing mother intuitively recognizing that the Christmas of that year was likely to be her last. With four of her five children and five grandchildren around her bedside, the family did, indeed, exchange gifts and enjoyed their last Christmas together. As Bryan described, "Mother sat up in bed and distributed the presents. I never saw her happier. . . . She died ten days before my nomination for the presidency. I went from her funeral to the Chicago convention. Often I have thought of the joy it would have given me if she could have lived to see me nominated."[6]

"THE LOGIC OF THE SITUATION"

In his capacity as editor of the *Omaha World-Herald*, Bryan attended the Republican National Convention, which opened in St. Louis on June 15, 1896. It was a convention dominated by "gold bugs," which, at the bidding of the shrewd political svengali, Marcus Hanna, nominated William McKinley on a gold and high-tariff platform. Bryan's task was to report on the convention to his newspaper and, at the same time, to see what he could do to strengthen the hand of the silver Republicans. Because of Hanna's dictatorial approach, Bryan could do little.

Compared with the disciplined Republican National Convention, the Democrats seemed more of a mob than a political party. Among the train-loads of delegates pouring into Chicago toward the end of June were a host of fringe groups, each hoping to influence the upcoming Democratic National Convention. Prohibitionists, Coxeyites, Debsites, Socialists, Suffragists, and followers of Utopian Socialist Henry Bellamy were all competing for at least a hearing for their special concerns. While the Democratic platform would eventually deal with issues of trusts, the income tax, regulation of railroad rates, banking reform, and the use of the injunction in labor disputes, the issue of silver dominated the convention, as many, if not most, looked upon the wider use of silver as a panacea for needed reform whatever the specific grievance. As historian and Cleveland biographer Allan Nevins wrote, "The Democratic movement toward silver in the last six months before the Chicago convention was like an avalanche: a mere whisper at first, then a half-imperceptible shift in the landscape, and suddenly a roar, a crash, an irresistible cataclysm."[7] Silver became a metaphor for reform and a cure-all for what ailed America. Little wonder, then that participating delegates were "greeted by silver demonstrations that perhaps equaled in pyrotechnics any celebration since 1776."[8]

The Democratic National Convention of 1896, one of the more remarkable conventions in the history of American politics, opened on July 7 in Chicago's Coliseum, which, with a floor space of five and a half acres and a seating capacity of twenty thousand, was the largest permanent exhibition hall in the world. There were 906 delegates, who were seated in a fan shape, in a space approximately one hundred twenty-five feet wide and eighty feet deep divided into five sections. An American flag one hundred feet in length and sixty feet wide hung from the main vestibule of the Coliseum. Adding to the decor were the coats of arms of every state and territory. In a futile attempt to demonstrate that Grover Cleveland was in charge of the convention and the leader of the Democratic Party, the president's portraits were ubiquitous. Besides the numerous flags, twenty thousand yards of streamers were likewise on hand to help create an environment of patriotism and enthusiasm.

Behind the delegates were chairs for official spectators, and among the seemingly unending sea of gallery visitors was Mary Bryan, the wife of the man who would win the nomination. In anticipation that this might be an emotional convention, a functionary charged with ordering chairs for the delegates insisted that ordinary, frail folding chairs would not do. Instead, he specified, "solid, oak-bottomed chairs, that three hundred pound men can jump on all day without weakening them."[9] As yet without electronic amplifying equipment, the hall was the perfect backdrop for a man like Bryan, whose barrel chest and voice training meant that he, almost alone in that convention hall, could clearly be heard in the farthest row despite the din of rowdy delegates.

While the convention's leadership was still dominated by Cleveland's gold Democrats, it was badly split, with the vast majority of the convention delegates supporting some form of bimetallism. The problem for the silverites was to wrest control of the machinery of the convention from Cleveland's acolytes. But President Cleveland stubbornly held to the idea that the convention, still under his nominal leadership, could yet be bent in the direction of sound money. To this end he prevailed upon William C. Whitney, former secretary of the navy and close friend of the president, to cancel a vacation in Europe, travel to Chicago, and lead the charge for gold. Whitney and his party left New York aboard a luxurious three-car train on Thursday afternoon, July 1, and reached Chicago at 4:40 p.m. the following day. En route to Chicago, he and other prominent sound moneymen discussed their chances of steering the convention away from silver and to gold. In the comforting sound of the train whistle, in the regular clatter of the wheels upon tracks of steel, in the euphoria of luxurious accommodations, superb food, and vintage beverages, the group naively brought themselves to believe that they could yet win. Whitney and his party left the train amid a blizzard of posters, buttons, and bunting all in support of silver. Their plans for a sound money rally set for Saturday, July 3, "fizzled out like a wet firecracker before the dawn of July 4."[10]

Little wonder, then, that the *New York Times* of July 7, 1896, blared the headlines:

"The Silver Fanatics are Invincible"

"Wild, Raging, Irresistible Mob Which Nothing can Turn from Its Abominable Foolishness."

"Sound-Money Men Surely Doomed to Defeat."[11]

The *Times* assured its readers, however, that it was "improbable" that the silver people would enjoy their power.[12]

Among the Democratic presidential hopefuls were the front-runner Representative Richard P. "Silver Dick" Bland of Missouri; Claude Matthews, Governor of Indiana; Senators Joseph Blackburn of Kentucky, John Daniel of Virginia, and Stephen White of California; and former Vice President Adlai Stevenson. The raucous "Pitchfork Ben" Tillman of South Carolina also thought he had a chance at the Democratic nomination, as did Governor Horace E. Boies of Iowa.

Bryan showed his political savvy by urging that delegates go to the convention committed to the principle of silver at sixteen to one but not committed to any one candidate. If enough Democrats supported silver, the convention would be wrested from the Cleveland establishment and Bryan would have a chance of winning the nomination for himself. As Bryan's Kansas friend John Atwood attested, "Boies is too new a convert [to silver], Bland is too old and not brilliant enough. Blackburn is too far south; you alone have every quality that goes to make up my ideal of the candidate; you are young, clean and brilliant."[13]

Bland, the best-organized candidate, remained on his farm in Lebanon, Missouri, and let his elaborate organization mount an opulent campaign as befits a front-runner. But this was a mistake in that Bland had too many negatives to overcome. He was considered too old by many, his wife was Catholic, he had lost reelection to the House of Representatives, and he was not acceptable to the Populists.

Bryan, a dark horse, would take no chances. He and the Nebraska silver delegation and their zealous supporters, journeyed from Nebraska to Chicago in a special train of fourteen cars emblazoned: "Keep Your Eye on Nebraska," "The William Jennings Bryan Club," "Nebraska Democracy 16 to 1," and "Nebraska First to Declare 16 to 1." They had come spoiling for a fight.

The first matter to be tackled by the convention when the national party chairman, William F. Harrity, called the noisy delegates to order on July 7 was the choice of a temporary chairman. Following tradition, according to which the national committee chooses the temporary chairman, Senator David B. Hill of New York was nominated. Hill was a prudent choice in that he had been a rival of Cleveland in New York and was believed to be flexible on monetary issues. Still, on balance, Hill was thought to be too closely associated with the gold crowd and so was unacceptable to the silver majority. Instead of Hill, the silverites proposed Senator John W. Daniel, the "Lame Lion" of Virginia. A glorious debate followed, but the silverites would not be swayed, and when the final vote was counted, Daniel received 556 votes, Hill, 349, and Harrity passed the gavel to Daniel.

Although Daniel had been decisively elected, the gold Democrats took some comfort from the fact that the silver Democrats could not yet muster the two-thirds of the 906 delegates needed to nominate a Democratic candidate. But the politically powerful Governor John Peter Altgeld, who led the forty-eight members of his Illinois delegation and was a strong silver advocate, used his muscle to assure the convention that when the serious voting took place, the silverites would have the two-thirds needed to nominate.

Preliminaries continued the next day when the silver-dominated Credentials Committee took the spotlight and center stage. To shore up the strength of silver, the Credentials Committee promptly disqualified four Michigan gold men, so that state was sure to be in the silver column when votes for the presidential nomination were counted. In addition, they replaced the Nebraska gold contingent with the silver men led by William Jennings Bryan, who promptly secured a post on the Resolutions Committee and moved out of sight to devise a pro-silver platform.

On the morning of Thursday, July 9, Arkansas Senator James K. Jones, chairman of the Resolutions Committee, briskly approached the rostrum and read the majority report. Included in the platform was the convention's position on silver. Written by Bryan, it repudiated President Cleveland and demanded "the free and unlimited coinage of both silver and gold at the present legal ratio of 16 to 1." The minority report, however, asserted that bimetallism "would impair contracts, disturb business, diminish the purchasing power of the wages of labor, and inflict irreparable evils on our nation's commerce and industry." The stage was set for a freewheeling debate on the platform.

All other details of the platform were subordinated to the silver planks, which urged that there be no interference with the tariff until the money question was settled. It took a swipe at federal interference in local affairs, an oblique criticism of Cleveland's sending troops into Illinois without Altgeld's permission, as he did in the Pullman strike. The platform demanded (as always) economy in government, a tariff for revenue only, abolition of government by injunction, a federal amendment to the Constitution allowing the imposition of an income tax, improvement of internal waterways, and protection of American labor against foreign labor. It urged the early admission of Oklahoma, Arizona, and New Mexico, all likely silver states; supported the Monroe Doctrine; and opposed a presidential third term—another swipe at Cleveland, should he have the intention of running yet again. The platform was a clear repudiation of Cleveland for his use of the injunction against labor and his hard line on monetary reform, but it was hardly radical and proved more important for what it did not demand. There was no proposal to nationalize the railroads or the banks and no criticisms of commerce, industry, or the accumulation of wealth. In outlook it anticipated in many ways the New Freedom of Woodrow Wilson, the New Deal of Franklin Roosevelt, and the Fair Deal of Harry Truman.

The gold democrats were determined to debate the platform, and under the permanent chairmanship of Senator Stephen White of California, a debate with historical consequences followed. Each side would have an hour and twenty minutes. "Pitchfork Ben" Tillman and Bryan would speak for silver, while Hill, Vilas, and Russell would make a last-ditch try for gold. In his canny way, Bryan arranged to speak last.

William Jennings Bryan could not have garnered the presidential nomination of the Democratic Party in 1896 through oratory alone; neither did he win it during a reckless moment with the unruly convention emotionally carried away by a skilled political evangelist. Instead, like a deft musician, he played the strings of the convention to make of the political cacophony the music he wanted to hear, namely, the convention's support of his presidential ambitions. He had worked effectively during the interlude between his exit from Congress and the July convention, and he had carefully prepared, practiced, and tested his famous speech. But if Bryan was to win the presidential nomination, he had to emerge from the crowded field of "favorite son" candidates, and he had to bring Illinois Governor Altgeld around. By the time the convention met, he had not done so.

Since Altgeld was a potential "presidential-nomination-maker," Bryan courted the Illinois governor with excessive zeal. He had to wean Altgeld away from Bland and convince the governor of his own merits. Bryan sent the governor representative speeches and invited comment, which he might then use to show that Altgeld was favorably disposed to a Bryan candidacy. But Altgeld's response was unhelpful. "These speeches," he wrote Bryan, "will give you a much more enduring and brilliant fame than has been made by most presidents."[14] No warm endorsement could be read into this statement. In the days leading up to the convention, Bryan paid a visit to Chicago to get Altgeld's support. Once again, he failed. "The Governor patted Bryan on the shoulder saying, 'You are young yet. Let Bland have the nomination this time. Your time will come.'"[15]

Bryan was disappointed but not distressed when Altgeld sent him a telegram asserting that in a survey of the "presidential situation" there was "an overwhelming sentiment that you are not available for president at this time."[16] Altgeld assured Bryan that once Democrats had won he would be welcome in a new cabinet. Nor was Bryan deterred when Altgeld raised the possibility of a vice presidential nomination. Altgeld, moreover, confided in his friend William Sulzer, who would later become governor of New York, and to the distinguished attorney Clarence Darrow, that Bryan never really understood the fundamentals of the money question.

The failure to get Altgeld's unqualified support did not derail Bryan's presidential ambitions, however, because Altgeld was suspected by many of being too radical, while those who knew Bryan recognized his innate conservatism. A writer for *Harper's Weekly* described the Illinois governor as a man with a "sharply chiseled French Revolution face, his high ringing voice, his bitter vehemence in manner, and his facility for epithet."[17]

In any event, Bryan would not so easily be brushed off by his failure to get Governor Altgeld's unqualified support. Youthful, brash, egotistical, politically wily, perpetually optimistic, Bryan recognized that none of the other widely mentioned presidential nominees could muster the required two-thirds vote to win the nomination. Bryan, serene and comfortable in his own skin, pursued his destiny. He was, he said to astonished friends, "the logic of the situation."[18]

On the eve of the convention, Alfred Henry Lewis described him in the *New York Journal* and reprinted in the *Literary Digest*:

> Bryan is a person of middle height, strongly, and without giving any one a fatty impression, stockily built. His shoulders are broad enough to excite the approval of a Norse viking; his chest is as deep as that of a race-horse. Nor is he overabundant about the waist, and he looks what he is— a man of perfect health and immense physical power. . . . There is nothing soft, yielding, or effeminate about Bryan, nothing of the willow. His eye is dark, his complexion swarthy, with the British, not the Spanish swarthiness; his nose an emphatic curve, his mouth well-widened and firm, and the whole face founded on a jaw, the very seat of power and as square hewn and indomitable as if cut from the living rock.[19]

"Pitchfork Ben" Tillman opened debate on the party platform. "Dark face suffused with blood, hair unkempt, collar wilted, necktie askew, jacket wrinkled, his pitchfork emblem on one lapel and a Cuban flag on the other, and a strange gleam in his one eye, he glanced from left to right, placed one hand on his hip, rocked on his heels, and threw his head back." He made few friends when he reminded delegates, "I come from a state which is the home of secession." Tillman's references to secession and sectionalism drew hisses from the crowd of delegates. Cries of "Time," and "Boil it down."[20] Tillman's speech on behalf of the platform was ineffective because of its vitriol. Bryan would have to single-handedly move the convention to adopt the platform. Cleveland Democrats, including Senator David Bennett Hill, Senator William F. Vilas, and Governor William E. Russell, spoke against the adoption of the majority report with its advocacy of silver.

The *New York Times* dismissively described Bryan when he mounted the dais to speak in behalf of the Democratic platform: "[He] wore trousers which bagged at the knees, a black alpaca coat, and a low cut vest. A black stud broke the white expanse of his shirt bosom. His low, white collar was partially hidden by a white lawn tie."[21] What the *Times* failed to recognize was that the moment was ripe for making history. "Wait till Bryan speaks," had been widely whispered among the conventioneers. They had waited long enough:

> Mr. Chairman and Gentlemen of the Convention: It would be presumptuous, indeed, to present myself against the distinguished gentlemen to whom you have listened if this were a mere measuring of abilities. But this is not a contest between persons. The humblest citizen in all the land, when clad in the armor of a righteous cause, is stronger than all the hosts of error. I come to speak to you in defense of a cause as holy as the cause of liberty—the cause of humanity. . . .
>
> Approaching the zeal which inspired the crusaders who followed Peter the Hermit, our Silver Democrats went forth from victory unto victory until they are now assembled, not to discuss, not to debate, but to enter up the judgment already rendered by the plain people of this country. . . .
>
> When you (turning to the gold delegates) come before us and tell us that we are about to disturb your business interests, we reply that you have disturbed our business interests by your course.
>
> We say to you that you have made the definition of a business man too limited in its application. The man who is employed for wages is as much a business man as his employer; the attorney in a country town is as much a business man as the corporation counsel in a great metropolis; the merchant at the cross-roads store is as much a business man as the merchant of New York; the farmer who goes forth in the morning and toils all day—and who begins in the spring and toils all summer—and who by the application of brain and muscle to the natural resources of the country creates wealth, is as much a business man as the man who goes upon the board of trade and bets upon the price of grain; the miners who go down a thousand feet into the earth, or climb two thousand feet upon the cliffs, and bring forth from their hiding places the precious metals to be poured into the channels of trade are as much business men as the few financial magnates who in a back room, corner the money of the world. We come to speak for this broader class of business men (wild cheering from the silver delegates). . . .
>
> Ah, my friends, we say not one word against those who live upon the Atlantic coast, but the hardy pioneers who have braved all the dangers of the wilderness, who have made the desert to blossom as the rose— the pioneers away out there (pointing to the West), who rear their children near to Nature's heart, where they can mingle their voices with the voices of the birds—out there where they have erected schoolhouses for the education of their young, churches where they praise their Creator, and cemeteries where rest the ashes of their dead—these people we say,

are as deserving of the consideration of our party as any people in this country. It is for these that we speak. . . . We have petitioned, and our petitions have been scorned; we have entreated, and our entreaties have been disregarded; we have begged, and they have mocked when our calamity came. We beg no longer; we entreat no more; we petition no more. We defy them. . . . What we need is an Andrew Jackson to stand, as Jackson stood, against the encroachments of organized wealth. . . .

We go forth confident that we shall win. . . .

It is the issue of 1776 over again. Our ancestors, when but three millions in number, had the courage to declare their political independence of every other nation; shall we, their descendants, when we have grown to seventy millions, declare that we are less independent than our forefathers? No, my friends, that will never be the verdict of our people. Therefore, we care not upon what lines the battle is fought. If they say bimetallism is good, but that we cannot have it until other nations help us, we reply that, instead of having a gold standard because England has, we will restore bimetallism and then let England have bimetallism because the United States has it. If they dare to come out in the open field and defend the gold standard as a good thing, we will fight them to the uttermost. Having behind us the producing masses of this nation and the world supported by the commercial interests, the laboring interests, and the toilers everywhere, we will answer their demand for a gold standard by saying to them:

You shall not press down upon the brow of labor this crown of thorns, you shall not crucify mankind upon a cross of gold.[22]

With the histrionics of the "political evangelist," as biographer Paolo E. Coletta labeled him, Bryan, with his golden voice, asserted, "You shall not press down upon the brow of labor this crown of thorns." He raised his two hands to the sides of his head, with his fingers spread inward. Bryan moved them slowly down and close to his temples so that the spectators were almost hypnotized into seeing the thorns piercing the brow and the blood trickling from the wounds.

When he said, "You shall not crucify mankind upon a cross of gold." Bryan's hands left his head and followed his arms out at right angles to the body. There he stood the crucified man in the flesh! He retained his position for about five seconds. Then he placed his arms at his sides and took a step backward. With the delegates transfixed and profoundly silent, he started toward his seat. The awkward silence, however, did not last.

By the time police escorted him to his seat, the first catcalls and Indian war whoops could be heard. "The demonstration for Bryan," declared the *New York Times*, "struck terror to the hearts of the Bland and Boies and

McLean and Stevenson Boomers." His speech "was a signal for an avalanche of cheers which speedily developed into a measureless outburst."[23] On the shoulders of some gleeful delegates Bryan was paraded through the convention hall while others screamed, "Down with gold!" "Down with the hooked-nosed Shylocks of Wall Street! Down with the Christ-killing gold bugs."[24] Little wonder that American Jews were convinced that Democrats as well as Populists were anti-Semitic. Did Bryan care?

While the outnumbered gold Democrats stonily observed the utter defeat of their cause, the convention proceeded in orderly fashion with the adoption of the platform. When it was over, the platform was overwhelmingly adopted by a vote of 628 ayes to 301 nays, and Bryan's potential as the nominee of the Democratic Party could not be ignored.

But would Bryan be the nominee? Bryan was certain of it, but others were not. When Murat Halstead, a prominent reporter, called William McKinley to tell him that Bryan would be nominated, the Republican nominee replied, "That's rot." Perhaps wishful thinking got the better of Governor Altgeld, who wrongheadedly believed that by the time nominations began the following day the Bryan bubble would "be as dead as a door nail."

Bryan had packed into that speech every oratorical and debater's trick he had learned in college. He spoke for the Democratic platform with a magnificent voice and earnestness of manner. He was not plagued by doubt, nor, for that matter, bothered too much by the facts. He alone was among the righteous. Those who disagreed were not so much wrong as evil. Altgeld, still carrying the banner for Bland, was impressed, "That is the greatest speech I ever listened to. I don't know but its effect will be to nominate him." Yet he later turned to the distinguished attorney Clarence Darrow and asked, "I have been thinking over Bryan's speech. What did he say anyhow?"[25]

"WHAT DID HE SAY?"

What Bryan said is on the record. But what his listeners heard depended upon the political baggage they brought to the convention. Conservative Democrats found Bryan's speech too radical, nearly bolted the convention, and briefly thought of forming a third party. In Bryan's cry for "free silver" they saw a popular movement for fairness in the workplace and marketplace going too far and becoming too hostile to people of property. The *New York Times* scoffed, "Bryan's chief qualifications as an orator is his splendid voice.

His views on public affairs are those of a wild theorist filled with a desire for personal advancement. No better evidence of the diseased condition of the minds of the silver delegates could be desired than that furnished to-day by their endorsements of Bryan's utterances."[26]

To the poet-reporter Edgar Lee Masters, however, Bryan's speech marked "the beginning of a changed America." Masters thought that for the first time since Andrew Jackson, a major political party identified itself with the poor and was prepared to wage a political campaign against privilege, power, and financial oligarchs.[27]

Josephus Daniels of North Carolina, journalist and close confidant of Bryan, found that Bryan stirred the hearts of men. "They believed that Bryan was a young David with his sling, who had come to slay the giants that oppressed the people and they felt that a new day had come and, with it, a new leader. Clean of limb, clean of heart, and clean of mind, he was a vital figure . . . like the others, I had been swept away on a tide of hero worship."[28]

To Willis Abbott, the journalist from William Randolph Hearst's *New York Journal*, the high point of Bryan's speech was not the eloquent peroration, but the cry of defiance: "We defy them!" To Abbott this was a fist shaken at Tammany and all it stood for, some of whose representatives were in the audience, including Richard Croker, Tammany boss of New York, and it was a challenge to the plutocrats and monopolists, some of whom, such as August Belmont and William C. Whitney, were also in the audience. This defiance, Abbott declared, came right from the orator's heart.[29]

Precisely because what his listeners took away from his speech depended on the political spectrum from which they came, what Bryan said mattered. What he sought to do at the convention was to stir up an emotional tide in his quest for the nomination. And this he did. It mattered little that some thought he was a latter-day David taunting Goliath and others thought he was a wild-eyed zealot whose time had not yet come. What did matter was that delegates to the convention were talking about Bryan and were no longer inquiring, "Who the hell is Bryan?" With each passing hour, he thought that he might just pull off the upset of the century and win the nomination. And he did.

"SAUL AMONG THE ISRAELITES"

Following his "Cross of Gold" speech, the outburst of enthusiasm among the delegates and in the gallery lasted for nearly half an hour, and because some delegates were urging that the nominating balloting begin at once, William Jennings Bryan could have had the nomination of the Democratic Party that very night. Again, he shrewdly refrained from pressing his advantage, as he recognized that following his nomination there would be a campaign to conduct and the postponement would test the depth of his support among the delegates. Some of Bryan's supporters thought he was making a mistake inasmuch as Richard Bland still had the support of John Peter Altgeld and was still the front-runner. But Bryan risked the delay. It was not until 8:30 p.m. of the day following Bryan's hypnotic speech that the actual nominations began.

An obscure delegate, Henry T. Lewis from Georgia, who initially had been assigned the chore of seconding the nomination for Bland, started the surge that led to the nomination of Bryan. "I do not intend to make a speech," Lewis declared, "but simply, in behalf of the delegation from the State of Georgia, wish to place in nomination as Democratic candidate for the Presidency of the United States a distinguished citizen, William Jennings Bryan who has stood on the field of battle among the leaders of the Democratic hosts like Saul among the Israelites, head and shoulders above all the rest."[30] Lewis was out of order, but the enthusiasm with which his words were met surely anticipated the final outcome. Journalist Edgar Howard, an admirer of Bryan, said of the Lewis remarks, "[I]t was the prettiest nominating speech of the day. It was short, pointed, patriotic, happily free from the objectionable features peculiar to the average nominating speech."[31]

The names of seven candidates were eventually put forth. When balloting began "Silver" Dick Bland led, with Governor Horace Boies of Iowa closely following. On the second ballot, Bland moved up but Bryan overtook Boies. On the fourth ballot, the Illinois delegation caucused and by five votes decided in favor of Bryan. Governor Altgeld reluctantly agreed to vote for Bryan and, bound by the unit rule, the forty-eight-member Illinois delegation broke the logjam. Bryan moved into the lead and Bland withdrew. Thus was the way paved for a stampede to Bryan, and his nomination was declared unanimous.

The vice presidential nomination was essentially an afterthought. With Bryan actively participating in a caucus to choose the nominee, men like Boies and Bland were bandied about but neither expressed an interest. It soon became clear that what Bryan needed to balance the ticket was a man of wealth, since Bryan had relatively little, and he needed a man of conservative bent to attract gold democrats. Arthur Sewell, a sixty-one-year-old multimillionaire shipbuilder from Maine, soon appeared to be a reasonable

Figure 3.1. William Jennings Bryan and Arthur Sewall, Democratic nominees for president and vice president, 1896. Library of Congress, RN: LCUSCZ2-6263.

choice. He sat on the board of many corporations and was a director of the Maine Central Railway. Although his background was in the corporate sector, he was a man with a public conscience in behalf of social justice and believed in silver as a way of helping the less fortunate. He also believed that bimetallism would help America out of the depression in which it was still bogged down. With Bryan's enthusiastic support, Sewall won the vice presidential nomination on the fifth ballot.

THE ONE-HUNDRED-DOLLAR NOMINATION

With the convention over, William and Mary Bryan checked out of their hotel. Bryan's penchant for strict economy had been served as he chortled that he had spent but one hundred dollars to secure the nomination of the Democratic Party for the presidency of the United States. If money did not win the nomination for Bryan, what did?

A 1953 poll of 277 professors of American history or government ranked the "Cross of Gold" speech among the fifty most significant documents in American history.[32] In his biography of Lyndon Johnson, Robert Caro compares the impact of Hubert Humphrey's civil rights speech on the 1948 National Convention of the Democratic Party only to William Jennings Bryan's "Cross of Gold" oration at the Democratic National Convention of half a century before.[33] There can be little doubt that Bryan's still famous "Cross of Gold" speech of July 9, 1896, made him a front-runner among potential nominees of the Democratic Party. However, many other factors went into the making of the candidate.

For one thing, Bryan, although initially a dark horse as a presidential nominee, was by no means unknown. Quite the contrary. He had toiled in the vineyards of state silver organizations and worked with the American Bimetallic Union. Moreover, as a means of making a living by giving speeches along the stops of the chautauqua circuit, he kept his name before the public; made many influential friends; established his niche as a politician devoted to silver; and practiced and sharpened the words, metaphors, and cadences that eventually found their way into the speech that earned him a leadership role in the Democratic Party. In making his rounds of the speaking circuit, giving free and paid political speeches, he demonstrated a grasp of practical politics and established himself among Democrats and Populists as an advocate for the free and unlimited coinage of silver. Those who recognized his talents and his potential for leadership sought to tie their tails to the high-flying kite of his soaring ambition.

As Bryan recalled in his *Memoirs*, his "Cross of Gold" speech was part extemporaneous, part spontaneous, and part well-planned and pretested many times before he used it at the Democratic National Convention on July 9, 1896. The speech was, in fact, a pastiche of remarks he already had made literally thousands of times, before audiences large and small, in and out of Congress. He had practiced opening and closing lines; framed appropriate metaphors; and rehearsed voice projection, dramatic pauses, body language, and hand and arm gestures, trying them out in private and often before Mary Bryan as his perceptive critic and admirer.

In his remarks in Congress against protectionism, for example, Bryan had used the same opening lines as in his "Cross of Gold" speech: "If this were a mere contest in oratory no one would be presumptuous to dispute the prize with the distinguished gentleman from New York . . . but clad in the armor of a righteous cause I dare expose myself to the shafts of his genius."[34] In the early afternoon of December 22, 1894, Bryan had taken the floor to oppose Cleveland's plan for a large issue of gold bonds. In that speech he had asserted, "I shall not help crucify mankind upon a cross of gold. I shall not aid the pressing down upon the bloody brow of labor the crown of thorns!"[35] He recalls also using the "cross of gold" metaphor only a week before his famous speech, during a debate at Crete, Nebraska, in which he took the side of silver while his opponent, John Irish of Iowa, supported gold.

To win the presidential nomination of the Democratic Party Bryan "built shrewdly."[36] He had mastered the arcane rules of the Democratic Convention so that he was able to save for himself a coveted place in the seemingly unending roll call of those wishing to address the convention. He was canny enough to resist the opportunity of being temporary chairman of the convention, a place that would have assured him a significant speaking opportunity, and cleverly became, instead, the last speaker to urge the adoption of the political platform of the Democratic Party.

As Bryan recalled in his *Memoirs* twenty-five years after the "Cross of Gold" speech:

> From the first sentence the audience was with me. My voice reached the uttermost parts of the hall, which is a great advantage in speaking to an assembly like that.
>
> I shall never forget the scene upon which I looked. I believe it is unrivaled in any convention ever held in our country. The audience seemed to rise and sit down as one man. At the close of a sentence it would rise and shout, and when I began upon another sentence the room was as still as a church. There was inspiration in the faces of the delegates. . . .
>
> The audience acted like a trained choir—in fact, I thought of a choir as I noted how instantaneously and in unison they responded to each point I made.[37]

In the election campaign, Bryan's first task was to unite the forces of silver under his standard. The journal *National Bimetallist* led the charge in behalf of Bryan and the free coinage of silver at the ratio of sixteen ounces of silver to one of gold. On July 12, the executive committee of the Bimetallic League endorsed Bryan enthusiastically, prompting Senator Henry M. Teller, the leader of the silver Republicans, to remark, "I consider the nomination an exceptionally strong one. Bryan is an able man of high character, a strong friend of silver, and close to the people. He will make an excellent president."[38] Although other silver Republicans were not as enthusiastic about Bryan, he managed to bring several under his capacious political tent.

On Wednesday, July 22, 1896, a ragtag group of fourteen hundred reformers and cranks, silver Republicans and silver Democrats, began arriving in St. Louis for the convention of the People's Party. Some came on foot. Most prepared to stay in shabby hotels as they could afford no better. Many took advantage of the nickel lunches and dinners that were available at cheap restaurants. With Palmetto fans they tried to stir the still air, and with the help of a big-voiced delegate from Wisconsin who served as a "repeater," they sought to overcome the poor acoustics in the convention hall.[39] Populists all, they had come prepared to nominate a candidate who was more than a flashy silverite but one who would endorse a Populist platform.

The Populist platform of 1896 included much that had been adopted in the Omaha Platform of 1892 and included sympathy for Cuban independence and criticism of the denial of voting opportunities to black Americans. Government ownership of railroads and telegraph systems, but not telephones, was advocated, as was reform of the nation's banking and monetary system. The platform urged the direct election of the president, vice president, and United States senators. And it had the courage to assert that "in times of great industrial depression, idle labor should be employed on public works as far as practicable."[40]

Just as it was possible for some politicians such as vice presidential candidate Sewall or the Republican Teller to be pro-silver but not necessarily for economic and political reform, so it was possible for some to be for the latter but not be especially supportive of free and unlimited coinage of silver. One such was socialist Henry Demarest Lloyd, who asserted that "free silver was the 'cow-bird' of the reform movement." It was his belief that the silver supporters waited until reform had built its nest and then placed its own eggs in the reform nest that others had built and pushed out other aspects of reform.[41]

Yet free and unlimited coinage of silver had been on the agenda of agrarian reformers since 1870 and by the presidential campaign of 1896 remained an important aspect of economic reform. "Neither the leaders of the Populists nor the Bryan Democrats initiated the clamor for free and unlimited coinage of silver, rather they were led by popular sentiment to emphasize the issue."[42] Populists were, therefore, divided on how much of their reform agenda should be subordinated to the demands of silverites. Populists from the West, where mining of silver was an important industry, far more than others, placed their hopes on silver and would eagerly forego other aspects of economic reform. Southern Populists were more interested in economic reform but saw silver as the wedge issue permitting other reforms to be adopted. The Populists understood well enough that should there be more than one candidate supporting silver, a united Republican Party strongly supporting gold would win and economic reform would die. However, if the Populists were simply to rubber-stamp the candidates of the Democrats, did that not mean the end of an independent People's Party? And was Bryan enough of a reformer to merit the nomination of the Populists? The dilemma before the Populists was whether they could dare tie their reform agenda to Bryan's high-flying kite of silver. To many Populists, Bryan seemed a "spoiler." It would not be easy for Bryan to mobilize the Populists on behalf of his candidacy.

Sewall, Bryan's vice-presidential running mate, for example, was a silver man. But he was also a plutocrat and an industrialist. He was a man who stood for nearly everything the Populists found abhorrent and corrupt with corporate America. Inasmuch as Sewall was clearly unacceptable to the Populists, the convention delegates on Saturday, July 25, 1896, first nominated their hero, Thomas Watson of Georgia, as vice president. They then reluctantly joined the bandwagon for Bryan and nominated him for president. Among the Populists, Bryan won the votes of 1,042 delegates, while 321 went to Colonel S. F. Norton. Although Bryan won the Populist nomination handily enough, the fact is that the arranged marriage between Bryan and the Populists was only a marriage of convenience.

THE "GREAT COMMONER" CAMPAIGNS

The presidential election of 1896 took place against a backdrop of a severe depression that had begun three years earlier, to which President Cleveland seemed unwilling or unable to respond. Thus, he did not respond to high unemployment, low farm prices, or the bankruptcy of railroads and the collapse of banks. About a quarter of the nation's railroads claimed bankruptcy, as did six hundred banks and sixteen thousand businesses. Unemployment ranged from one to three million and in Chicago one-sixth of its labor force was out of work.[43]

Bryan nevertheless approached his campaign for the presidency with his customary cautious optimism. But circumstances had to fall his way. According to historian Robert W. Cherny, "*If* he could hold the ethnic core of the Middle western Democratic Party, *if* he could attract economically distressed farmers and workers, *if* southern Democrats and Populists could set aside local differences during the campaign, *if* the western mining states would deliver votes as anticipated, then he would win. Early in October, a survey by the *New York Herald* indicated that Bryan held 237 electoral votes, a clear majority."[44]

At Mark Hanna's urging, William McKinley conducted his campaign for the presidency from the "front porch" of his home in Canton, Ohio. William Jennings Bryan, by contrast, traveled more than eighteen thousand miles by train, campaigned eighteen hours a day, and made thousands of speeches at whistle-stops throughout the country. He often carried his own luggage and frequently walked from the railroad station to his destination. He was tempted to take advantage of a generous offer from a major railroad to make a comfortable, private Pullman car available, but Willis Abbott, Bryan's friend from the Hearst newspapers who was present when the offer was made, interjected his advice: "Mr. Bryan, you should not accept this offer. You are the Great Commoner, the people's candidate, and it would not do to accept favors from the great railroad corporations." Bryan readily agreed. This decision took a toll on his health, and he paid a stiff price in discomfort endured, and efficiency compromised. But the sobriquet "Great Commoner" was forever associated with William Jennings Bryan.[45]

As the campaign took its toll of Bryan's ability to campaign effectively the national committee did provide Bryan with a special railroad car named, ironically, "The Idler." But Bryan was by no means idle. He made a triumphal tour through Illinois, but as he moved east, his audiences became more hostile. The official launching pad for his campaign was to be on August 10, 1896, in Madison Square Garden where he was officially to accept the presidential nomination of the Democratic Party. With a night's rest, he was on the hustings the next morning. "Night after night he rolled across the country, prayed to his God kneeling on the floor of his sleeping-car, slept soundly, and arose refreshed to address himself, during twenty or thirty halts, to as many as 100,000 persons a day. He spoke spontaneously, with his wonted earnestness and power, and often with native wit. To the crowds he appeared 'godlike' as he placed himself at the head of the greatest rising of the poorer classes and the equally numerous middle classes which the country had ever known."[46] He visited twenty-six states, more than two hundred fifty cities, and addressed more than five million people. He gave three thousand formal speeches, and gave thirty of them in one day. In addition, whenever the train stopped and people gathered he made innumerable informal remarks.[47] To the hog farmers of Ohio and the wheat growers of Illinois, he decried mortgage foreclosures and castigated the legislators who had not come to the farmers' rescue. In St. Paul, Minnesota, where the railroad baron Jim Hill ruled his empire, he attacked railroad wreckers and coal barons. He assured small-town merchants that their prosperity would grow to the extent that bimetallism was adopted. He denounced the use of the army to break strikes and curried favor with labor unions by opposing the injunction, which limited labor's right to bargain collectively and to strike if necessary.[48]

He did, however, make a major mistake in the speech in New York City when he formally accepted the nomination of the Democratic Party. Recognizing that the backdrop of New York City was a hostile environ-

Figure 3.2. Cartoon showing William Jennings Bryan touting 16 to 1 from the back of his campaign train. "Blowing himself around the country," Puck, September 16, 1896. Library of Congress, RN: LC-USC62-95402.

ment, he prepared carefully. To be sure that his support of silver was not perceived as a crackpot idea, he cogently marshaled his silver views in a lawyer-like argument. He assumed that his task in New York was to convince his sophisticated listeners that he was neither a socialist nor a revolutionary nor a political maverick nor a starry-eyed idealist. "Our campaign," he said in New York, "has not for its object the reconstruction of society. . . . [W]e do not propose to transfer the rewards of industry to the lap of indolence. Property is and will remain the stimulus to endeavor and the compensation for toil."[49]

Nor was he above currying favor with New York's Tammany Hall. "Great is Tammany!" he extravagantly announced, "And Croker is its Prophet."[50] Richard Croker, Tammany boss, and Bryan would be the odd couple of the 1896 and 1900 campaigns. The relationship started out coolly enough, with Croker admitting that in 1896 his initial reaction to Bryan was hostile, but as he listened to his speeches and as the depression deepened, be became a convert. As one biographer described it, "Before the love-making between Croker and Bryan was over it was to cause considerable embarrassment to the anti-Tammany Nebraska leader, but it was a genuine attachment as long as Croker stayed in public life, and Bryan was not ashamed of it."[51]

Perhaps intimidated by New York's size and reputation and sensitive to the fact that he felt he was but a country politician in the heart of "enemy"

Figure 3.3.   Literal stump speech. Nebraska State Historial Society.

country, where his hostile audience might not respond favorably to the rhetoric of an evangelist, he read his remarks so that the press would not distort them. He should have been brief, especially as New York City was sweltering in ninety-degree heat, but he delivered himself of a dull, two-hour speech. As the *Washington Post* noted, "It was not the speech that should have been delivered. . . . It was too long, it was too academic, it was too metaphysical. . . . He missed the opportunity. Fifteen or twenty minutes of breezy, epigrammatic eloquence, a dozen graceful effective gestures, and one eagle's flight of peroration would have transformed that dismal failure into an apotheosis."[52] Little wonder that he made few converts in what was not yet called the "Big Apple."

But the unenthusiastic reaction in New York was the exception rather than the rule. In middle America he was received with warmth and eagerness. More than seven hundred babies were named for Bryan during the year, including three sets of triplets who were named, "William," "Jennings," and "Bryan."[53] Bryan ran his campaign with the zeal of an evangelical, casting his opponents as evil and his supporters as good. His was the voice of a missionary ordained to bring the word of silver to those who did not yet believe. But it is by no means clear that this style of speaking evoked a response among immigrant newcomers or the hoi polloi of urban America.

Election Day, November 3, 1896, "was an ideal autumn day throughout the whole of America."[54] Bryan slept a little later than usual, but by late morning Mr. and Mrs. William Jennings Bryan voted in Precinct F of the Fifth Ward of Lincoln, Nebraska, in a firehouse. The candidate was said to be a "model of serenity."[55] But he grew tired as the day wore on and retired for the night at 6:30 p.m. It was left to Mary Bryan to bring her husband the more important bulletins by Western Union and Postal Telegraph. By 11 p.m., he was convinced that he had lost.

"As the evening progressed," Bryan later wrote, "the indications pointed more and more strongly to defeat and by eleven o'clock I realized that, while the returns from the country might change the result, success of my opponent was more than probable. Confidence resolved itself into doubt, and doubt, in turn gave place to resignation. While the compassionless current sped hither and thither, carrying its message of gladness to foe and its message of sadness to friend, there vanished from my mind the vision of a president in the White House, perplexed by the cares of state, and in the contemplation of the picture of a citizen by his fireside, free from official responsibility, I fell asleep."[56]

Although turnout on election day was massive, with four out of five eligible voters going to the polls, including women voters in Wyoming and Colorado, he was right in anticipating defeat. In Iowa, Illinois, Indiana, Ohio, and Michigan, turnout of eligible voters reached 95 percent. Of the votes cast, 6.5 million, more than any previous candidate had ever won, were for Bryan. But 7.1 million votes were cast for McKinley, who won twenty-three states and 271 electoral votes while Bryan won twenty-two states and 171 electoral votes. A remarkably good showing to be sure, but not good enough.

Late on the morning of November 5, Bryan wrote the first message of congratulations a presidential candidate ever sent his victorious opponent: "Senator Jones has just informed me that the returns indicate your election, and I hasten to extend my congratulations. We have submitted the issues to the American people and their will is law." McKinley wired Bryan: "I acknowledge the receipt of your courteous message of congratulations and thanks, and beg you will receive my best wishes for your health and happiness."[57]

A Kansas editor declared, "McKinley won because the Republicans had persuaded the middle class . . . that a threat to the gold standard was a threat to their prosperity."[58] During the last days of his campaign, Bryan had a severe cold, which the pressures of electioneering made impossible for him to overcome. Yet it was not the cold that had defeated him. It was, instead, employers coercing their employees, lenders their creditors, and ministers their congregations. Yale students heckled him for so long and so vigorously that he could not speak. When President E. Benjamin Andrews of Brown University invited Bryan to speak on his campus, he was fired by his board. Steel magnate Andrew Carnegie disparagingly called him a "conjurer."

Among representative examples of coercion was that of the president of a large factory in Steinway, New York, who assembled his employees on the night before the election and said: "Men, vote as you please, but if Bryan is elected tomorrow the whistle will not blow Wednesday morning."[59]

Or as reported in the *Morning News* of Wilmington, Delaware: "The Harlan and Hollingsworth Company of this city have received a contract for a boat costing $300,000. One clause in the contract provides that in the event of Bryan's election the contract will be canceled. If the boat is built here, $160,000 of its cost will be paid to Wilmington workmen for wages. The corporation wanting the boat feel that it would not be justified in having it constructed if Bryan should become president."[60]

In addition to coercion, there was corruption. John Peter Altgeld, for example, asserted in a letter to Chairman Jones, "There were fully 100,000 fraudulent votes counted in Illinois this fall . . . the states of Indiana, Kentucky and California were stolen."[61] Election irregularities were rampant in Ohio and Indiana. Josephus Daniels was convinced that Bryan was the victim of fraud on a scale similar to that which kept Samuel J. Tilden out of the White House twenty years earlier. Bryan took a more objective view of his defeat. "I have borne the sins of Grover Cleveland," he said. But political postmortems, of which there were many, concluded that while there was widespread fraud, McKinley would have, nevertheless, eked out a victory.

During the campaign Bryan was regarded by many who should know better as an anarchist, a radical, and a "crackpot"—a man too dangerous to entrust with the levers of presidential authority. Bryan was also defeated since he was largely viewed as a stand-in for Altgeld, perceived by conservatives as a dangerous radical and a potentially violent anarchist.[62] Bryan was often whipsawed by his two vice presidential running mates, who did little to help. Watson was too radical for Democratic conservatives, and Sewall was too conservative for Democratic reformers.

The clergy were particularly hostile to Bryan, "The platform," declared Reverend Cortland Myers in Brooklyn, "was made in hell." The Reverend Thomas Dixon Jr. at the Academy of Music in New York denounced Bryan as "a mouthing, slobbering demagogue, whose patriotism was all in his jawbone."[63]

The McKinley campaign was well organized by Mark Hanna and financed by American industrialists, who proved to be generous. It is estimated that the Republican expenditures at national, state, and local levels was between ten to sixteen million dollars. William Jennings Bryan had but three hundred thousand, a sum supplemented modestly at state and local levels.[64]

Bryan had little time for remorse or second-guessing. Instead, he proceeded with dispatch to gather material for his book about his campaign. While Bryan could and did make inspiring speeches, he was dull as a writer. Yet his book, *The First Battle*, sold two hundred thousand copies. And as the title suggests, in Bryan's mind the fight for silver was not yet over.

NOTES

1. William Jennings Bryan, *Speeches of William Jennings Bryan*, vol. 2 (New York: Funk and Wagnall's Company, 1913), pp. 384–88.

2. Quoted in Louis W. Koenig, *Bryan: A Political Biography of William Jennings Bryan* (New York: G.P. Putnam's Sons, 1971), p. 147.

3. Ibid., pp. 156–57.

4. Samuel Eliot Morison and Henry Steele Commager, *The Growth of the American Republic*, vol. 2 (New York: Oxford University Press, 1937), p. 254.

5. Ibid., p. 255.

6. William Jennings Bryan and Mary Baird Bryan, *The Memoirs of William Jennings Bryan* (Chicago: John C. Winston Company, 1925), p. 31.

7. Allan Nevins, *Grover Cleveland: A Study in Courage* (New York: Dodd, Mead and Company, 1932), p. 689.

8. Ibid.

9. Quoted in Koenig, *Bryan*, p. 182.

10. Paul W. Glad, *McKinley, Bryan, and the People* (New York: J. B. Lippincott Company, 1964), p. 132.

11. *New York Times*, July 7, 1896.

12. Ibid.

13. Quoted in Koenig, p. 181.

14. Quoted in ibid., p. 169.

15. Quoted in ibid., p. 170.

16. Quoted in Harvey Wish, "John Peter Altgeld and the Background of the Campaign of 1896," *Mississippi Valley Historical Review* 24 (March 1938): 515.

17. "The Democratic Convention," *Harper's Weekly* 40 (July 18, 1896): 714.

18. Quoted in Koenig, p. 192.

19. *Literary Digest* 12 (August 8, 1896): 452.

20. Paolo E. Coletta, *William Jennings Bryan*, vol. 1, *Political Evangelist, 1860–1908* (Lincoln: University of Nebraska Press, 1964), p. 135.

21. *New York Times*, July 10, 1896.

22. Excerpted from William Jennings Bryan, *The First Battle*, vol. 1 (Port Washington, NY: The Kennikat Press, 1971, c1896), pp. 199–206.

23. *New York Times*, July 10, 1896.

24. Coletta, *William Jennings Bryan*, vol. 1, p. 141.

25. Quoted in Koenig, p. 199.

26. *New York Times*, July 10, 1896.

27. Coletta, p. 148.

28. Quoted in Koenig, p. 199.

29. Willis J. Abbott, *Watching the World Go By* (Boston: Little, Brown and Company, 1934), p. 167.

30. Quoted in Bryan, *The First Battle*, p. 213.

31. William E. Christensen, ed., "The Cross of Gold Refurbished: A Contemporary Account of the 1896 Democratic Convention," *Nebraska History* 77 (Fall/Winter 1996): 122.

32. Robert W. Cherny, *A Righteous Cause: The Life of William Jennings Bryan* (Boston: Little, Brown and Company, 1985), p. 61.

33. Robert Caro, *The Years of Lyndon Johnson: Master of the Senate* (New York: Alfred A. Knopf, 2002), p. 445.

34. Quoted in Charles Morrow Wilson, *The Commoner William Jennings Bryan* (Garden City, NY: Doubleday & Company, 1970), pp. 188–89.

35. Quoted in ibid., p. 190.

36. James A. Barnes, "Myths of the Bryan Campaign," *Mississippi Valley Historical Review* 34 (December 1947): 379.

37. Bryan, *Memoirs*, p. 115.

38. *New York Tribune*, July 12, 1896.

39. Robert F. Durden, "The Cow-Bird Grounded: The Populist Nomination of Bryan and Tom Watson in 1896," *Mississippi Valley Historical Review* 50 (December 1963): 400.

40. Quoted in Gene Clanton, *Congressional Populism and the Crisis of the 1890s* (Lawrence: University of Kansas Press, 1998), p. 113.

41. Durden, "The Cow-Bird Grounded," pp. 397–98.

42. Ibid., p. 413.

43. See Cherny, *A Righteous Cause*, p. 64.

44. Ibid., p. 68.

45. Koenig, p. 211. See also Coletta, p. 152. However, Abbott recalls this conversation as happening at the beginning of the 1900 campaign. "I wouldn't do that. You neither want to be under obligation to a railroad or travel in luxury. You must be like William Pitt, 'The Great Commoner,'" p. 242.

46. Matthew Josephson, *The Politicos, 1865–1896* (New York: Harcourt, Brace and Company, 1938), p. 690.

47. Cherny, p. 66.

48. Josephson, *The Politicos*, p. 690.

49. William Jennings Bryan, *The First Battle*, vol. 2 (Port Washington, NY: Kennikat Press, 1971, c1896), p. 316.

50. Quoted in Josephson, p. 689.

51. Wayne C. Williams, *William Jennings Bryan* (New York: G.P. Putnam's Sons, 1936), p. 220.

52. Quoted in "Bryan's Speech of Acceptance," *Literary Digest* 12 (August 22, 1896): 516.

53. Cherny, p. 67.

54. Williams, *William Jennings Bryan*, p. 191.

55. Koenig, p. 251.

56. Bryan, *The First Battle*, vol. 2, p. 605.

57. Quoted in Coletta, vol. 1, p. 190.

58. Quoted in Cherny, p. 70.

59. Quoted in Williams, p. 195.

60. Ibid.

61. Quoted in Paul W. Glad, *McKinley, Bryan, and the People* (Philadelphia and New York: J. B. Lippincott Company, 1966), p. 196.

62. See Koenig, pp. 252–54.

63. Quoted in ibid., p. 243.

64. Cherny, p. 65.

4

"I HAVE KEPT THE FAITH"

You may dispute whether I have fought a good fight, you may dispute whether I have finished the course, but you cannot deny that I have kept the faith.

William Jennings Bryan at the
1904 Democratic Convention

In 1896, William Jennings Bryan was but thirty-six years old and head of a great political party. Although he had lost what he called "the first battle," his political future should have been bright, and his political trajectory should have taken an upward course. But 1896 marked the zenith of his potential, and the remaining twenty-nine years of his life were ones of defeat, decline, and frustration. He would serve for sixteen years as the leader of the Democratic Party but would get the credit for little, either during his political lifetime or in the annals of history. What is remarkable is that he seemed to take disappointments without losing his essentially sunny disposition, optimistic outlook, and faith in God and the American people.

In 1896 Bryan spoke for a great many, perhaps even for a majority of Americans, in the stand he took for bimetallism and for the principle that political leadership requires, above all, an ability to listen to the will of the people, to interpret their needs, to lean against the winds of adversity that altogether too often rage against them, and to do something to ease their burdens. But increasingly his voice became less relevant. Because he had staked out an impossible position—namely, conservatism in religion and activism in politics—he would "inherit the wind," that is, the opprobrium of people of faith who did not trust his activism as well as the hostility of people of action who were skeptical that his was the voice that would carry them to victory.

But in 1896, undeterred by defeat, sympathetic to the cause of a Cuba under the heel of Spanish oppression, Bryan continued to seek out useful political roles to play.

"CUBA LIBRE"

In 1925 William Jennings Bryan, the Great Commoner and greater man of peace, was buried among the military heroes at Arlington National Cemetery. What had he done to merit such an honor?

Early in the morning of February 16, 1898, the USS *Maine* blew up in the harbor of Havana, Cuba, and 258 of the crew were killed. Whether it was an internal explosion from aging equipment on the vessel, or whether the explosion was from a submerged explosive device planted by Spanish or Cuban terrorists, was uncertain. However, the "sinking of the *Maine*" rallied Americans to aid Cuban rebels in their struggle to end Spanish tyranny in Cuba, while also providing an opportunity for America to join the parade of imperial powers and stake a claim for itself beyond the continent. The opportunity to thrust America on the world scene was fanned by the sensational journalism practiced by William Randolph Hearst in the *New York Journal* and Joseph Pulitzer in the *New York World*.

On April 25, 1898, when Congress declared war on Spain, William Jennings Bryan in New York led the cheers of a crowd of more than twenty thousand people.[1] But his judgment to support McKinley in the war against Spain derived not from any spirit of expansionism, but from the certitude that it was America's obligation to help the oppressed of an island nation so close to its shores. At a Jefferson Day dinner in Washington, D.C., Bryan declared, "Humanity demands that we should act. . . . A neighbor must sometimes incur danger for a neighbor, and a friend for a friend."[2] To prove that the war was not for imperial enhancement or an exercise to further America's "manifest destiny," Congress adopted, and the vast majority of Americans approved, the Teller Amendment to the Joint Resolution of April 20, 1898, authorizing the use of American troops to liberate Cuba. The amendment disclaimed any "disposition or intention to exercise sovereignty, jurisdiction, or control over said Island, except for the pacification thereof, and asserts its determination, when this is accomplished, to leave the government and control over the Island to the people." Thus, with a clear conscience, and with John Philip Sousa's "Stars and Stripes Forever" ringing in their ears, America and William Jennings Bryan embarked on what John Hay later described in a letter to Theodore Roosevelt as "a splendid little war; begun with the highest motives, carried on with magnificent intelligence and spirit, favored by that fortune which loves the brave."[3]

On the very day war against Spain was declared, Bryan offered his services to President McKinley. "I hereby place my services at your command during the war with Spain and assure you of my willingness to perform to the best of my ability any duty to which you, as commander-in-chief of the Army and Navy, may seem fit to assign me."[4] But the president, unwilling to give a likely opponent in 1900 an opportunity for gallantry, was in no hurry to accept the Great Commoner's offer.

Instead, the Populist governor of Nebraska and a good friend of Bryan, Silas A. Holcomb, thought it would help the morale of the still young but defeated presidential candidate by inducting Bryan on July 13, 1898, into the army with the rank of colonel of the Third Nebraska Volunteer Infantry. More than thirty independent companies were organized over the state, eager to serve in Bryan's regiment. Yet because of his total lack of military expertise, Bryan's appointment did not escape criticism.

What experience Bryan lacked was more than made up by the appointment of his Belgian-born friend, the estimable Victor Vifquain, as lieutenant-colonel. Trained at the military academy in Belgium, Victor Vifquain emigrated to America before the Civil War and established his home in Saline County, Nebraska. In June 1861 he enlisted as a private in the Fifty-Third New York Infantry. He rose rapidly through the ranks and was made brevet brigadier general by President Lincoln. He was awarded the Congressional Medal of Honor for heroism at Fort Blakely, Alabama. After the war he served as United States consul in Colon and Baranquilla and as consul-general in Panama. That Vifquain was willing to take a position subordinate to Bryan despite his military record is testimony, on the one hand, of his devotion to Bryan, and on the other, of his willingness to put service to country ahead of ego or service to self.

As with Theodore Roosevelt's "Rough Riders," William Jennings Bryan's Third Nebraska, the "Silver Regiment," as it was unsurprisingly known, was under constant scrutiny and in the klieg lights of public attention. While Roosevelt's leadership of the "Rough Riders" is the stuff from which legends may be made and contributed to the future president's political career, McKinley made sure that Bryan's military service would be spent in the swamps of Camp Cuba Libre just north of Jacksonville, Florida, where the main enemy would not be the Spaniards but malaria, typhoid, and diarrhea. When the war ended on August 12, McKinley released seventy-five to one hundred thousand troops. Bryan was not among them.

Instead, his regiment kept fighting intestinal diseases, to which Bryan, in due course, succumbed.

Spain had no choice but to agree to the harsh terms of the December 10, 1898, Treaty of Paris, whereby it ceded to the United States the Philippines, Guam, Puerto Rico, and additional islands in the Caribbean under the rule of Spain. The United States was to pay Spain some twenty million dollars in compensation for the Philippines. Clearly what had been a war for humanitarian goals had become a war for imperial expansion. Two days later, on December 12, Bryan was honorably discharged, and he would eventually take up a new message—anti-imperialism.

Bryan had joined the war effort against Spain out of the conviction that he was helping to free Cubans from the iron fist of Spanish tyranny. He left the military without having been given an opportunity for gallantry and convinced that a war that supposedly had been waged to oppose oppression had become imperialistic and had ended in imposing American authority on both the Philippines and Cuba.

However, Bryan endorsed the Treaty of Paris and urged Democratic senators to vote for it. Few episodes in Bryan's political career reflect more negatively on his naïveté and muddled thinking than this strange position on the treaty. It was his view that adoption of the Treaty of Paris would oust a malevolent power from the Philippines and replace that power with a benign American outlook, which, in turn, would lead to prompt independence for the Philippines. From Savannah, Georgia, where he first articulated his support for the Treaty of Paris, he rushed to Washington, D.C., there to use his considerable clout in persuading Democratic senators to support treaty ratification. Bryan's position was a shock to the anti-imperialist views of the Democratic Party. Foolishly, Bryan missed an opportunity to lead and unite the anti-imperialist forces of both parties and thereby, perhaps, win the election of 1900. On February 6, 1899, the Senate ratified the Treaty of Paris by a vote of fifty-seven to twenty-seven, thus providing a one-vote margin for the two-thirds majority necessary for the Senate's ratification of treaties with foreign countries.

Bryan's fight for the treaty was a huge mistake. J. Rogers Hollingsworth, in his study *The Whirligig of Politics*, asserts, "His attempt to rally support for it caused many Americans to turn against him as the potential leader of the anti-imperialist movement."[5] He alienated Andrew Carnegie, who opposed both imperialism and bimetallism. David Starr Jordan, president of Stanford, reprimanded Bryan forcefully: "Twice you have failed us. Once when you justified the war with Spain and once when you advised ratification of the Treaty of Paris. . . . Will you lead or shall we turn your face to the wall, counting you only as one of the opportunists of whom one is just as good as another."[6]

As the journalist Willis J. Abbott, a Bryan sympathizer, conjectures, since the Treaty of Paris won by but a single vote, McKinley would have been forced to go into the 1900 campaign with unfinished business. He would be unable to claim that the war had been won, Spain humbled, and that America stood proud. Defeat of the treaty would have meant McKinley's abandonment of important segments of his own party, thereby encouraging others to seek the Republican presidential nomination.[7] Bryan's support of the Treaty of Paris may have cost him the presidency.

What accounts for Bryan's muddled thinking and political blundering? Bryan was not seeking to hasten the independence of the Philippines, although that is what he would have preferred. In his view, the campaign of

Figure 4.1. Depicting Bryan chipping away at imperialism while McKinley raises the flag of imperialism. *Judge,* May 12, 1900. Library of Congress. RN: LCUSZC4-5392.

1900 would be a replay of the campaign of 1896, in which bimetallism was the overarching issue. By 1900, however, imperialism not bimetallism was to be the resounding issue of the campaign. Initially, Bryan did not or would not see that, and only reluctantly and certainly belatedly did he begin to adopt a more logical anti-imperialist stand and to try to assume leadership of anti-imperialist politics. It would be too little too late.

SETTLING IT RIGHT: THE SECOND BATTLE

Once the results of the 1896 election were in, Bryan addressed his supporters by congratulating them on their efforts, exhorting them to strengthen their silver clubs for another day, and assuring them that "No personal or political friend need grieve because of my defeat. My ambition has been to secure remedial legislation rather than to enjoy the honors of office; and therefore defeat brings to me no feeling of personal loss." Obviously, Bryan needed no consultant to put this "spin" on his defeat. He then went on to quote a poem written by Mrs. Ella Wheeler Wilcox, the first stanza of which asserts:

> However the battle is ended,
> Though proudly the victor comes
> With fluttering flags and prancing nags
> And echoing roll of drums,
> Still truth proclaims this motto
> In letters of living light,
> No question is ever settled
> Until it is settled right.[8]

In 1900, Bryan was determined that the silver question would, at last, be "settled right."

At forty Bryan was still energetic, his stride still swift and sure, his grin still broad and friendly, and the hand he extended was large, warm, and firm. To wage his campaign for the presidency Bryan changed his military uniform to a civilian one. The latter consisted of a white shirt, alpaca suit, black string tie, and heavy-soled shoes. But because of illness while in the army, he was thinner than he had been four years ago, and his clothes hung loosely on his frame. Bryan unselfconsciously continued a role that came naturally to him, namely that of the "Great Commoner."

Even as his prosperity grew, he still met constituents and callers at home in his shirtsleeves. He looked after his horses and was uncertain whether the automobile would be good for America. For a time he avoided using one. He mowed the lawn, chopped wood, and brought in the kindling for the fireplace. When he was at home, Bryan led his family in prayer daily, and Sunday was set aside for worship and good works. One could see, however, that the "mountain lion" was aging none too gracefully. His hairline was clearly receding, and he was not as photogenic as four years before. It was evident "that the Boy Orator was no longer a boy."[9]

Bryan signed up with the Redpath Agency for a series of paid lectures on the chautauqua circuit. The chautauqua movement had began in New York State on Lake Chautauqua as a training ground and inspirational opportunity for Sunday school teachers. Its goal, succinctly expressed in its literature, was "Religious-Democratic Faith in the Popularization of Knowledge." This goal matched Bryan's religious instincts as a "political evangelist." The chautauqua movement was well-suited to Bryan's emotional and financial needs, and he would remain committed to it for most of his life.

THE CAMPAIGN OF 1900

To mark the arrival of the new century Bryan invited about a hundred neighbors to his home for an evening of prayer and thanksgiving. He shared with his guests his good fortune in having a loving wife, devoted and lovely children, and an adequate share of worldly goods. But Bryan evidenced little awareness of the rapidity of change in his country and in the world, and he seems not to have contemplated what unanticipated gyrations the turn of the century might take. Three years earlier, Woodrow Wilson, then a Princeton professor, asked, "Where do we go from here? What we want to know is what the nation is going to do with its life, its material resources, and its spiritual strength?"[10] Bryan asked no such questions.

An English observer, friendly to America, commented in 1900, "Life in America is one perpetual whirl of telephones, telegrams, phonographs, electric bills, motors, lifts, and automatic instruments."[11] But Bryan seemed neither to note the potential impact of an industrial revolution on a growing America nor to assess the impact of technological advance on the development of cities, the upheaval of rural America, and the rise of suburbia, all of which the new technology implied. He asked few "big" questions of himself or of his country.

Instead, Bryan looked to the "celestial crown" of Christian ethics and wrapped his reform impulses in what he believed to be God-given principles that required no further justification. "Moral certitude left him poorly

read in the growing literature of the social sciences and his arguments un-
fettered by its findings."[12] As he was about to launch his second presidential
campaign, Bryan's failing was to regard the new with suspicion, to find
truth only in the Bible, and to prefer that the world stand still. But neither
America nor the world would oblige.

In 1900, because of his political leadership in the Democratic Party, it
was a foregone conclusion that Bryan would be nominated by the Democrats as their presidential standard-bearer. The expectation was, however,
that Bryan would lose the election to McKinley, who had gained in popularity by the return to prosperity (the "full dinner pail"), by massaging
America's jingoism, and by promising new overseas adventures. Moreover,
in the presidential campaign Bryan would be at a disadvantage in that imperialism, not silver, would be the dominant issue. Bryan was a zealous anti-
imperialist yet he embraced its cause only reluctantly, while mistakenly
clinging to silver even when it was clear that such arcane questions as the
virtues of bimetallism vs. monometallism, the ratio of silver to gold, were
fading from public awareness, to be replaced by an interest in exotic places
previously read about only in the pages of *National Geographic.*

Had he attended the national convention of the Democratic Party in
1900 in Kansas City, Bryan's moral sense would have been affronted by the
abundance of beer and beer hall girls, who freely displayed their wares and
assured one and all that what was seen was also for sale. Gambling, including cards and roulette, was ubiquitous. Jesse James's cigar store, operated by
the bandit's son, was the most notorious sight in town, and in a barbershop
on Walnut Street barbers danced to the tune of a young black on the piano.[13] But so confident was Bryan in his nomination that he took the high
ground and, unlike four years ago, remained at home.

Bryan was aware that the silver issue could be an albatross around his
neck, but he resisted all pleas that he compromise. It was silver at sixteen to
one, he declared, or he would not be a candidate. In an interview to a reporter of the *New York World,* he summarized his platform: "I want the Fil-
ipinoes to have a chance to celebrate the Fourth of July and I want every
private monopoly destroyed, but I also want silver restored at the ratio of
16 to 1 and I want the national banks deprived of the power to issue paper
money. I also want the Constitution amended so as to authorize an income
tax and the election of senators by the people. In addition to these I want
to see the system known as government by injunction abolished and arbitration between labor and capital established."[14]

There was logic to Bryan's position on silver. Although he had lost the
1896 campaign, he had run a good race and for four years had been the

Figure 4.2. Political cartoon showing William Jennings Bryan as a Populist Party python swallowing the Democratic donkey. *Puck,* July 11, 1900. Library of Congress. RN: LCUSZC4-1473.

leader of his party. Bryan was certain that he would be renominated. He could not retreat from a platform that had almost elected him president and that contained principles his conscience would not let him readily abandon. But the very certainty of his renomination contributed to his zealotry.

Bryan kept in touch with what was going on at the Democratic convention by telephone and telegraph and confided to the numerous visitors to his home in Lincoln, Nebraska, that he would hold to his course. Although he insisted that sixteen to one be an explicit part of the Democratic platform, he reluctantly accepted an anti–imperialist stand as a higher priority. Democrats hoped that by making anti–imperialism the paramount issue of the campaign they could persuade anti–imperialist and anti–silver Republicans to vote for a Democratic candidate.

Bryan was readily nominated by the Democrats, but the selection of a vice presidential candidate presented some problems. To offset the glamour of "Rough Rider" Theodore Roosevelt, McKinley's vice presidential candidate, some Democrats sought to nominate William F. Cody, "Buffalo Bill," but Bryan signaled his dissent by his silence. Instead, Bryan reluctantly accepted the distinguished and incorruptible Adlai Stevenson of Illinois, who had been Grover Cleveland's vice president during his second administration.

As Bryan scholar Paolo E. Coletta observes, "Bryan had been honored singularly, only twice before had a major party renominated a candidate originally defeated. He was in addition the choice of all the anti-McKinley parties worth mentioning. Without spending a dollar, without the support of newspapers with large circulations, and without financial backing, he had kept the leadership of the Democracy."[15]

While Bryan's second run at the presidency lacked the dynamic enthusiasm of 1896, it nevertheless had some highlights and moments of drama. Unlike 1896, Bryan selected Indianapolis, not New York, as the city in which he would make his speech accepting the nomination. The twelve-car train that made the journey from Lincoln to Indianapolis was a triumphal journey. The Bryan family was accompanied by enthusiasts, celebrities, political supporters, well-wishers, and members of the press. A crowd of fifty thousand assembled on August 8 at a thirty-acre site, Military Park, near the center of Indianapolis. With his own family and that of Adlai Stevenson looking on, Bryan stirred the crowd with oratory that seemed undiminished by advancing years.

Although the twentieth century had dawned, Bryan waged his 1900 campaign serene in the belief that the campaign tools of yesteryear would be good enough to lead him to victory. And so no one should be surprised at the rather uninspired campaign song:

> Voters, come and hear my ditty,
> What was done at Kansas City;
> David Hill, the New York lion,
> Nominated Billy Bryan.
> (Chorus)
> Get out of the way, you Grand Old Party,
> Get out of the way, you Grand Old Party,
> Get out of the way, you Grand Old Party,
> You're so old, you're getting warty.
> For running mate there was a pull,
> But 'twas no use, the woods were full;
> And then there to still the noise
> They give the job to Illinois.
> (Chorus)
> Still your boss in Mark A, Hanner,
> He looks just like a stockyard's tanner,
> In the ring our hats we're shying,
> Whoop! Hurrah! for Billy Bryan.
> (Chorus)

Keep the banners ever flying;
Follow always Billy Bryan.
Onward now and all keep steady,
'Cause we're after Mark and Teddy.
(Chorus)[16]

Recognizing that his political campaign would be waged with a background of international conflict in the Boer War in South Africa, the Boxer Rebellion in China, and revolutionaries led by Emilio Aguinaldo in the Philippines, Bryan, with sensitive political antennae, emphasized that the battle between plutocracy and democracy would be fought over the subject of imperialism. To support his anti-imperialist position he drew upon America's heroes, including Patrick Henry, George Washington, and Abraham Lincoln. As was his wont, he likewise drew God to his side by asserting that imperialism was not supported by the Bible. Perhaps the most startling element in his 1900 acceptance speech was his formal embrace of pacifism. It was perhaps the first and only time a presidential candidate had done so. "It is our duty," he declared, to avoid killing a human being, no matter where the human being lives or to what race or class he belongs."[17]

Although much less known than his "Cross of Gold" speech of 1896, Bryan's acceptance remarks of 1900 must be regarded as one of the great speeches of American political campaigns. He laid out his arguments carefully and expressed them with flair, touching the hearts of his audience and winning the plaudits of friend and foe alike. Senator George Hoar of Massachusetts, by no means an uncritical supporter of Bryan, recognized the "power and dexterity" with which he made his case. And Mark Hanna, McKinley's gray eminence and campaign manager, grudgingly acknowledged that as a campaign issue anti-imperialism had political "legs." The "country took the bait," Hanna declared.[18]

If his acceptance speech in Indianapolis was the zenith of his 1900 campaign, his subsequent remarks in New York may be viewed as its nadir. The key to a victory for Bryan was to win New York's electoral votes. With his anti-imperialist stance finding favor in that state, Bryan thought he had a chance. And if he could secure support from New York' s Tammany machine, his chances would be even better. Richard Croker, Tammany's notorious political boss, arranged for Bryan to make two significant speeches in New York City, one of which would be delivered in Madison Square Garden, the other in the run-down but still venerable hall in Cooper Union where Lincoln once spoke. At Madison Square Garden, on October 16, Bryan held his audience of fifteen thousand by castigating McKinley and

Theodore Roosevelt, his vice presidential running mate, as lovers of trusts, gold, and imperialist wars of aggression. Speaking without notes, with humor as well as conviction, he painted the Democrats as the party of liberty and compassion.

But the enthusiasm he created at Madison Square Garden he eroded at Cooper Union on October 17 by an unqualified endorsement of Tammany boss Richard Croker. Instead of building on the virtues of democracy Bryan, inexplicably carried away by rhetoric, abruptly intoned, "Great is Tammany and Croker is its Prophet." Tammany loved it, but still he lost New York and his own virtue as well. Urban reformer Carl Schurz was disgusted with this pandering for votes at the expense of principle from a man who made a fetish of the latter. "Bah," he cried, "Wasn't it awful."[19] And it was.

In the 1900 presidential campaign, Theodore Roosevelt, running for second place on the Republican Party ticket, stole the show from Bryan and perhaps from McKinley as well. Two years older than Bryan, "Teddy" Roosevelt's exploits in Cuba as leader of the "Rough Riders" had already become the subject of myth, and this brash, young, egotistical politician took advantage of every opportunity to confront Bryan. Sometimes he spoke immediately before the Great Commoner was expected to speak and sometimes immediately afterward. While McKinley campaigned mainly from his "front porch," Theodore Roosevelt became the Republican spear-thrower. To the consternation even of Republicans, Roosevelt's name was soon better known than that of McKinley, and he had the gall to refer to Bryan as "my opponent." With a mouthful of teeth, a broad smile, a high and piercing voice, and a talent for self-publicizing, he badgered, harried, taunted, and provoked Bryan at nearly every stop on the campaign trail. Bryan retained his personal magnetism, and compared to Roosevelt, his speeches sought the high ground. However, to no avail.

With 6,358,737 popular votes, Bryan lost the election to McKinley, who polled 7,217,525 votes. In the electoral college, McKinley received 292 votes and Bryan 155. The Republicans carried all the states that had voted Republican in 1896 with the exception of Kentucky. Bryan lost his home state, Nebraska, as well as most of the silver states including Kansas, South Dakota, Utah, Washington, and Wyoming. Bryan only carried the silver-producing states—Colorado, Idaho, Montana, and Nevada. McKinley received 52 percent of the popular vote and 65 percent of the electoral vote.

Why did Bryan lose?

Mostly he lost because McKinley could ride the wave of returning prosperity. He promised American voters "a full dinner pail." Since prosperity was likely to continue under McKinley, they reasoned, why make a change for someone who was as yet untested as president. But a closer look at the election returns of 1900 revealed Republicans lost several hundred thousand votes in the Middle Atlantic states compared to 1896. Moreover, in urban centers, in industrial complexes with large forces of often immigrant laborers, Democrats had gained in strength, thus suggesting that the future for the Democrats was not so bleak as the initial review of the results would appear to indicate. Bryan lost in 1900 because the issues were unclear. Silver and imperialism were the dominant issues, but there were those who were anti-imperialist as was Bryan but opposed his pro-silver stance. There were others who supported imperialism, as did McKinley, but were reluctant to vote for the incumbent because of his anti-silver preference. Without clearly defined issues to guide them, many voters simply did not vote. Voter apathy in 1900 was no small reason for Bryan's second defeat. Moreover, in 1900, unlike 1896, "the country was busy and prosperous, too fat and contented to be aroused to a high pitch of crusading zeal."[20] And, perhaps above all else, Bryan was a crusader. If crusading could not move the voters what could?

THE GREAT COMMONER: THE BATTLE CONTINUES

Bryan's defeat in 1900 was hailed by Bryan-haters as the repudiation of all that Bryan stood for. The anti-Bryan press gloated that Bryan is "dead and buried beyond hope of resurrection." He was freely called a "quack nostrum doctor," a "fake prophet," a "Dr. Jekyll and Mr. Hyde," a "court jester," an "anarchist," an "artful dodger," a "Divvicrat," a "brazen footman to the rapacious Tammany Tiger." He was a "blatant demagogue," a "constitutional pessimist," a "traitor," an "apostle of sedition and class hatred." The nation has "buried him under an avalanche of votes."[21] Yet this was more wishful thinking than balanced reporting.

Among many of the political cognoscenti of his time, William Jennings Bryan was widely viewed as a "has been" whose time had come and had (mercifully) passed. But not just yet. His political clout would fade, the light he shed would dim, but Bryan did not know how to quit. He would remain a prominent political figure until his death.

Despite his defeat, Bryan was still the darling of farmers, workers, and small business, and he remained especially popular west of the Mississippi. To express his ideas and to keep his name before the people he turned to journalism and established a weekly newspaper called the *Commoner*. His idea was that such a journal, in effect a chautauqua in print,[22] could be sold cheaply so as to be within the financial means of less affluent Americans. In the columns of the *Commoner* Bryan could test his ideas before he ventured to air them from the speakers' platform. The journal would serve as a consistent call for reform, and with revenue from subscriptions and advertising, it would provide him with a modest income. The paper appeared for the first time on January 23, 1901, and consisted of eight 10 x 13 inch pages. A year later it consisted of sixteen pages. In the first year the paper sold seventeen thousand subscriptions at a dollar each and the total sales of the first issue were fifty thousand copies. Dedicated to aiding "the common people in the protection of their rights, the advancement of their interests, and the realization of their aspirations,"[23] the *Commoner* pursued these ideals for twenty-two years. The last issue ran in April 1923.

Defeat gave William and Mary Bryan the opportunity to travel abroad, absorb world culture, and study alternative political systems. "We went several times to Europe," wrote Mary Bryan, "twice to Canada, three times to Old Mexico, three times to the West Indies. We spent a year going around the world and a winter traveling in South America. During all our journeys Mr. Bryan's chief concern was the operation of governments, and it is interesting to note the political changes that have taken place which have elapsed since our last tour."[24]

In 1902, Bryan attended the inauguration of the first president of the Republic of Cuba, and upon his return, after a detour in Mexico, he prepared for a nine-week trip to Europe on which he would be accompanied by his son, William, now fifteen. Father and son left in mid-November on the White Star liner *Majestic*. As a prominent American political leader and twice a candidate for president of the United States, Bryan was accorded VIP treatment wherever he went. He met privately with Arthur Balfour, the British prime minister, listened to debates in Parliament, and met with leaders of the new British Labour Party including Sidney and Beatrice Webb. In London, on the American Thanksgiving Day, he delivered an address on the theme "Love, Not Hate, Will Control." He met with Ireland's freedom fighters John Redmond and John Dillon. He met Pope Pius X and rather undiplomatically lectured Czar Nicholas II on the virtues of freedom of speech and the press. But no encounter was more influential for Bryan than his meeting with Leo Tolstoy.

While dining with American diplomats Mr. and Mrs. Henry White, his hosts from the American embassy in London, Bryan expressed an interest in visiting Russia and to meet Count Leo Tolstoy, whose views he greatly admired. Characteristically, however, when Mrs. White inquired as to which of Tolstoy's writings he had read, Bryan admitted, "Oh, I have not read Tolstoy's works; but I have read a great many articles in magazines and the Sunday newspapers about him."[25] Bryan never found it especially important to read very deeply, even on subjects about which he was passionate and had deep convictions. "Only the bible was more important as spiritual inspiration for Bryan."[26]

At Yasnaya Polyana, about one hundred thirty miles south of Moscow, the Bryans spent several days as guests of Count Leo Tolstoy. Surprisingly, the American Christian fundamentalist and the Russian philosophical atheist and theoretical anarchist developed a special rapport. In his discussions with Russia's "intellectual giant" Bryan's developing pacifist views were confirmed. In many issues of the *Commoner* Bryan would refer to his visit with Tolstoy and share the latter's views with his readers, using him to support his own positions on domestic and global affairs. When on November 25, 1910, the *Commoner* announced Tolstoy's death, Bryan wrote: "The night is darker because his light has gone out: the world is not so warm because his heart has grown cold in death."[27]

Bryan returned from Europe in early 1904, and in September 1905 he left America with his family for an around-the-world tour. He visited Asia as well as Europe, hailed the 1905 Russian Revolution as the beginning of Russia's progression toward democracy, and attended a session of the Russian Duma. He wrote about his travels abroad in *Under Other Flags* and *The Old World and Its Ways*. "Bryan's Travels Have Made Him Known the World Over" was the headline in the *Chicago Daily Tribune*.[28] But was he any better known in America, was he a more informed American, and did he know America any better?

Although Bryan was recognized as a world figure, his role in American politics remained uncertain. When Bryan returned from Europe, the 1904 presidential campaign was already well under way, and it was the Republicans who were ascendant. Theodore Roosevelt, who had become president upon McKinley's assassination, was the obvious candidate of the Republicans and seemed to be a likely winner inasmuch as he took a stand against trusts in restraint of trade, supported the formation of labor unions, and established the Bureau of Corporations as an administrative mechanism to bring corporate predatory practices to light. He had a glittering personality that made him widely known, generally respected, and very popular among Americans.

Bryan determined not to run for the presidency in 1904 but withheld support from other potential Democratic candidates. Newspaper tycoon William Randolph Hearst initially emerged as the leading Democratic candidate, but Bryan refused to support Hearst or any other candidate. Instead, he came to the Democratic National Convention, which was held in St. Louis, to endorse principles not candidates, a technique he had used so successfully in 1896 when he made his initial run at the presidency. His adversaries at the Democratic National Convention were the so-called "reorganizers," who were determined to destroy "Bryanism" and return the party to the conservative thrust of President Cleveland. The candidate of the "reorganizers" was the able but conservative Judge Alton B. Parker of New York.

Though handicapped by what doctors diagnosed as pneumonia, Bryan was successful in getting a platform adopted that contained the Bryan stamp. It expressed opposition to high tariffs and imperialistic ventures, supported Philippine independence and the direct election of United States senators, and condemned trusts and monopolies. Free silver was no longer an issue, even for Bryan. Although quite sick, he stayed up all night to fight for his platform and to second the nomination of Senator Francis Marion Cockrel of Missouri, a little known candidate who had no chance of winning the nomination. In a hoarse voice, yet one which the delegates could clearly hear, he reminded his fellow Democrats that despite his defeats, "I have kept the faith." Fifteen thousand conventioneers cheered and Bryan, once again, became a hero to his party.

At the conclusion of his speech he was helped from the platform and put to bed in his hotel room. Still in bed the next day he was disappointed that Parker won the nomination on the first ballot, but loyal Democrat that he was, he endorsed the Democratic ticket of Parker and eighty-year-old former senator and millionaire Henry Gassaway Davis of West Virginia.

Roosevelt won a great victory with 56.2 percent of the popular vote to but 37.6 percent for Parker. Even in Bryan's home state of Nebraska, Roosevelt was gloriously successful.

Bryan nevertheless made the best of the 1904 debacle. He had discovered that although he had lost favor with many in the party and despite being essentially ignored at the St. Louis convention, he had retained the ability to move Democrats. He had fought successfully for his platform even if he lost in choosing a presidential nominee. On more than one occasion during the St. Louis convention he had received the grudging admiration of Democrats, and he could still hear their cheers. Although he was not the presidential nominee of the Democratic Party, Bryan biographer Louis W. Koenig describes him as the "hero of the 1904 convention."[29]

According to Josephus Daniels, he had "converted a convention hostile to him to one that gave him a larger measure of applause than he ever received before or afterwards."[30] And, a formidable political foe, August Belmont, reluctantly admitted, "My God! Now I understand the power of the man."[31] Republican senator Albert J. Beveridge hailed him as "the hero of conscience."[32] And, Walter Wellman, a distinguished newspaper correspondent of the day asserted, "The leadership of men by Mr. Bryan is the finest thing in American public life."[33] With ample reason to believe that he still had widespread support among Democrats, Bryan laid long-term plans for 1908. In the short term, he decided upon a year-long globe-trotting tour with Mary and the entire family, except for Ruth, who was pregnant.

Figure 4.3. William Jennings Bryan, a portrait, 1907. Library of Congress. RN: LCUSZ62-95709.

To pay for the trip Bryan contracted to do a series of articles for the *Commoner* and for the Hearst newspapers.

The distinguished group left San Francisco in the fall of 1905, made a brief stop in Hawaii, and went on to Tokyo, where Bryan met the emperor. The Bryan group continued on to Korea, China, and the Philippines, where he received a warm welcome for his support of Philippine independence. In the Philippines he met with the rebel leader Aguinaldo, but to the disappointment of the Philippine people he did not elaborate strongly upon his view that the islands ought to be free and independent. The Bryans then traveled to Singapore, Java, Ceylon, Burma, and India. In India, he was critical of the British for what he considered the exploitation of that subcontinent for the benefit of the mother country. From India, the ambitious journey continued to Egypt, Beirut, Damascus, on to the Holy Land, then Greece and Turkey.

The seemingly endless itinerary continued to Bulgaria and to the Austrian-Hungarian empire where they enjoyed the cities of Budapest, Prague, and Vienna. From these cities the family traveled to St. Petersburg, where Bryan felt he could sense the stirrings of the foundation for a "free, self-governing and prosperous nation." The Bryan family travels neared its end with a visit to King Oscar II of Sweden, who won his praise for agreeing to the peaceful separation of Norway from Sweden. The Bryans, so as to balance things out, then went to Norway to witness the coronation of a new monarch for that country. But Bryan's comments at the conclusion of the coronation of the Norwegian monarch perhaps best sum up his distinct preference for democracy. He declared, "The more one sees of [royal pomp and pageantry] the more one appreciates the simplicity of public life in his own country."

In Great Britain Bryan was received by the king. He also met with liberal leaders and, at a fourth of July celebration given by the American ambassador, he had the opportunity of meeting Winston Churchill. In London, Bryan met with the distinguished American financier J. P. Morgan. But travel for the Bryans was not yet at an end. Instead of turning homeward, they visited Holland, Germany, Switzerland, Italy, France, and Spain.

The Bryans finally arrived in New York in late August of 1906, where they were greeted by an encouraging turnout of Democrats and Nebraskans. At Madison Square Garden, at an engagement sponsored by the Commercial Travelers Anti-Trust League, he spoke to a supportive audience of some twelve thousand. It must have been reassuring to his supporters to hear Bryan once again inveigh against the trusts, support additional legislation to curb their excesses, and urge that at least the trunk lines of railroads be federally owned and operated. He told his audience that America's flirtation with imperialism had made this country less, rather than more popular, in the countries he visited. He acknowledged that the silver issue was dead inasmuch as a substantial increase in the availability of gold meant that those who wanted to retain the gold standard and those who wanted a larger volume of money in circulation had both won. He was convinced that during the 1908 campaign the dominant issue would involve how best to control trusts. Thus, following a dizzying world tour Bryan signaled that he was ready to enter another political fray. He did so with gusto.

"SHALL THE PEOPLE RULE?"

The year 1907 was one of financial panic for America and a year of opportunity for William Jennings Bryan. John D. Rockefeller, pessimistic over the speedy return of prosperity, blamed Theodore Roosevelt's attacks on business for the nation's financial panic. Despite falling stock prices and the bankruptcies of some financial institutions, President Roosevelt counterattacked and blamed the economic downturn on "malefactors of great wealth." With the country in economic disarray, and with Theodore Roosevelt having adopted the mantle of a "trust buster," Bryan forged a strategy that would lead to his presidential nomination by the Democratic Party and, hopefully, eventual victory in the presidential elections of November 1908.

Bryan's opponent would be the Roosevelt-anointed William Howard Taft, his secretary of war. He had served as a judge in Ohio's Superior Court, and as a federal circuit federal court judge. He had also served as United States solicitor general, president of the Philippine Commission, and governor general of the Philippines. For Taft, the presidential race was his first effort at electoral office. That he would have Roosevelt's support was something of a surprise, as Taft was far more conservative, far more pro-business, and anti-labor. Perhaps the conservatism of his opponent made Bryan likewise more conservative than he had otherwise been. But T.R. was sure that Taft would carry out his policies, and the presidential wish could not be thwarted. Roosevelt wrote the Republican platform and chose the Republican presidential nominee. On July 16, 1908, the Republicans met in Chicago and did as the president wished.

As Theodore Roosevelt dominated the Republican Convention of 1908, William Jennings Bryan likewise dominated the Democratic Convention, and by the time the Democratic National Convention opened in Denver, Bryan was assured that two-thirds of the delegates were with him

Figure 4.4.   William Jennings Bryan addressing the 1908 convention of the Democratic Party. Library of Congress. RN: LCUSZC2-6258.

and that his nomination was certain. But having nominated their presidential candidate, how would the Democrats amuse themselves?

Because Denver was the first time that either party had gone west of Kansas City to hold a convention, delegates from urban centers were startled to find people making a living in the great American West. As one Tammany stalwart remarked as he looked out the window of the dining car as the train moved across the plains: "Look at that . . . Actually human beings in them fields . . . human beings like me and you, living way out here and working!"[34] Moreover, Denver boosters sent freight trains into the mountains and brought in trainloads of snow, which was then deposited on shady streets in Denver so that the delegates could have a grand time throwing snowballs at one another![35] Although Bryan was to be the nominee, the official business of the convention still had to go on. And under the able leadership of Charles Bryan, brother of the nominee, it did.

While Bryan remained at his home in Fairview, a suburb of Lincoln, where he had built a new house, the Democrats readily nominated him amid cheers that lasted sixty-five minutes. A Bryan platform was easily adopted, and Bryan agreed to the convention's selection of Senator John W. Kern of Indiana as his running mate. Even New York's Tammany under the leadership of Charles F. Murphy, now a Bryan foe, was forced to declare for Bryan.

During an otherwise rather placid convention, discord became evident over a resolution proposed as a memorial tribute to former President Grover Cleveland, who had recently died. Judge Alton Parker, Democratic nominee in 1904, was chosen to eulogize Cleveland. He asserted that Cleveland had "maintained the public credit and honor stood firm as a rock in defense of sound principles of finance."[36] Bryan supporters saw this as a slap at their favorite candidate and had none of it. They accordingly drafted a resolution that paid honor to a deceased president without casting even implied criticism of the man they would shortly honor with the Democratic nomination for president.

The platform, essentially dictated by Bryan, carried the title "Shall the People Rule?" In it the Democrats urged independence for the Philippines, low tariffs, direct election of senators, civil service reform, conservation of natural resources, and "cooling off" treaties among countries to try to turn back the outbreak of war. Most important were the provisions for organized labor, which Bryan hammered out with Samuel Gompers of the American Federation of Labor after the latter had been rebuffed by the Republican Party. The labor provisions urged a Department of Labor with cabinet rank and limitation on the use of the injunction to break strikes. Included in the Bryan platform was a proposal for government backing for bank deposits and a postal savings system. The platform attacked what it considered Republican failure to exercise prudence in the expenditure of tax dollars. The platform welcomed Oklahoma as a new state and praised its progressive constitution, which Bryan had recently helped draft.

The Bryan platform is more significant, perhaps, for what it left out than what it included. As a platform it was a model of political pragmatism and demonstrated Bryan's grasp of practical politics. In a spirit of compromise, for example, the platform was silent on government ownership of railroads. Although rhetorically asking "Shall the People Rule?" the platform was noteworthy for dramatically excising the heretofore almost untouchable issues of initiative and referendum, to the dismay of many of Bryan's liberal adherents. Nor was any mention made of bimetallism, to which Bryan had committed himself in campaigns past. The Bryan platform was adopted without debate and, as his political biographer suggests, the 1908 platform was Bryan's most conservative and represents the views of a man now in his "political middle age."[37]

On August 12, 1908, Bryan gave his third speech accepting the presidential nomination of the Democratic Party. From Fairview, Nebraska, Bryan spoke to his party and the nation on the theme, "Shall the People Rule?" Bryan accused the Republicans of serving as a "front" for monop-

Figure 4.5.   Fairview, Bryan's home on D Street in Lincoln, Nebraska. Nebraska State Historical Society.

olies, trusts, banks, and railroads. Having been servants of the moneyed groups, Bryan argued that they must now take responsibility for the financial panic of 1907, into which, he asserted, the Republicans had plunged the nation. He urged campaign finance reform to limit the influence of the malefactors of great wealth and, as he did in previous years, again urged an amendment to the Constitution of the United States calling for the direct election of senators. He denounced the authoritarian rule of Speaker Joseph Cannon and urged that reforms be made so that that body could become, as it was intended to be, deliberative in character.

Despite a vigorous campaign, Bryan lost decisively to William Howard Taft. The voters' interest could not be sustained, and they were largely unmoved by either of the candidates. Indeed, Charles Gates Dawes, a lifelong Republican and Bryan's neighbor in Lincoln, thought that the most interesting thing about the campaign was the ample girths of the presidential contenders. "Whoever is elected this year . . . it will be a lush year for the White House grocer!"[38]

Taft's popular majority was in excess of a million votes: 7,679,006 for Taft to 6,409,106 for Bryan. In the Electoral College Taft won 321 votes out of the 483 total electoral votes. Bryan had won in the solid South and had carried Kentucky, Oklahoma, Nebraska, Colorado, and Nevada. In the *Commoner* he admitted that he could not understand the reasons for his loss, and in an article entitled, "The Mystery of 1908" he urged readers to write to him on the subject.

The most important reason for Bryan's defeat was Theodore Roosevelt's popularity, which weighed heavily in Taft's behalf. The president was absolved in the public mind for the depression of 1907, and if, as the president promised, Taft would follow in Roosevelt's footsteps, that was good enough for the voters.

Bryan lost because his 1908 campaign was unfocused. Unlike 1896, when the focus of the presidential campaign was the free and unlimited coinage of silver at a ratio of sixteen to one, or in 1900 when anti-imperialism was an important platform plank, Bryan's 1908 campaign lacked political focus altogether and never found an overarching issue by which to attract voters. "Shall the People Rule?" was ambiguous, rather vapid, and self-serving. Who could be against allowing the people to rule?

He compromised on crucial issues and remained adamant over relatively trivial ones. Thus, he compromised on government ownership of railroads but was unwilling to compromise on prohibition. The latter, not so big an issue as it later became, nevertheless may have been crucial in marginal states. Bryan's oratory was as moving as ever, but people were reading more and listening less, and the Republicans controlled most of the mass media of the time. Charles F. Murphy's Tammany failed to deliver the New York City vote, and while Bryan could complain, he could never get Murphy to explain.

Bryan was substantially outspent by his Republican opponent. He was among the first to urge that campaign contributions to political campaigns be regulated. In his 1908 campaign, for example, Bryan would accept no contributions from corporations nor accept contributions over $100 later than three days before elections. He set $10,000 as the limit for individual contributions and promised the publication of the names of donors of $100 or more.[39] Bryan used some $4,046 from the profits made by the *Commoner*, but according to newspaper editor and Bryan friend and political loyalist, Josephus Daniels, Bryan's money came mostly "from people with little education, men who wrote from the farms saying they were sending a dollar with their prayers, laboring men, preachers, and men in colleges especially small colleges, who thought there was a moral issue involved and that Bryan was the preacher of righteousness."[40]

Although he worked with Samuel Gompers and hammered out a platform favorable to organized labor, the latter did not vote for Bryan in the numbers expected from them. In many cases factory workers were intimidated by their employers, who threatened loss of jobs or cancellation of plans for industrial and plant expansion if Bryan was elected.

Catholics, who had ordinarily voted Democratic, switched in significant numbers to William Howard Taft, who was credited with negotiating favorable payment terms with the Vatican for important farmlands in the Philippines, known as the Friar Lands, which Aguinaldo had seized in the revolution. Nor did Bryan's essentially fundamentalist Protestantism square with his overtures to Catholic voters. He appeared insincere when, in a speech to the Ancient Order of Hibernians, he reminded Irish-Americans of his pride in his Irish blood and congratulated them on their contributions to American progress. And he failed to impress Jewish-Americans when, in a speech to the Young Men's Hebrew Association of New York, he faintly praised Jews for their contributions to the nation's advancement. Surprisingly, he was not helped by Taft's Unitarian affiliation, which, according to the devout, meant that he was not a Christian in that he did not believe in the divinity of Jesus and was, therefore, not fit for the presidency.

Among African Americans his approach was tepid to say the least. In fear of alienating Southern voters he remained ambiguous about human rights and voting infractions in states below the Mason-Dixon line. He could have capitalized on the notorious incident in 1906 in Brownsville, Texas, when members of the Negro Twenty-fifth Infantry were falsely accused of shooting up the town, thereby killing one and wounding two others. The real culprits were never found. President Theodore Roosevelt endorsed the recommendation of the inspector general and dismissed three Negro companies without honorable discharges. Although W. E. B. DuBois, the distinguished African American intellectual, supported Bryan and urged others of his race to do so, blacks voted, yet again for Republicans. Bryan, in short, failed to persuade African Americans that he did not share the bigoted mind of the South.

The Haskell affair likewise hurt him, since, once again, it seemed to reflect on the sincerity in his fight against trusts. Charles N. Haskell was governor of Oklahoma and treasurer of the Democratic Party. Hearst's newspapers began a series of attacks on Haskell for having allegedly conspired with the railroads and with the Standard Oil Company for favorable treatment. Hearst charged that Haskell had received $50,000 for helping to organize the Federal Steel Company. "This Haskell," complained Hearst in his newspapers, "is not only a Standard Oil tool and the promoter of crooked railroads but also an organizer of trusts."[41] In his belligerent way, Theodore Roosevelt took up the charges against Haskell and threw them in Bryan's face. Initially reluctant to respond, Bryan eventually asked for and received Haskell's resignation. But the seeds of doubt about Bryan's commitment to fighting trusts had been sown.

As Coletta comments, Bryan did more for the cause of reform than he did for himself. That is, he lost each of the presidential elections in which he was a candidate, yet nearly all of the reforms for which he campaigned were eventually adopted.

Despite defeat, Bryan anticipated much of the platform of the Democratic Party as it evolved under Woodrow Wilson, and even more so under Franklin D. Roosevelt as he grappled with the depression of the 1930s. Bryan anticipated reforms such as direct election of senators, guaranteed bank deposits, the imposition of an income tax, and the regulation of business.

Bryan was ever a gracious loser. He declared after the biggest defeat of his three campaigns that his only regret was that his wife would never be first lady. Although he was only forty-eight years old after the presidential campaign of 1908, William Jennings Bryan decided that he would not seek the presidency again. He would never again be a candidate for elective public office. But he had politics in his blood, and he continued to work for the causes closest to his heart.

NOTES

1. David D. Anderson, *William Jennings Bryan* (Boston: Twayne Publishers, 1981), p. 98.

2. Quoted in ibid., p. 99.

3. Quoted in Samuel Elliot Morison and Henry Steele Commager, *The Growth of the American Republic* (New York: Oxford University Press, 1937), p. 335.

4. Quoted in ibid.

5. J. Rogers Hollingsworth, *The Whirligig of Politics: The Democracy of Cleveland and Bryan*, (Chicago: University of Chicago Press, 1963), p. 153.

6. Quoted in ibid., p. 155.

7. Willis J. Abbot, *Watching the World Go By* (Boston: Little, Brown, and Company), pp. 229–30.

8. William Jennings Bryan, *The First Battle: The Story of the Campaign of 1896*, vol. 2 (Port Washington, NY: Kennikat Press, 1971, c1896), pp. 626–30.

9. Charles Morrow Wilson, *The Commoner William Jennings Bryan* (Garden City, NY: Doubleday and Company, Inc.), p. 257.

10. Quoted in William Miller, *A New History of the United States* (New York: James Braziller, Inc. 1958), p. 285.

11. Quoted in Louis W. Koenig, *Bryan: A Political Biography of William Jennings Bryan* (New York: G.P. Putnam's Sons, 1971), p. 355.

12. Ibid., p. 367.

13. Ibid., p. 318.

14. Quoted in Paolo E. Coletta, *William Jennings Bryan*, vol. 1, *Political Evangelist 1860–1908* (Lincoln: University of Nebraska Press, 1964), p. 251.

15. Ibid., p. 263.

16. Roger J. Welsch, ed., *A Treasury of Nebraska Pioneer Folklore* (Lincoln: University of Nebraska Press, 1941), pp. 78–79.

17. Quoted in Koenig, *Bryan*, p. 326.

18. Quoted in ibid., p. 327.

19. See Coletta, *William Jennings Bryan*, vol. 1, p. 274.

20. Thomas A. Bailey, "Was the Presidential Election of 1900 a Mandate on Imperialism," *Mississippi Valley Historical Review* 24 (June 1937): 48.

21. Quoted in William H. Allen, "The Election of 1900," *Annals of the American Academy of Political and Social Science* (1901): 56.

22. Anderson, *William Jennings Bryan*, p. 124.

23. Ibid., p. 122.

24. William Jennings Bryan and Mary Baird Bryan, *The Memoirs of William Jennings Bryan* (Chicago: The John C. Winston Company, 1925), p. 308.

25. Quoted in Coletta, p. 317.

26. Kenneth C. Wenzer, "Tolstoy and Bryan," *Nebraska History* 77 (Fall/Winter 1996): 140.

27. Quoted in ibid., p. 143.

28. Quoted in ibid., p. 142.

29. Koenig, p. 391.

30. Quoted in ibid., p. 389.

31. Quoted in ibid.

32. Quoted in ibid.

33. Quoted in Wayne C. Williams, *William Jennings Bryan* (New York: G.P. Putnam's Sons, 1936), p. 268.

34. Quoted in Abbot, *Watching the World Go By*, p. 263.

35. Ibid.

36. Quoted in Koenig, p. 434.

37. Ibid., p. 439.

38. Quoted in Kendrick Alling Clements, *William Jennings Bryan and Democratic Foreign Policy, 1896–1915* (PhD diss., University of California, Berkeley, 1970), p. 110.

39. Coletta, p. 412.

40. Daniels, Editor in Politics, p. 543.

41. Quoted in Koenig, p. 451.

5

HERO OF LOST CAUSES

> If any one thinks that I am disappointed because the leader-
> ship fell to another, let him disabuse his mind of that thought.
> I rejoiced that there was one who could win where I lost. And
> I was so much more interested in the cause than in any title
> that would come with it that I am sure the president was not
> happier than I was.
>
> William Jennings Bryan, *New York Times*, May 9, 1913

In 1909, six hundred guests helped the Bryans celebrate their silver wedding anniversary in their home at Fairview. There were no gifts, but floral arrangements filled the house, while guests who might have enjoyed
something more stimulating had to do with frosted cakes, lemonade, punch,
and other nonalcoholic beverages. In 1910, William Jennings Bryan was in-
stalled as an elder of the Westminster Presbyterian Church. As a speaker on
the chautauqua circuit, he was much in demand and, inasmuch as he was a
good traveler who could sleep in the sleeping cars of ricocheting trains and
survive on bad food, he crossed and recrossed the country expounding
Bryanism and Christian morality.

It is interesting to conjecture what might have happened had Bryan
elected to sit out the campaign of 1908 and to bestir himself as a presidential candidate in 1912 when a divided Republican Party would put a Democrat in the presidential mansion. Had Bryan, rather than New Jersey governor Woodrow Wilson, won the presidency, it is unlikely that America
would have entered the first World War and the course of America's history
might have taken a decidedly different turn.

Yet in the political wilderness Bryan was in some sense truer to his
ideals than Bryan the always-eager presidential candidate and leader of his

Democratic Party. He could, and he did, wear his "causes" on his sleeve, and for better or for worse his place in history is more effectively measured by what he did and said and how he conducted himself after his political life was over than it is by his runs for the presidency. Like President Jimmy Carter, who won the Nobel Peace Prize in 2002 and who admitted that he was a better ex-president than president, William Jennings Bryan may be said to have been a better man when he was no longer seeking political office.

Evidence that the Democratic Party was slipping out of his grasp may be gleaned from the menu of the Jackson Day dinner of 1911, during which Bryan was one of the principal speakers. The opulent dinner menu: oysters, diamondback terrapin soup, Jersey capons of highest quality, canvasback ducks and Smithfield hams, 1,000 cocktails, 552 quarts of champagne, and 400 quarts of sauterne, was not the Bryan style. Had Bryan retained the leadership of the Democrats, no such sumptuous repast with alcoholic accompaniment would have been allowed. A Democratic Party hungry to occupy the White House once again would make life a political misery for the Commoner.

"AT HIS HEROIC BEST"

In his book *The Hero in America*, historian Dixon Wecter writes of Bryan: "Unperceived by the country at large, Bryan was at his heroic best in 1912."[1] What had he done to merit this judgment of history?

In 1912, the Democratic Convention met in Baltimore, but Bryan, its most popular delegate, now no longer a presidential candidate, was still ardently courted by those who yet wished him to make the race. With the Republicans in disarray, 1912 may well have been the year Bryan finally made it to the presidency. But by then the fire in his belly appeared to abate, and he resisted the blandishments of his supporters.

Among the Democrats, Woodrow Wilson, the governor of New Jersey and former president of Princeton University, and James B. "Champ" Clark, Speaker of the House of Representatives, soon pulled away from the pack of presidential hopefuls. In heated competition between Wilson and Clark, the latter had a majority of the delegates but not the two-thirds required by the rules of the Democratic Convention. William Jennings Bryan, previously pledged to Clark, switched his support from Clark to Wilson, thereby giving him the votes needed to win the nomination. Bryan's last minute support of Woodrow Wilson was his finest hour. But why did he do it?

That he chose not to make the presidential race for a fourth time is more understandable than why he came to Wilson's support. The two men had never been close; indeed, the scholarly and aloof Wilson had often been critical and unkind to the man he had publicly intimated was essentially a country bumpkin. In 1896, when the Democrats were praising Bryan's "Cross of Gold" speech, Wilson called it "ridiculous." In 1904, he had publicly demanded that the Bryan wing "utterly and once and for all be driven from Democratic counsels."[2] In 1908, not only did Wilson refuse to share a platform with Bryan, but he asserted that Bryan was "the most charming and lovable of men personally, but foolish and dangerous in his political beliefs."[3] He even refused to give Bryan permission to deliver a speech at Princeton during the 1908 campaign. Moreover, an old letter was released by Adrian H. Joline, a Princeton trustee, to whom Wilson had confided, that he wished to find a way, "at once dignified and effective, to knock Mr. Bryan once and for all into a cocked hat."[4]

Bryan overcame his personal pique in recognition that over the years Wilson had become far more progressive and had come around to most of his own political positions. Moreover, "Champ" Clark had become the darling of New York's Tammany Hall, and Bryan had pledged that he would not support any candidate endorsed by New York's corrupt political machine. Thus, on a July night in the Fifth Regiment Armory in Baltimore, William Jennings Bryan, now fifty-two years old, threw his support to Wilson.

During the 1912 campaign against Republican incumbent William Howard Taft and the latter's erstwhile political supporter, Theodore Roosevelt, who had formed a third party, Bryan energetically campaigned for Wilson, making four hundred speeches in seven weeks, and so contributed to Wilson's victory. "It is a great triumph," he declared without apparent envy. "Let every Democratic heart rejoice."[5]

Bryan observed that the three great reforms of the age were peace, prohibition, and woman suffrage.[6] During his brief and turbulent tenure as secretary of state, a position to which Wilson appointed him as a reward for his service in making Wilson's election possible, Bryan would stake his reputation and the nation's prestige by taking concrete steps to advance the cause of world peace.

THE PRESIDENT AND THE SECRETARY

On December 21, 1912, in his office at the New Jersey state capital, President-elect Wilson, despite objections from trusted aids as well as his own misgivings, offered William Jennings Bryan a distinguished place in his cabinet, namely, that of secretary of state. Bryan had few qualifications for such a position. He was a well-traveled man. He had visited cities of renown the world over and even been hailed as a world leader in many of them. But in truth, what he saw and gleaned from his European travels were the insights of a tourist not a statesman. Bryan was not a man of global vision. His view of America remained provincial, nativist, and Christian.

Wilson recognized that domestic, not foreign, affairs would dominate his administration initially, and inasmuch as Bryan was far better known than he, Bryan could lead the lobbying for the legislation of the "New Freedom," about which both were in accord. Moreover, while Wilson would give Bryan wide latitude in matters of foreign affairs, he felt that as president of the United States he would, during periods of international crises, be his own secretary of state, and he was.

Bryan did not accept the proffered cabinet office unconditionally. Instead, he warned the president-elect that he and Mrs. Bryan objected to alcoholic drinks at public receptions and as secretary of state he would not serve them. He hoped that this would not embarrass the president. Wilson assured him that it would not. Bryan's second condition was that he wanted to use his position as secretary of state to pursue a pacifist agenda by initiating a series of "cooling off" treaties according to which nations would step back from the brink of war and attempt arbitration before plunging into armed conflict. With these conditions acceptable to the president-elect, Bryan eagerly accepted the position of secretary of state. Thus, with some apprehension on the president's part, Bryan was appointed to the highest cabinet office.

Humorist Peter Finley Dunne's "Mr. Dooley," had this to say about the Bryan appointment: Wilson preferred to have Mr. Bryan "in his bosom than on his back." The cartoonist had it right. President Wilson did not want Bryan in his cabinet. But could he do without him? Bryan knew more Democrats personally than Wilson, and the latter's leadership role in the Democratic Party could not be easily put aside. Colonel Edward House believed that it was inevitable and probably better, on balance, for Bryan to be a member of the Wilson "team" rather than out of it as Wilson critic.

But Bryan's initial wavering and conditions should have been a warning to the president-to-be. Here was his proposed secretary of state putting his teetotaling preferences on the same plane as the affairs of state. Surely there must be a difference in the way a moral man conducts personal affairs and the way a moral nation conducts international affairs. Bryan seemed to be saying that a nation is nothing more than an extension of a moral individual and that clues to the proper conduct of affairs with other countries can be gleaned from individual relationships. In Bryan's view, a single, immutable standard of morality pertained to interpersonal as to international affairs. The new secretary of state would propose a national course of action or inaction based on what he felt was morally right or morally wrong without much analysis of short- or long-term consequences for the nation. Historian Merle Curti observes that Bryan carried over into the field of international relations "the conviction that the behavior of nations was exactly analogous to that of individuals."[7]

On Tuesday, March 4, 1913, at 9:00 a.m., Woodrow Wilson took the oath of office as president, and fifty thousand people cheered, but Bryan was not a little embarrassed when the cheers for him were even louder. Bryan's appointment as secretary of state was approved by the Senate, and he appeared to be at the height of his popularity. Although he never became president, he seemed to be a politically fulfilled man.

As secretary of state, William Jennings Bryan got to ride in a government-provided carriage driven by an Irish chauffeur who had been driving secretaries of state around for nearly a quarter of a century. As he was likely to do, Bryan befriended the coachman. According to William Bayard Hale's account for *World's Work*, a day or two before Bryan was to give the 1913 St. Patrick's Day speech, Bryan asked his driver whether or not he was going to the St. Patrick's Day dinner: "No, the driver wasn't going. 'Well. I should like to have you go,' said Mr. Bryan, 'and I'll see that you get an invitation.' Accordingly, on the night of March 17, 1913, the banquet at which the secretary of state spoke was graced by the presence of his coachman, who was conspicuously placed not only at the head table, but on the program: for being a guest of honor and, bearing the name 'Barry' which takes alphabetical precedence over 'Bryan' and 'Belmont,' the coachman found that lo! his name led all the rest."[8]

Initially it appeared that the president of the United States and his secretary of state would be an "odd couple." The former—patrician, elegant, scholarly, analytical, ascetic, and former president of Princeton University—seemed a far different person from his secretary of state. But they were similar in many respects. Both were of Scotch-Irish ancestry; they likewise shared a common interest in literary and debating societies. Both were brought up in religious environments, received religious instruction from their parents, and as Presbyterians believed in a personal God and prayed daily. As Mary Bryan noted, both were lawyers, elders in the Presbyterian Church.[9]

But Wilson the scholar sought to understand all sides of a question and studied issues on their merits. He demonstrated a capacity to grow politically and reinterpret reality in the light of his own idealism. Bryan could never do this. Now a paunchy, fifty-three-year-old, balding, midwestern, shirtsleeved bear of a man, whose clothes were rumpled and who still wore a string tie about his neck, he appeared smugly unchanged and unchangeable. Despite a staff and an office that befits an American secretary of state, official state papers, sometimes with memoranda scribbled thereon, could be found in his bulging pockets. If one dug into those pockets deeply enough, likely as not, one could come up with a radish or two, his favorite snack.

Yet the astonishing thing is that the president and the secretary worked effectively on both domestic and foreign affairs during the years Bryan remained in office. During the first two years of the Wilson administration a mutual friendship and admiration developed between the two men. Wilson, for example, wrote to Bryan, "I have learned not only to value you as a friend and counselor, but, if you will let me say so, I have found a very strong affection for you growing in my heart."[10] And Bryan appeared content to be a loyal retainer to the president and so supported Wilson's domestic agenda.

Bryan lobbied successfully for the adoption of the Sixteenth Amendment (ratified February 3, 1913), which provided for an income tax, and for the Seventeenth Amendment (ratified April 8, 1913), which mandated the direct election of U.S. senators. He lobbied for the Underwood Tariff (October 3, 1913), which lowered the tariff on imported goods, as Wilson and Bryan sought and incorporated a modest income tax, which the Sixteenth Amendment made possible.

More difficult, but still successful, was Bryan's lobbying for the Glass-Owen Banking Bill establishing the Federal Reserve System (December 23, 1913). In doing so he was gratified that only the government and not private bankers would be responsible for the nation's currency and its banking system. In the pages of the *Commoner*, Bryan continued to endorse the much-amended Glass-Owen bill and urged his readers to let Congress hear from "the folks at home."[11]

In a farewell luncheon for Ambassador James W. Bryce of England on April 21, 1913, the secretary of state, as promised, served no wine. The astonished guests, nevertheless, applauded this man of principle. Protestant church groups and the Women's Christian Temperance Union congratulated him. But his attempt to serve grape juice in lieu of wine became something of a joke, which rose to serious proportions when some of his

Figure 5.1.   President Woodrow Wilson and his new secretary of state, William Jennings Bryan, 1913. Library of Congress. RN: LCUSZ62-68294.

diplomatic initiatives were derided as "grape juice" diplomacy. History buffs were reminded of "Lemonade Lucy," the wife of President Hayes who, likewise, refused to serve wine or whiskey at the White House.

His request, granted by President Wilson, to augment his personal income by continuing to lecture at chautauquas, was met with considerable scorn. Many thought it unseemly that the administration's most distinguished cabinet officer should share a platform with magicians, ventriloquists, belly dancers, and other exotic entertainers. In 1911, the salaries of cabinet officers had been increased from $8,000 to $12,000, and to most observers, a salary of $1,000 a month was sufficient to keep a highly placed and distinguished cabinet officer from demeaning himself by lecturing for money. But Bryan was not swayed. He loved to lecture at chautauquas, and he felt that he could not support himself on his cabinet salary alone. Criticism forced him to cut in half his lecturing on the circuit, however; no matter how few fee-paid lectures he gave, he was in the public eye, and every time he was away from Washington lecturing, sometimes for money but often without compensation, there was a great outcry about it.

The voices loudest in condemning him were often those who were political opponents, and they exaggerated the claim that by lecturing for pay on the chautauqua circuit he was demeaning his position as secretary of state. But Bryan did not handle his critics well. He was insensitive to the depth of their charges and unaware that his critics were destroying his effectiveness. By defying them, their rancor only escalated. Bryan was a warm, friendly, and optimistic man. But he remained blind to the depths of the criticisms. Here was an area where he could have retreated with grace. But he failed to do so.

Just as he insisted upon lecturing for pay, albeit at a reduced level, he likewise insisted that he continue publication of the *Commoner*. There was much less criticism of this enterprise. He earned five thousand dollars annually, and the *Commoner* became an important political journal that supported the Wilson program. As a political tract, the journal had increased in size, reached half a million readers, and reflected a positive view of Wilson's first two years in office. Unlike his obtuseness in the matter of lecture fees, Bryan was careful that the *Commoner* not be a self-serving opportunity to showcase the secretary of state.

At State Bryan was head of a department consisting of seven assistant secretaries and a department counselor, seven bureau heads, four division

Figure 5.2.   William Jennings Bryan speaking to a crowd at a state fair in Sante Fe, 1913. Library of Congress. RN: LCUSC62-50422.

chiefs, and two law clerks. Serving in Washington, D.C., there were 157 people. In 1914 the diplomatic staff had 121 persons abroad and 291 in the consular service, or a grand total of some 447 employees.[12] With so many positions to fill, it is little wonder that Bryan was besieged by those who felt they deserved a job.

In Bryan's day, few of the positions in cabinet departments were under civil service requirements, and so Bryan had a good opportunity to appoint those to whom he believed he owed political favors. His Jacksonian instincts became evident in that he appointed people who had few special qualifications. Like a good Jacksonian, serene in his confidence that any person of goodwill whose virtues were Christian and self-evident could perform effectively in any assigned task, however delicate the diplomacy, he shamelessly appointed "deserving" Democrats as a reward for their service to the party rather than for any extraordinary diplomatic talent they possessed. Party hacks and political warhorses thus were often appointed to positions requiring at least a modicum of delicate diplomacy.

Those who were called to his attention primarily because they were rich were likewise suspect. Viewed through his populist vision, candidates of means were flawed because they were believed to be permanently tied to Wall Street, to trusts, or were or had been among the malefactors of great wealth.

Illustrative of Bryan's attitude toward filling positions was the case of John Bassett Moore. When a vacancy opened for a State Department counselor, Wilson took the advice of Colonel House that the world-renowned legal scholar Moore be named to the position. Moore reluctantly accepted the appointment, provided it was understood that he would do it for but one year and would serve as acting secretary in Bryan's absence. When Moore joined the department Bryan reportedly said, "Moore? Moore? Yes I had a letter about you. By the way have you made any special study of international law?" When he went off on the chautauqua circuit, he called Moore in, turned the department over to him, and waved toward the bookshelves saying, "I'm told that if there's anything you don't know you can find it in those volumes over there."[13] They were Moore's own *International Adjudications*.

BRYAN AND WORLD PEACE

William Jennings Bryan, assured his friend and cabinet colleague Josephus Daniels, the secretary of the navy, "There will be no war while I am secretary of state."[14] But could a pacifist secretary of state succeed? Was a pacifist secretary of state good for the nation? Could a nation's foreign policy be driven exclusively by Christian virtue? Would Bryan be able to move the world with a peace-at-any-price policy? Would such a policy enhance American security around the world? Bryan thought so. And thirty nations thought they would give it a try.

In his chautauqua lectures, the theme of peace was a frequent subject. In his set piece, "The Prince of Peace," a speech that proved extremely popular with his audiences and that he gave many times, he declared, "I am glad that He, who is called the Prince of Peace—who can bring peace to every troubled heart and whose teachings, exemplified in life, will bring peace between man and man, between community and community, between State and State, between nation and nation throughout the world—I am glad that he brings courage as well as peace so that those who follow Him may take up and each day bravely do the duties that to that day fall."[15]

Emerson wrote, but Bryan probably did not read, that "the power of love, as the basis of a State, has never been tried." However, now that he was secretary of state, he was, as historian Merle Curti reminds us, "the first man in public office to try to put such a doctrine into practice."[16] As with so much in Bryan's work, what he advocated was unachievable and how he went about trying to do it was contradictory. For example, although a man of peace, he was also a man of justice, and so he had favored intervention by America on behalf of the Cubans even though it meant war. "Far from endeavoring to stem the popular clamor, Bryan blessed it."[17]

In the early twentieth century, the peace movement was vibrant, and Bryan assumed a leadership role in it. At the Interparliamentary Union conference held in London in 1906, Bryan spoke of his belief that before nations engage in war there should be a cooling-off period to make war unnecessary. As passions cooled and rationality returned, there would be an investigation as to the sources of the quarrel and attempts at arbitration. Bryan's leadership in the Interparliamentary Union conference made his peace proposals seem more realistic to Americans, and with Wilson's blessing he made them the keystone of his foreign policy. When, in March 1913, Bryan was appointed secretary of state, the peace movement rejoiced that one of their number was now in a position to inject practical procedures for avoiding war. "Having won the ear of the world for his plan, Bryan lost no opportunity for presenting it in and out of season."[18]

By August 17, 1913, El Salvador signed the first of the arbitration treaties, while the Netherlands became the first European country to do so. Painstaking negotiations followed, and in due course thirty countries negotiated treaties, while twenty were ratified. Bryan skillfully secured the two-thirds approval from the Senate, as required by the United States Constitution. But it was Bryan's fate not to have a period of grace during which his arbitration treaties could be tested, as the pacifist secretary of state had a world war thrust upon him.

William Jennings Bryan, again with the support of President Wilson, sought to achieve peace in Latin America. Appalled by the Rooseveltian policy of "speaking softly but using a big stick," and William Howard Taft's cynical use of "dollar diplomacy," Wilson, the scholar as president, and Bryan, the pacifist as secretary of state, sought higher ground and a more humane approach.

During the two years that Bryan was secretary of state was he a player in these emerging foreign crises? It is ironic, declares Paolo Coletta in volume two of his three-volume study of Bryan, that the pacifist secretary of state should have been confronted "with more threats of war than had confronted any secretary of state in American history and served during some of the bloodiest years in history to date."[19] While Bryan sought to find moral and just approaches to the diplomatic problems, central to the thinking of both Wilson and Bryan was a realism that dictated that America must protect the new Panama Canal and retain hegemony in the Caribbean. As a result, Bryan, with his usual inconsistency, resorted to both dollar diplomacy and the "big stick" when all else failed. But Bryan, in his inimitable way, could look two ways at the same time, in that he spoke against the foreign policies of his predecessors while he continued to pursue them. That he did so did not appear to bother him very much.

Bryan's policies with regard to both Latin America and Asia were laced with both paternalism and racism. When he favored intervention, when he endorsed the take over of the finances of weak countries, he did so serenely confident that America knew best, that its democratic traditions could be imposed on countries not yet prepared for them, and that whites were clearly superior to Asians and Hispanics. The president of the United States and his secretary of state were mindless about how racism marred their decision making and strained American relations with emerging nations of the world. With Kipling, America still viewed non-Europeans as "half devil and half child" and paternalistically treated them that way.

A SECRETARY OF STATE RESIGNS

At the outbreak of World War I, President Wilson expressed the hope that Americans would remain "impartial in thought as well as in action." Bryan took the president at his word. Because Bryan felt that Wilson's actions did not match his rhetoric, Bryan ultimately resigned from the president's cabinet.

The question of how best to keep America out of the war in Europe tested the bond between the president and his unlikely secretary of state. Both urged "neutrality," but they differed on what this meant and how best to achieve it. For example, was a loan that France requested from American banker J. P. Morgan a violation of the spirit of neutrality? Bryan thought it was. Wilson was at first undecided but finally agreed that a loan did violate the spirit of American neutrality, although the extension of "credits" to the allies did not. Was this a semantic or substantive difference?

Bryan urged Wilson to attempt international arbitration as established by treaties that Bryan had concluded with thirty or so nations. Surprisingly, Wilson agreed to do so, but it was his political advisor Colonel Edward House, and not Bryan, he sent to Europe to attempt to restore peace. Bryan was disappointed that he had not been chosen for this delicate and intricate assignment, but like a good soldier he did not complain. Colonel House, however, approached his assignment with a distinct pro-British bias, which contributed to his failure.

Early in the war Great Britain, as mistress of the seas, established a blockade against German shipping. Germany responded with a threat to unleash unrestricted submarine warfare against ships that were carrying contraband of war should such a measure become necessary—and no one doubted that it would. The list of what constituted contraband grew longer, and it soon became clear that Americans would be caught in the crossfire.

In late March 1915, a German submarine torpedoed the British ship *Falaba* and one American on board was drowned. Wilson was torn between the advice of his secretary of state to take a "soft" approach to Germany and that of Robert Lansing, who replaced John Bassett Moore as his new counselor in the State Department, who urged a vastly harder line with Germany. Bryan felt that the president had an obligation to warn the American people to stay out of harm's way, as the nation may not be able to protect them. Lansing insisted that according to international law, inasmuch as America was not at war, its citizens could go anywhere they wished and the nation would intercede in their behalf should their safety be threatened. But as the president groped for a course of action that would be in the best interests of the nation, Americans were shocked by the sinking of the *Lusitania* on May 7, 1915.

The *Lusitania* was torpedoed by a German submarine and went to the bottom of the sea in less than fifteen minutes. Among the 1,153 passengers aboard were 128 Americans who went down with the ship. British and American officials and citizens were quick to blame the "uncivilized" behavior of Germany, who had flaunted the rules of combat. It was later revealed that the *Lusitania* was carrying munitions, which were ignited by the torpedo, and this explained why the ship sank so rapidly.

How America ought to respond to the sinking of the *Lusitania* was the anvil upon which whatever links still existed between the president and his secretary of state were severed. Although Bryan had urged that no precipitous protest over the *Lusitania's* sinking be lodged, he nevertheless joined Wilson in a terse but strongly worded response to Germany. Wilson reasserted the right of Americans who, as neutrals, should have the right to sail during wartime where they wished. Wilson went on to demand that the Germans repudiate the act of their submarine commander and pay America reparations. In this, the first admonition to Germany, Bryan reluctantly joined the president.

Germany, for its part, was equally adamant and asserted that its action in sinking the *Lusitania* was a fair act of war. Wilson, while consulting with Bryan but heeding Lansing's advice, issued an ever more sharply worded letter protesting Germany's belligerency. This time Bryan felt he could not go along with Wilson and submitted his resignation.

Much of the truth about the incident was not known at the time. Instead, American and British public opinion was stirred, and the cry that America should enter the war on the side of the Allies was heard with ever greater stridency. Wilson betrayed his neutrality by declaring, "There is such a thing as a man being too proud to fight." Thus, the president of the United States wavered in his neutrality, but his secretary of state held fast. As the war in Europe became ever more bitter and as the possibility of applying Bryan's doctrine of "cooling off" and arbitration to international conflict became remote, Bryan felt increasingly isolated in Wilson's cabinet, nearly all the members of which quickly abandoned neutrality and became ever more closely associated with the Allied nations. Not so William Jennings Bryan.

In his letter of resignation Bryan declared, "I . . . respectfully tender my resignation. . . . Alike desirous of reaching a peaceful solution of the problems arising out of the use of submarines against merchantmen, we find ourselves differing irreconcilably as to the methods which should be employed." Bryan went on to say, "It falls to your lot to speak officially for the nation; I consider it to be none the less my duty to endeavor as a private citizen to promote the end which you have in view by means of which you do not feel at liberty to use."[20]

Although Wilson accepted Bryan's resignation with "profound regret," the regret was probably tinged with some relief. Wilson did send a modified note to Germany, which Bryan asserted he never saw, and because it was more conciliatory in tone than the note initially being considered, it might have satisfied Bryan.

While rumors of Bryan's probable resignation from the Wilson cabinet had been meat for the Washington gossip factory for some days, the first person to hear of it directly was Mrs. Bryan, who did not at all like what she heard. Mary Bryan had grown accustomed to the nation's capitol. Unlike their first stint in Washington, when her husband was a member of the House of Representatives, she now took a lively interest in the cultural life of the nation's capitol, the availability of music and theater, and she was loath to leave it. Moreover, she had a wide circle of influential friends in which, as the wife of the secretary of state, she was much respected.

There may have been other motives at work in Bryan's unprecedented decision to resign as secretary of state. The strain of being a cabinet officer took a toll on his health. In March 1914, Bryan's doctor diagnosed his distinguished patient as having diabetes and put him on a strict diet. Bryan still chafed when he was criticized for lecturing for pay on the chautauqua circuit, and he missed the additional income from such lectures. William and Mary Bryan also looked forward to developing their new home, *Villa Serena*, in Florida. Bryan felt, too, that he would be in a better position to work for peace among nations without the burden of an official position. Like former President Jimmy Carter, Bryan sought to develop the instruments through which global conflict resolution might be achieved.

Bryan's resignation came after twenty-seven months in the State Department, but was he right to resign? Could he have been more effective as the lone voice against the war by continuing to serve his country as secretary of state, or did he do the right thing to resign and continue his peace efforts as a private citizen?

The judgment of history is still inconclusive, but initial reaction among Americans, especially among Democrats, was essentially hostile: Bryan had made a "beaut" of a mistake. There were those who felt that the resignation was cowardly in that Bryan was abandoning his president when the latter needed him most. There were others who thought that Bryan was a deserter to his country because he favored peace at the price of liberty, and a deserter to his party because he was undermining the Democrats by making Wilson's reelection more difficult. He was called a "white livered scoundrel," and viewed as a "second Benedict Arnold." He was called a "mountebank," "fakir," "political wire-puller," "Billy Sunday humbugger," "grape-juice clown."

The *Louisville Courier-Journal* of June 12, 1915, was particularly vicious in its judgment: "Men have been shot and beheaded, even hanged, drawn and quartered, for treason less heinous. The recent secretary of state commits not merely treason to the country at a critical moment, but treachery to his party and its official head. . . . With the mind of a Barnum and the soul of a Tittlebat Titmouse he waited for the opportune moment, and when it arrived he struck wantonly and shamelessly." And, taking a swipe at Bryan for speaking for money at chautauquas and elsewhere, the editorial continued, "Already the summer shows pant for him. The circus tents flap for him. His treason to his country and his chief will be worth quite an hundred thousand dollars cash in hand."[21]

Walter Hines Page, the American ambassador to the Court of St. James was venomous in his outburst against Bryan, who as secretary of state had been his boss. In a letter to his son, Page's outburst was unrelenting in its harshness: "W. J. B . . . has made a good measure of himself—his crankiness-one-sided, crazy, fanatical mind—of his vanity and (unhappily) his selfishness and disloyalty; and of course the old mania for the applauding multitude and for the first-page advertisement asserted itself as yearning for grog in a topper. Happy riddance." And in a later comment to his son, Ambassador Page asserted: "Of course he's a traitor; he always had a yellow streak, the yellow streak of a sheer fool."[22]

Former President William Howard Taft equally undiplomatically asserted: "Bryan as usual is an ass, but he is an ass with a good deal of opportunity for mischief."[23]

On the other hand, Charles Willis Thompson, writing for the *New York Times* of May 30, 1915, asserted the view that Bryan contributed mightily to the success of Wilson's domestic program and expected, in return, a greater opportunity to work for peaceful resolution of international conflict. Instead, he found that on the matter of the *Lusitania*, the president was not listening to him. Mr. Thompson continued:

> Mr. Bryan is smarting—smarting because of the fear that his hope of becoming famous as the statesman of peace may be thwarted. . . . He is smarting because of the incessant daily picturing himself as a nonentity and a figurehead. . . . He is smarting because he suspects hostility to himself in quarters close to the president. He is smarting because he no longer has the feeling of being one with the president. . . . He no longer

feels that pat on the back from the presidential hand that used to do so much to deprive even poisoned arrows of their venom.[24]

After attending his last cabinet meeting, Bryan asked the cabinet to have a "last supper" with him at the University Club. Albert Sidney Burleson, postmaster general; Josephus Daniels, secretary of the navy; Lindley M. Garrison, secretary of war; David F. Houston, secretary of agriculture; Franklin K. Lane, secretary of the interior; and W. B. Wilson accepted. But it was hardly a lighthearted group that gathered. As the luncheon neared its end, Bryan spoke: "Gentlemen, this is our last meeting together. I have valued our association and friendship. I have had to take the course I have chosen. The president has had one view, I have had a different one. I do not censure him for thinking and acting as he thinks best. I have had to act as I thought best. I cannot go along with him in this note, I think it makes for war." He continued, "I believe that I can do more on the outside to prevent war than I can on the inside. . . . I can work to control popular opinion so that it will not exert pressure for extreme action which the president does not want. We both want the same thing, Peace."[25]

Bryan held a series of tearful farewell meetings with his staff, and many wept to witness the abrupt departure of their chief. He made the rounds of other offices and spent ten minutes with Assistant Secretary of the Navy Franklin D. Roosevelt. Finally, Bryan and President Wilson met in the Green Room where each extended a hand and said to one another, "God bless you."

NOTES

1. Dixon Wecter, *The Hero in America: A Chronicle of Hero Worship* (New York: Charles Scribner's Sons, 1972), p. 373.

2. John A. Garraty, "Bryan: Exhibit One in a Gallery of Men Who Fought the Good Fight in Vain," *American Heritage* 12 (December 1961): 112.

3. Ibid.

4. Ibid.

5. Ibid.

6. Lawrence W. Levine, *Defender of the Faith: William Jennings Bryan: The Last Decade* (New York: Oxford University Press, 1965), p. 102.

7. Quoted in Merle Eugene Curti, *Bryan and World Peace* (Northampton, MA: Smith College, 1915), p. 115.

8. William Bayard Hale, "Mr. Bryan," *World's Work* 26 (June 1913): 157.

9. William Jennings Bryan and Mary Baird Bryan, *The Memoirs of William Jennings Bryan* (Chicago: The John C. Winston Company, 1925), p. 328.

10. Quoted in Louis W. Koenig, *Bryan: A Political Biography of William Jennings Bryan* (New York: G.P. Putnam's Sons, 1971), p. 530.

11. Coletta, *William Jennings Bryan*, vol. 2, p. 135.

12. Ibid., p. 111.

13. Ibid., pp. 110–11.

14. Quoted in Levine, *Defender of the Faith*, p. 4.

15. Quoted in David D. Anderson, *William Jennings Bryan* (Boston: Twayne Publishers, 1981), p. 153.

16. Curti, *Bryan and World Peace*, p. 116.

17. Ibid., p. 117.

18. Ibid., p. 148.

19. Coletta, vol. 2, p. 147.

20. Bryan, *Memoirs*, p. 407.

21. Quoted in Arthur S. Link, *Wilson: The Struggle for Neutrality, 1914–1915* (Princeton, NJ: Princeton University Press, 1960), p. 426.

22. Quoted in ibid., p. 427.

23. Quoted in ibid.

24. Quoted in "Mr. Bryan's Split with the President," *Literary Digest* 1 (June 1915): 1452.

25. Quoted in Coletta, vol. 2, pp. 342–43.

6

"I DIDN'T RAISE MY BOY
TO BE A SOLDIER"

Will has been absolutely loyal—let that fact be firmly recorded.

Mary Bryan[1]

Resignation from the Wilson cabinet took its toll on Bryan's health. After his final meeting with President Wilson, Bryan returned home in
a state of near physical collapse. According to his daughter, "His face was
flushed as in a high fever, his eyes clearly showed the great emotional agony
he was enduring, and his gait was that of a person suffering from a great
weakness."[2]

Recognizing that the nation was woefully unprepared for war, Wilson
embarked on a program of military preparedness that greatly alarmed
Bryan, who saw in rearmament a threat to his peace initiatives. In press re-
leases and at huge public rallies Bryan, released from the cares of office, was
free to express his views. It is to his credit that he did not attack President
Wilson but saw in the president the best and the brightest opportunity
through which the warring parties might be brought to the arbitration
table. With his accustomed moral clarity, Bryan's view was that war is un-
equivocally evil and peace always good. Why, he wondered, if a hundred
Americans were killed on the *Lusitania*, was necessary to go to war in which
thousands would be killed?

Late in 1915, Bryan was invited to join the Henry Ford–sponsored
peace initiative that took the form of a "peace ship" bound for Europe.
Ford leased the *Oscar II* from the Scandinavian line and invited prominent,
peace-oriented guests to join. The merchant John Wanamaker was one,
Cardinal Gibbons of Baltimore was another; also included was Judge Ben
Lindsey of Denver. Bryan boarded the vessel with Ford on the day the ship

was to sail, but he declined the opportunity to sail with her, as he preferred remaining in America, where he believed he could be a better spokesman for peace. Bryan, and Ford's close friend Thomas Alva Edison, watched as the *Oscar II*, which Bryan likened to Noah's Ark, sailed out of Hoboken harbor to the tune of "I Didn't Raise My Boy to Be a Soldier."

But little came of the peace initiative. The peace delegation was not welcome in Norway when the *Oscar II* arrived on December 18, and Ford himself left the vessel as soon as he could. Bryan likewise returned home and received a gratifying welcome when he and Mary got off the train at Lincoln, Nebraska. To a crowd of five thousand he pilloried the "eastern press," congratulated his listeners on living thirty-six hours from New York, and hailed the Alleghenies as a dike that saved the rest of the country from a flooding of New York's "prejudice, insolence, and ignorance." He declared that in office he had been "hand-tied and tongue-tied," but now he was free. "I have a larger work outside the cabinet, than I ever had within it."[3]

The Bryans headed for Fairview, their Nebraska home. The house had been sorely neglected. But instead of repairing it, they felt that Mary Bryan's severe, crippling arthritis would benefit from a winter's stay in Miami, Florida, and summers in Asheville, North Carolina. The Bryans still had a home in Washington, D.C., which they would give up before long. Fairview would become nothing more than the Bryans' official home, where they would vote.

Of course, Bryan was growing older, and none too gracefully at that. He was paunchy and nearly bald, his face heavy, mottled, and lined. Yet friend and foe alike were impressed with his seemingly indefatigable energy, undiminished optimism, and commitment to the causes that seemed "righteous" to him. According to William Allen White, with whom Bryan visited during the summer of 1915, "his voice was fresh and his eyes were keen."[4] While his political powers were fading, and his health deteriorating, he still played an important role in what he believed to be the three great reforms of his age: peace, prohibition, and woman suffrage.

"HE KEPT US OUT OF WAR"

As Democratic delegates assembled in St. Louis, Missouri, for the presidential nominating convention set to open on June 14, 1916, it was evident that Wilson would be renominated without opposition and that the convention, compared to the backdrop of the international situation, would be a dull affair.

Bryan, for the first time in twenty years, was neither a leading candidate nor an important delegate, having been defeated by Nebraska Democrats for the position of delegate at large. This was the revenge of the sullen "wets," who sought to punish their distinguished "dry." As Mary Bryan described the opposition in the *Omaha World Herald* of April 14, 1916, it was "a union of breweries, saloons, drinkers, [and] gamblers."[5] This defeat left a bitter taste, and William Jennings Bryan lost his moorings in Nebraska and looked to establish roots elsewhere.

As a reporter for the *Commoner*, Bryan nevertheless was present at both the Democratic and the Republican Conventions. At the latter he witnessed the nomination of Charles Evans Hughes and at the former the renomination of President Woodrow Wilson. Although but a journalist, he was by no means entirely forgotten by the Democratic Convention. He occupied a prominent seat in the press gallery, and the cheers for him were "spontaneous," "generous," and "warm." Although he had no official role in the dull convention, the *New York Times* called him an "outstanding figure."[6]

Temporary convention chairman, Martin Glynn, delivered the keynote address. Since he had informally discussed its contents with Bryan, the speech had Bryan's "word prints" all over it. That is, Glynn praised President Wilson because he had kept America out of war. This was a theme Wilson had tried to avoid, inasmuch as he was aware that a call to arms might not be far away. But the theme resonated with the delegates, who seemed to draw their sustenance more from Bryan's relentless search for peace than from the president's efforts to rearm America. Glynn recounted episode after episode in which America responded to diplomatic taunts and humiliation with negotiation rather than war. Before long, Glynn had the crowd of delegates chanting after each episode and the query:

Glynn: "What did we do?"

Delegates in chorus: "We didn't go to war."

The response was unwanted and unexpected. Wilson's floor managers and supporters did not expect their candidate to run on a peace-at-any-price platform, but they could not disavow the quest for peace. They had little choice but to join the rising sentiment. To Wilson's discomfiture, the theme of the convention had become "He kept us out of war."

Although he had no official assignment at the Democratic Convention, the delegates demanded a speech from Bryan, and he was glad to oblige. To the vast relief of Wilson supporters, Bryan praised his former boss as a fearsome fighter for peace. "I join with the American people in thanking God that we have a president who does not want this nation plunged into war."[7] He acknowledged that he has had some differences with President Wilson, but asserted, "I join the people in thanking God that we have a president who does not want the nation to fight."[8] Once the convention was over, Bryan campaigned for Wilson in nineteen mainly western states, carrying a message of peace.

On election night the Bryan family, some fourteen in all, sat down to a turkey dinner, which included a huge fruitcake marking the thirty-second wedding anniversary of Mary and William Jennings Bryan. But the evening turned somber as the returns did not point to a Wilson victory. While the final vote would take some days to ascertain, the dark omens were that victory would go to Charles Evans Hughes. It wasn't until California's vote was counted that it became clear that Wilson would be reelected. Clearly, Bryan's campaigning in the West overcame Hughes's lead in the East, and once again, Wilson was in Bryan's debt.

Aware of the sentiment in America for peace, Wilson, to Bryan's joy, let the warring powers know that he stood ready to mediate the conflict. But it was now too late. The positions of the warring nations had hardened, and the mediation proposal only seemed to exacerbate tensions. The British were "mad as hell"[9] at the Wilson mediation effort. To Bryan's deep disappointment, Wilson broke off diplomatic relations with Germany on February 3, 1917.

Bryan was desperate to thwart the rush to war. He issued "An Appeal for Peace to the American People," in which he outlined specific steps to avoid a costly war. Among his proposals were these:

1. Keep Americans off belligerent ships.
2. Postpone until after the war any question that cannot be settled now by peaceful means.
3. Refuse clearance to American and other neutral ships carrying passengers and contraband.
4. Withdraw protection from American citizens who travel as seamen with contraband on American or other neutral ships.
5. Keep all American vessels out of the danger zone.
6. Any Congressional declaration of war should be submitted to a national referendum.
7. Send telegrams to the president and to members of Congress expressing the national desire for peace.[10]

As a result of the last proposal the White House and Congress were flooded with antiwar messages. But Bryan recognized that his efforts would not be fruitful, and he returned to Miami in a dejected mood.

When German U-boats sank three unarmed American merchant vessels with the loss of thirty-six lives, Bryan continued to fight for peace. When German submarines torpedoed the French cross-channel steamer, *Sussex*, with Americans aboard, although no Americans died, Bryan demanded that Americans be prohibited from sailing on belligerent ships.

When, in March 1917, the Zimmerman note revealed Germany's efforts to make Mexico its ally against the United States, Bryan continued to urge peace.

In an appeal to Congress on March 30, 1917, Bryan pleaded:

> Let Congress remember that wrongs you would punish, cruel and unjustifiable as they are, are not intended primarily against this country, but are acts of desperation, directed against other nations with which the offenders are at war. Our land is not threatened with invasion, but that we are asked to go three thousand miles for a chance to fight. . . . If Congress should prefer war, let it first consult by referendum those who must defend the nation's honor with their lives.[11]

But as the war drums beat ever louder and became more insistent, Bryan was branded by many as a "shyster," a "traitor," and another "Benedict Arnold." Wilson, deaf to Bryan's pleas, on April 2, 1917, asked Congress to recognize a state of war. He asserted that "the world must be made safe for democracy" and, in approaching the conclusion of his war message, made the point that "the right is more precious than peace." On April 6, Congress declared war.

And Bryan's pacifism ended. "Now . . . the discussion has ended and the people of the entire country will stand undivided behind the president. In no other country should the people be so willing to make extreme sacrifices as in the United States."[12] In a telegram to the president, Bryan offered his services, "Please enroll me as a private wherever I am needed and assign me to any work that I can do."[13] Graciously but firmly Wilson rejected Bryan's offer.

As with so many aspects of Bryan's political behavior, it is almost inexplicable that he should, at one stroke, give up his pacifist leanings and offer himself for the war effort. If his words have any meaning, he was apparently prepared to serve on the battlefields as a "private" if necessary. Obviously, this would not have happened because of Bryan's age and physical infirmities. But while his patriotic desire to support his president and rally round his nation in a time of peril is laudable, one must ask why did he not take up the struggle for peace as a conscientious objector to war? "The logic of his position," wrote Paxton Hibben, was "conscientious objection. Instead he became the pacifist in arms."[14]

When the war ended, Wilson also resisted Bryan's overtures that he be appointed to the peace commission. Wilson had determined that he would go to Paris and personally head the American delegation. Among those who would accompany him were Colonel Edward House, Secretary of State Robert Lansing, his two nephews Allan and John Foster Dulles, and experienced diplomats Henry White and General Tasker H. Bliss. It was not, to be sure, the best "peace team" America could offer, but Wilson could readily dominate this delegation, and had Bryan been a member of it, the latter's fierce ideological inflexibility would make him a difficult person with whom to work. Having once been burned by Bryan, the president would not be burned again.

On December 4, 1918, Wilson, his peace delegation, and a shipload of experts and specialists boarded the *George Washington* and sailed for Europe. Bryan was not among them. Nevertheless, on March 12, 1919, Bryan wrote a newspaper article in which, with some qualifications, he expressed his support for the League of Nations, which Wilson included in his Fourteen Points as a basis for restoring a peaceful world. Bryan asserted that the League of Nations was "the greatest step towards peace in a thousand years."[15] Oddly enough, Bryan, who was considered prone to oppose compromise, urged compromise on Wilson so as to get the principle of a structured body that would work to deflect the onset of war. He drew on his experiences with the arbitration treaties he had negotiated while serving as Wilson's secretary of state. President Wilson, on the other hand, was adamant in opposing any sort of compromise on the League, with the result that the Senate never adopted the League.

In a twist of roles, Bryan had resigned as secretary of state because of the hard line President Wilson took with Germany over the sinking of the *Lusitania*, but at a Jackson Day dinner in January 1920, Bryan publicly opposed the president because of the hard line he was taking in an all-or-nothing approach to the covenant of the League of Nations. In the matter of the *Lusitania* it was Bryan who refused to compromise; in the matter of the League of Nations it was the president of the United States who refused to compromise.

While Bryan was disappointed, he was not idle. Instead, he plunged into the fight for prohibition and for woman suffrage.

"DRY CLEANING": BRYAN AND PROHIBITION

Bryan was a teetotaler, but during his presidential campaigns he finessed the issue of prohibition in recognition that most of his immigrant supporters enjoyed drinking beer and spirits. Far from feeling it a sin, they thought it a requisite for relaxation and socialization after long hours on the job. For many, liquor was still viewed as medication, and some thought alcohol to be "the good creature of God."[16]

On May 24, 1893, the Anti-Saloon League was founded at Oberlin College to fight against liquor and saloons in Ohio. In other states, temperance fighters likewise organized themselves, and in 1895 a national Anti-Saloon League held its initial meeting in Washington, D.C. Before long it became the leading force in America urging the prohibition of alcohol and the closing of saloons. With major support from mostly Protestant Evangelical churches, with women playing a role equal to or even greater than that of men, the Anti-Saloon League became a political force in America with which those seeking office would have to come to terms in a manner not unlike the power and political influence of the National Rifle Association in our own time.

By 1910, as evidence of the growing power of the Anti-Saloon League, thirteen states, the District of Columbia, Alaska, and Puerto Rico had become dry. William Jennings Bryan slowly, but with growing enthusiasm, assumed a leadership role in the campaign to bring prohibition first to Nebraska and later to the nation. Bryan plunged into the campaign against liquor and the saloons with his customary gusto, sure that moral Christianity demanded no less of him.

During the early years of the twentieth century, the fight about prohibition was a struggle that made the political juices flow among voters. Prohibition became an emotional issue and aroused the passions of men and women as few other aspects of American life did. While most Republicans were "dry" and most Democrats "wet," prohibition was more divisive among Democrats than among Republicans. Bryan knew that should he intervene in the debate on prohibition, political infighting among the Democrats would be intense and had the potential to split the party. With his ever alert political antennae carefully tuned in, Bryan inserted himself into the fray. Why did he do so?

With no presidential ambitions to feed, he could assert that his fight for prohibition in Nebraska was entirely in keeping with his Christian morality and long-held beliefs. But political ambition likewise played an important role. To the extent that he identified with a potentially vigorous cause, he had the opportunity, although not the certainty, of retaining the leadership of the Nebraska Democrats, a role he felt was slipping away from him. For a man with no small ego, it was an honor he felt he deserved, in view of his respectable showings in three presidential campaigns.

But could a "dry" retain leadership of a predominantly "wet" political party?

Nebraska regulated alcohol by allowing the voters of each of the state's towns or villages to determine for themselves whether to allow the sale of alcohol within its boundaries. Nebraska's Anti-Saloon League, however, formed in 1897, was determined to strengthen laws prohibiting the sale and distribution of alcoholic beverages. While still a potential presidential candidate, Bryan had dragged his feet.

In 1902, when Cary Nation raised her hatchet against the saloons in Nebraska, Bryan kept his distance. By 1908, four hundred fifty communities had chosen to stay or become dry. But this did not satisfy the zealots of the Nebraska Anti-Saloon League. Clever saloonkeepers could and did open shops in "wet" areas adjacent to "dry" neighborhoods, so that an easy walk across the street or down the road could bring a customer to a nearby bar. Since extremists of the Anti-Saloon League could not sleep soundly knowing that someone, somewhere, was having a good time, something more would have to be done.

In 1910, Bryan supported legislation allowing voters in Nebraska's counties to determine whether the county, not the town, would be "wet" or "dry." By substituting the county, a much larger political entity than the village, buying liquor would be far more difficult and saloons more easily driven out of business.

In 1908, the popular Ashton C. Shallenberger, a Democrat, had been elected governor with a popular vote larger than Bryan's vote for the presidency. Shallenberger had navigated a number of political reforms through the state legislature, but county option on liquor was not among them. Shallenberger was blamed for capitulating to the liquor lobby, the beer barons, and the tavern keepers. The liquor lobby was also blamed for defeating a reform proposal calling for an initiative and referendum that would have allowed the voters to bypass the state legislature and vote directly for or against county option on liquor. Governor Shallenberger and Arthur F. Mullen, his liaison with the legislature, sought to defuse county option, which they clearly knew to be political dynamite, by pushing through the legislature a law closing the saloons of Nebraska, with the exception of those in Omaha, from 8:00 p.m. to 7:00 a.m. When signed by Governor Shallenberger, "Nebraska's nights became as dry as Death Valley,"[17] as his aide, Arthur Mullen, quipped.

But this did not satisfy Bryan and his new prohibitionist allies, who wanted Nebraska's days as well as nights to be dry. By supporting the Nebraska Anti-Saloon League's county option, Bryan put himself on the side of the antiliquor angels while challenging the growing leadership of Governor Shallenberger in the Democratic Party.

In the Nebraska Democratic primaries, in which all eligible voters could vote, Bryan refused to support Shallenberger for reelection as governor and, in an unholy alliance with Republican "wets," defeated him. James C. Dahlman, mayor of Omaha, a committed "wet," won the gubernatorial nomination by just over three hundred votes over Shallenberger and was nominated by the Democrats.

Bryan rather abruptly announced that he was not satisfied with the Daylight Saloon Law and that he would introduce a county option plank in the 1910 convention of the Democratic Party, which was held that year at Grand Island, Nebraska. Nothing would do more to shatter the unity of the Democrats and to bring down upon Bryan the wrath of a still powerful liquor industry and of his ethnic supporters. Bryan exhorted his listeners: "Will you put the Democratic Party on the moral side or will you put it on the immoral side?" The answer of the Democrats was clear, his county option plank was rejected in the Democratic Convention by a humiliating 647 to 198.[18] The once influential Democrat was, on this issue at least, way off the mark. But, not for long.

Because of Dahlman's exuberant anti-prohibition stance, Bryan refused to support his former close friend and erstwhile political ally and victory went to the "dry" Republican candidate, Chester Aldrich, who strongly supported county option. Thus did Bryan, clad in the armor of principle, rather callously bury Shallenberger in the primaries and Dahlman in the election and eliminate two potential rivals to his leadership of the Democratic Party in Nebraska. The price he paid was the election of a Republican governor for Nebraska. But Bryan hid the political hatchet he wielded so clumsily behind his ode to water:

> Water, the daily need of every living thing. It ascends from the seas, obedient to the summons of the sun, and descending, showers blessing upon the earth; it gives of its sparkling beauty to the flagrant flower; its alchemy transmutes base clay into golden grain; it is the canvas upon which the finger of the Infinite traces the radiant bow of promise. It is the drink that refreshes and adds no sorrow with it—Jehovah looked upon it at creation's dawn and said—It is good.[19]

Advertising writers on New York's Madison Avenue could not do better.

Principle in Bryan's hands often became a two-edged sword. He could claim that his fight was for the principle of saving the souls of Christian

America from demon rum, while ruthlessly using those principles to demonstrate his political muscle to undercut his political enemies.

Bryan observed his sixtieth birthday at a "dry" party (March 19, 1920) given in his honor by six hundred friends at the Aldine Club in New York. "The liquor issue," Bryan told his friends "is as dead as slavery."[20] But, Bryan was wrong, again.

The Anti-Saloon League eventually exercised enough clout so that by 1920, with Bryan's considerable help, it could impose prohibition on America. The Anti-Saloon League gloated, "It is here at last—dry America's first birthday." The League's press release continued, "At one minute past twelve tomorrow morning a new nation will be born. . . . To-night John Barleycorn makes his last will and testament. Now for an era of clear thinking and clean living! The Anti-Saloon League wishes every man, woman and child a happy Dry Year."[21]

BRYAN AND WOMAN SUFFRAGE

The call to the movement for votes for women came late to William Jennings Bryan. When, as a first-term congressman, he was invited to attend a meeting in which the distinguished suffragette Julia Ward Howe was to be the speaker, the Bryans refused the invitation (see p. 31). Carrie Chapman Catt, president of the National American Woman Suffrage Association from 1900 to 1905, was likewise dismayed that Bryan did not come out strongly for the cause of woman suffrage.

Yet, during his 1896 campaign for the presidency in a speech in Minneapolis, Bryan took a rather forward-looking step in lecturing to a group of women on bimetallism. While the common outlook was that women could not possibly understand the arcane elements of this subject, Bryan's attitude was quite the contrary in that he felt that all the American people, the common man who had the vote and the common woman who did not, could share in understanding the complex issues in the campaign before them.

By 1914, he was hailing woman suffrage when the State of Nebraska was considering the matter. "I shall claim no privileges for myself that I do not ask for my wife."[22] The determination of women to secure the vote must have impressed him when he witnessed during the Republican Convention held in Chicago in 1916, which he attended as a journalist, the march of suffragettes through winds so strong and rain so heavy that it often took several women to hold their banners aloft. Aided by his wife, Mary Bryan, the couple became workers for votes for women.

During World War I, he prodded a reluctant President Wilson to support the Nineteenth Amendment to the Constitution providing female voting rights—a wartime issue, a patriotic expression, and an overdue reform. Bryan's support for the Nineteenth Amendment was influential enough to bring reluctant Democrats to embrace the issue. On August 26, 1920, the Nineteenth Amendment was added to the Constitution of the United States. The victory was Bryan's to savor, and in the pages of the *Commoner* he did. But Woodrow Wilson, who had been opposed to woman suffrage, at least through a constitutional amendment, claimed credit and heralded its adoption.[23]

NOTES

1. William Jennings Bryan and Mary Baird Bryan, *The Memoirs of William Jennings Bryan* (Chicago: The John C. Winston Company, 1925), p. 420.

2. Quoted in Lawrence W. Levine, *Defender of the Faith: William Jennings Bryan: The Last Decade* (New York: Oxford University Press, 1965), p. 15.

3. Quoted in Louis W. Koenig, *Bryan: A Political Biography of William Jennings Bryan* (New York: G.P. Putnam's Sons, 1971), p. 554.

4. Quoted in Levine, *Defender of the Faith*, pp. 22–23.

5. Quoted in Paolo E. Coletta, *William Jennings Bryan*, vol. 3, *Political Puritan, 1915–1925* (Lincoln: University of Nebraska Press, 1969), p. 34.

6. Quoted in Koenig, *Bryan*, p. 73.

7. Quoted in Coletta, *William Jennings Bryan*, vol. 3, p. 39.

8. Quoted in Koenig, p. 564.

9. Quoted in ibid., p. 567.

10. Ibid., p. 568.

11. Quoted in ibid., p. 569.

12. Quoted in ibid.

13. Quoted in ibid., p. 570.

14. Paxton Hibben, *The Peerless Leader: William Jennings Bryan* (New York: Farrar and Rinehart, 1929), p. 350. At Hibben's death the biography was completed by C. Hartley Grattan.

15. Quoted in Robert W. Cherny, *A Righteous Cause: The Life of William Jennings Bryan* (Boston: Little, Brown and Company, 1985), p. 161.

16. Herbert Asbury, *The Great Illusion: An Informal History of Prohibition* (Garden City, NY: Doubleday, Doran and Company, Inc. 1950), p. 1.

17. Quoted in Cherny, *A Righteous Cause*, p. 121.

18. Ibid., p. 122.

19. Bryan, *The Memoirs of William Jennings Bryan*, p. 295.

20. Quoted in Mark Sullivan, *Our Times: The United States, 1900–1925*, vol. 6, *The Twenties* (New York: Charles Scribner's Sons, 1935), p. 528.

21. Quoted in Koenig, p. 559.

22. Quoted in ibid.

23. Quoted in ibid., p. 582.

7

THE WANING YEARS

My heart is in the grave with our cause. It must pause until it comes back to me.

William Jennings Bryan at the conclusion of the
1920 Democratic National Convention

The times must have seemed out of joint to William Jennings Bryan, what with jazz and the blues in music, the Charleston in dance, the short and growing shorter skirt of the flapper. The automobile—and Bryan would soon own one—could take families for a Sunday drive in the country or to church, but to Bryan's dismay, they increasingly chose the former. With a host of new labor-saving machinery that made life easier for the American housewife in the postwar era, there was more time to listen to the radio. Sometimes Bryan did not like what they chose to hear.

While he had been reluctant to use radio at first or to use amplifiers at the conventions, in 1922 Bryan made his first radio address to sixty thousand people. He now hailed radio as "the gift of Providence" to the Democratic Party. Decades later when the head of RCA Laboratory in Hollywood heard recordings of Bryan's lectures, he exclaimed, "Look at that meter! Look at that voice! Why, it has absolutely no bass tones. We have recorded thousands of voices, but never a voice like this."[1]

Bryan was now a rather wealthy man. He commanded high fees for his lectures and was much sought after as a paid lobbyist, especially by those seeking to do business in Latin America, where as secretary of state he had been deeply involved in negotiations. He promoted sales in Florida lands, which were then reaching a speculative frenzy. Mostly, however, he was a religious evangelist, bringing a literal interpretation of biblical truth to the multitudes, who in turn brought financial rewards to their idol.

In the spring of 1921, Bryan announced that he would give up his home in Lincoln, Nebraska, and take up residence in Miami, Florida, a city whose climate appeared more suitable for his wife's health. The announcement immediately provoked suggestions that he make a race for the Senate from Florida. While the idea intrigued him, the appeal was short-lived, as it became clear that to win in Florida would not be easy and he did not wish to end a political career in still another defeat.

But in Nebraska, the Bryan name still cast a kind of political magic and was used to get Charles Bryan, William's brother, elected governor. Charles had spent much of his career in his brother's shadow, working in his brother's political campaigns, planning political rallies, and tending to the office chores of the *Commoner*. Now, as governor, Charles felt he could not do what was required of him to keep the *Commoner* afloat, and the last thing William Jennings Bryan wanted was to assume the nitty-gritty work of getting a political journal published. Thus, the *Commoner*, after twenty-one years, ended publication in April 1923.

To many "the old time religion" failed to satisfy. Organized religion appeared less than organized as when the formerly devout began to question religious fundamentals. Church attendance fell; modernity was squeezing out the faithful as secular studies, such as sociology, anthropology, and psychology, seemed to provide modern, rational, answers to eternal queries. Christian fundamentalists had fallen upon troubled times and found in William Jennings Bryan a constant voice of support. Bryan moved ever closer to the cause of religious fundamentalism and channeled his waning political powers into religious causes. From a moderate on prohibition he became a zealot, and from a moderate stance regarding the teaching of Darwinian evolution in public schools, he took an extreme position against doing so. But the torch that threatened to destroy religious fundamentalism appeared to be the now widespread knowledge about evolution. In the battle between Darwin and Bryan the latter would score but a Pyrrhic victory and would be consumed in the battle.

But although he would fight for God in 1920, he was not yet ready to give up altogether on the political battles that seemed to nourish him. Bryan, the eternal optimist, entered the political jousts once again.

BRYAN AND THE 1920 CONVENTION

The Democrats who gathered on June 28, 1920, in San Francisco to choose a presidential candidate realized that their chances of electing a president were remote if not altogether absent. The political titans were leaving or had already left the stage. Woodrow Wilson was very ill but still dominated the convention through his loyal surrogates. Bryan's vitality seemed undiminished, but while he still had much prestige, he wielded little power. Recognizing that their chances of retaining the White House were dim, the Democratic conventioneers who assembled at San Francisco settled in to have a good time.

Because women were convention delegates for the first time, in their honor the song "Oh You Beautiful Doll" became a popular refrain. Despite prohibition, the convention managers made forty barrels of whisky available, but in protest to the high price, the delegates were not bashful in proclaiming in song "How Dry I Am."[2] "The Sidewalks of New York" made its initial debut too, as Al Smith, the governor of New York and a potential candidate, used it as his political theme song.

Although he had been urged by many to make the race for the presidency once again, by the time of the convention, Bryan had effectively taken himself out of the running. He thought, however, that he still had sufficient political clout to frame the party platform for that year. The Democratic platform that was adopted, however, was Wilson's not Bryan's.

He proposed a plank that would encourage compromise on the League of Nations so that it would pass muster in the United States Senate where a two-thirds vote was needed for its adoption. Bryan lost.

He tried for a platform plank that would endorse prohibition. Bryan lost again.

His proposal against compulsory military training in peacetime was quickly voted down.

As usual, however, Bryan remained optimistic that he could win in the floor debates, where his still powerful voice could reach the rear seats without electronic amplification. Perhaps it was symbolic that for the first time at a national political convention a loudspeaker system was used so that other voices could now be heard in the rafters. Initially Bryan brushed aside the amplifiers; he had little to fear inasmuch as few, if any, speakers were more eloquent than he. But in 1920 eloquence failed him, and his proposals went down to decisive defeat. As historian Lawrence Levine put it, "the delegates voted against his proposals with the same abandon with which they had cheered his oratory."[3]

Divisions within the Democratic Party became evident when it took forty-four ballots to nominate James Cox of Ohio as president and Franklin D. Roosevelt as vice president. Cox, a wet, was a mediocre presidential candidate for whom Bryan cared little, if at all. To a reporter who asked him whether he would support the Democrats he answered evasively, yet with a tinge of sadness, "My heart is in the grave with our cause. It must pause until it comes back to me."[4] By acclamation, Bryan was offered the presidential nomination of the Prohibition Party, but he refused. Instead, he essentially sat out the presidential campaign of that year, other than to make a well-publicized trip from Florida to his home in Lincoln, Nebraska, where he announced that he would remain a loyal Democrat and vote for Cox. The latter lost the election decisively and a Republican-dominated decade began.

This had not been a good convention for William Jennings Bryan. As one journalist wrote, Bryan had been "flattened into a political pancake."[5] William Allen White wrote: "It was evident that his party had left him and he was a rather sad, lonely figure, surrounded by a new generation of Democratic politicians to whom 1896 was but a tale that is told."[6] The journalist/historian Mark Sullivan had this observation to make:

> One thought of Bryan at that 1920 convention as an elderly uncle who comes to visit us, wearing his black alpaca coat and his starched white shirt and his narrow black tie. He read us the Bible every night, he said grace at very meal, he quoted a good deal from Isaiah and the prophets, and he exhorted us to morality and virtue. We were all glad to see him; we listened to him very respectfully; we paid him the greatest deference; we treated him altogether with genuine and unstudied affection; but when he got around to telling us what we should do about our business, we gently, and kindly, but firmly, elbowed him aside.[7]

Health problems intruded into the lives of the Bryans. William's diabetic condition worsened, as did Mary's arthritis. But despite adversity, William Jennings Bryan exuded confidence in his future. For one thing, in March 1924, he bought a new automobile and within a few days, and without instruction, learned to drive it. During the 1923–1924 winter social season, Bryan was unusually active, and when Franklin Delano Roosevelt was carried ashore from his yacht, the *Laroco*, he and Bryan had "a nice talk." Moreover, not only did he assert that he was studying "principles" upon which to base the 1924 platform of the Democratic Party which would meet in New York City, but he put forth feelers that he might be interested in running for United States senator from Florida in 1926. In the meantime, he campaigned in every county so as to be sure to be elected Democrat delegate at large from Florida and pledged to vote for William G. McAdoo, a former treasury secretary in Wilson's cabinet and a 1924 presidential candidate. Although a newcomer to Florida, he won the election by a lopsided vote of 85,462 to barely 40,000 for the next highest candidate.

BRYAN AND THE CONVENTION OF 1924

On June 18, 1924, a few days before the scheduled opening of the convention in Madison Square Garden, William and his brother Charles Bryan went to New York. As a measure of both his still considerable political clout and of his financial affluence, he and his brother checked into a suite at the posh Waldorf-Astoria. No longer the dollar-a-day hotels of yesteryear. As he arrived in Manhattan, Bryan looked like the Floridian he had become. He wore a well-tailored, white Palm Beach suit with matching white shoes and a Panama hat. As if he really needed one, he also wore a name tag by way of identification. But his black string tie was still around his neck and the palm-leaf fan remained in his hand.[8] He made something of a splash when he contributed $7,500 to help reduce the Democratic Party's intractable debt.

Dubbed the "imperial" city by the press, New York went out of its way to make the delegates to the Democratic National Nominating Convention feel welcome. Whatever the outcome of the convention, and irrespective of the bitterness with which contentious issues were debated, New Yorkers made sure their visitors enjoyed themselves. The weather cooperated; the sweltering heat of previous days had vanished, and New York was able to strut its stuff.

As journalist Elmer Davis described the city in the *New York Times*:

What other city could spare for a mere street parade enough fire apparatus to put out a four-alarm fire? What other city could put on such a display of the machinery used in cleaning its streets, machinery novel and unfamiliar not only to visitors but to most of the inhabitants of the city? . . .

What other city could feed 3,500 delegates and alternates in a single restaurant at one sitting even if it does have to put them three deep and at the same time feed all the wives and husbands of delegates and alternates at another restaurant?

What other city could make the display of concentrated wealth that was on display in that single line of silk-hatted, morning-coated gentlemen following Police Commissioner Enright—enough wealth to have paid off the pre-war national debt of the United States?[9]

By noon on June 24 the crowd seemed to overwhelm the convention site. By the time of the official opening there were sixteen hundred delegates and alternates and an unknown number of spectators seeking to get in. Bryan remained serene and reveled in the opening rituals. While not as politically powerful as he once had been and aware, perhaps, that this would be his last convention, Bryan retained an enthusiastic band of followers. The convention meeting in Madison Square Garden was broadcast by radio, and Bryan, although a delegate, was well paid by a newspaper syndicate for providing firsthand accounts of the proceedings.

Bryan was shameless about money. He was the most highly paid speaker on the chautauqua circuit, he was a paid lobbyist, he made money speculating in Florida real estate, and he saw no conflict of interest in serving as a convention delegate while working for pay as a journalist. But his money-making activities never went over very well with other delegates, who viewed him as a reformer on the one hand yet hypocritically accepting high fees while performing official duties. Little wonder, then, that Bryan's oratory began to grate on the ears of his listeners, and among the boos and catcalls were those who taunted, "A thousand dollars a speech," "Who's paying you?" and often, "hypocrite."[10] Bryan's insensitivity to these money questions did not serve him well when the going got rough, as it especially did at the 1924 Democratic National Convention.

On the first day of the convention, keynote speaker Senator Pat Harrison of Mississippi eulogized President Wilson, who had died on February 3, 1924. But this was the high point of Democratic harmony, for the convention went on to prove the often asserted belief that Democrats would rather fight one another than fight Republicans. The Democratic conventioneers and those who observed the proceedings witnessed a "futile, furious, and fanatical convention," whose participants acted "like the inmates of a madhouse . . . and raised human folly to the highest potency."[11]

Bryan worked tirelessly for William McAdoo, but the hostile convention tired of Bryan's eloquence and refused this time to be swayed by his oratory. "Cut it short!" a heckler demanded. Sweaty and tired, Bryan retreated from the platform. Senator Henry Ashurst, who was present at Bryan's humiliation, expressed the thought that "twenty-eight years ago . . . at Chicago, W. J. B. with raven locks and frame of oak, spoke eloquently and won a presidential nomination. Tonight, emotionally sore, barren of hope, no longer handsome, eyes like occult jewels, he seemed to be a crotchety, crabbed, played out man."[12]

In the end, on the 103rd ballot, Democrats nominated John W. Davis as its candidate for president. Bryan could have supported Davis, a dry and an advocate of the League of Nations. He had been a member of the U.S. House of Representatives from West Virginia, solicitor general of the United States, Wilson's ambassador to Great Britain, and a distinguished constitutional lawyer. But in Bryan's eyes he had sinned grievously; he had put his legal talents in the service of the House of Morgan, and so, as a "Wall Street man," he was tainted and could not be supported.

Although he had worked behind the scenes to achieve it, Bryan was surprised when the convention chose Nebraska governor Charles Bryan, William's brother, as its candidate for vice president. "The age of miracles has not passed," Bryan exclaimed. He later wrote, "The convention was remarkable in many ways. Its conclusion beat anything I have ever known. To have a man whose nomination I opposed pick out my brother for his running mate demonstrates that this is a queer world."[13]

THE BIGOTRY OF BRYAN?

Among the more important debates of the 1924 convention was one about the position the Democratic Party ought to take with regard to the Ku Klux Klan. Every member of the eleven-man platform committee, of which Bryan was a member, agreed that the bigotry represented in the Klan should be denounced. But should the Klan itself be mentioned by name? Bryan was of the opinion that the platform should contain a vigorous endorsement of the principles of religious freedom and racial tolerance, but he felt that mention of the Klan by name would give it more prestige, recognition, and publicity than it deserved while alienating those voters who were Klan members. It was his feeling that opposing the Klan by name would only add venom to an already acrimonious Democratic convention.

Late in the evening on the fifth day of the convention, debate began on the KKK. And it was well past midnight when Bryan rose to close the debate. As William Allen White describes the scene: "He [Bryan] stepped upon the platform, a fine, upstanding man, but middle aged; no longer the boy orator, yet aflame with the ardor of his quenchless youth. . . . His agile movements, his almost buoyant step, his clear, soft resonant voice filling the entire hall with its electric power, cast him perfectly as the central figure of the second act."[14]

But this time, Bryan faced a hostile crowd. Boos and catcalls were prominent as he pleaded for unity and denied that it was necessary to call attention to the Klan. He said the Democratic platform was strong enough in its protection of religious diversity and asserted that the Klan "does not deserve the advertisement that you give them." He closed with, "It was Christ upon the Cross who said, 'Father, forgive them for they know not what they do!' My friends, we can exterminate Ku Kluxism better by recognizing their honesty and teaching them that they are wrong." When the final vote was taken, Bryan had scored a very narrow victory. But it was a victory for which Bryan would pay a heavy price.

Rabbi Stephen S. Wise deplored the fact that Bryan equivocated and was silent in the matter of Klan condemnation at the Democratic National Convention. But to Catholics and Jews who urged that the convention condemn the Klan by name, Bryan asserted that the Klan would fade away and that there were graver issues that required attention.

Bryan was convinced that by persuading the convention not to condemn the KKK by name he had helped restore the sorely lacking harmony among Democrats. "The action of the convention cleared the atmosphere. Storm clouds have disappeared and the delegates are again smiling at each other. We meet in a spirit of friendship and harmony to elect our candidates and when we present the nomination we will say it with flowers."[15]

Few, if any, of the Democratic conventioneers shared Bryan's view. His speeches in support of potential candidates were met with hostility and derision. "I saw Bryan at Madison Square Garden in 1924," writes Edgar Lee Masters, "not applauded but hissed, not carried on shoulders, but in danger of being booted; not smiling, young, trim, inspiring and inspired, but hard, set of mouth, dogmatic, shriveled, old and malicious."[16]

Bryan's stand at the 1924 convention on the Ku Klux Klan in many ways reflects his attitude toward other faiths and races. While not a Populist Party member, Bryan was closely connected with that movement and received much support from it. But in a contradictory way, the Populists were tainted with anti-Semitism, although to what degree remains a matter of scholarly debate. There is some evidence that Bryan parted with the Populist anti-Semitic tendencies, however. During the campaign of 1896, for example, he received from the Hebrew Democrats of Chicago, a beautiful badge that prompted Bryan to write a letter of thanks: "Our opponents," he said, "have sometimes tried not make it appear that we were attacking a race when we denounced the financial policy advocated by the Rothschilds. But we are not; we are as much opposed to the financial policy of J. Pierpont Morgan as we are to the financial policy of the Rothschilds. We are not attacking a race; we are attacking greed and avarice, which know neither race nor religion. I do not know of any class of our people who, by reason of their history, can better sympathize with the struggling masses in this campaign than can the Hebrew race."[17] As secretary of state he was supportive of Zionism. In 1916, he expressed enthusiasm for the appointment of Louis Brandeis to the United States Supreme Court and urged Secretary of War Newton D. Baker to appoint Catholic and Jewish Chaplains in the military.

In 1920, when Henry Ford, on the basis of the phony text *Protocols of the Elders of Zion*, charged that the Jews were planning world domination, Bryan fiercely denounced Ford and the *Protocols*. "It is astonishing," he wrote, "that anyone would build upon an anonymous publication an indictment against one of the greatest races in history."[18] He counted among his friends Supreme Court Justice Louis Brandeis, great lawyer Samuel Untermeyer, eminent jurist Nathan Straus, world-famous philanthropist Oscar Straus, fearless preacher Rabbi Stephen Wise, as well as Julius Rosenwald, Ambassador Morgenthau, Otto and Julius Kahn, and Bernard Baruch. Bryan was highly praised by the Young Men's Hebrew Association of Miami, now his home city. In 1920, he made a list of possible presidential candidates he could support that included Jews and Catholics. When asked in 1923 what he thought of Henry Ford as a possible candidate of the presidency, he wrote to one of Ford's sponsors, "I do not like his attacks upon the Jews. It does not indicate the breadth of view that we need in those who are to speak for the entire country."[19] He opposed forcing Jewish businesses to be closed on Sunday, the Christian Sabbath. "Those who worship any other day as a matter of conscience and religion should not be compelled to observe our Sabbath."[20]

In his opposition to the teaching of evolution in American public schools, he stressed that whether one was Jewish, Protestant, or Catholic, belief in God must be protected from atheists and evolutionists. A few days before his death, he wrote he was delighted "to have lived long enough to see an issue upon which all believers in revealed religion—that means all Christians, Protestant and Catholic, and all Jews as well—can unite, for the fight is against the Bible—both the old [*sic*] Testament and the New."[21]

On matters of race Bryan's views were carefully calibrated, and one may summarize by saying that by and large he endorsed the Jim Crow prejudices of his day. He opposed the immigration of Asians, including Chinese, Japanese, and Filipinos, and feared what he freely called the "Yellow Peril" as a menace to the country. His liberalism and progressivism, along with those of other progressives, could not cross the racial barrier. As to African Americans, Willard H. Smith, in a piece for the *Journal of Negro History*, concludes that "the Commoner's views on white-Negro relations constituted one of the weakest points in his armor."[22]

When President Theodore Roosevelt invited the African American leader Booker T. Washington to the White House in 1902, Bryan was aghast and insisted that rather than improve white-black relations it would make them worse. Bryan insisted that in legal rights blacks should have those belonging to other Americans. Yet, he asserted naively, in none of the Southern states, "has an attempt been made to take from the Negro the guarantees enumerated in our constitution and the bill of rights." As to education, African Americans were entitled to all the educational opportunities of other Americans, yet he let himself believe that indeed they possessed them. As to political and voting rights, Bryan supported white supremacy and felt that educational qualifications were "absolutely essential" to Southern welfare. Bryan believed that social equality between the white and black races was impossible and that the two races could probably never live amicably together, "Social equality should be opposed on the ground that amalgamation of the races is not desirable, and is not the solution of the race problem."[23]

Bryan opposed Theodore Roosevelt's appointments of African Americans to selected offices and opposed President Wilson's desire to appoint an African American as ambassador to Haiti. Bryan felt that inasmuch as all European countries had whites serving as ambassadors, the United States would be at a disadvantage should an African American serve in such a post. He feared that in view of the importance of the Panama Canal to the United States and Haiti's strategic geographic position in relation to the Canal, a white person ought to be appointed. African Americans believed that Wilson would more effectively address their problems than other presidents. But Wilson made little effort to do so and was supported in doing little by his secretary of state. Indeed, by the end of Wilson's administration, Washington, D.C., the nation's capitol, became more segregated than ever.

On the subject of lynching, Bryan was more than obtuse—he was blind to the problem. While he deplored lynching, he believed that because of some of the "hideous offences" held by some African Americans, lynching was sometimes justified as the only way to deal with black provocation. Bryan believed that among the provocations that justified lynching was the appointment of blacks to public office and efforts to achieve some social interaction among whites and blacks. When in 1922 an antilynching bill was before Congress, he thought its passage would be a "grave mistake which the North would regret as much as the South."[24]

In view of his positions on race, racial integration, and lynching, it is not surprising that many voters thought Bryan a member of the Ku Klux Klan. There is no evidence that such was the case, but there was nevertheless so much overlapping between his views and those of the Klan that even Klan members believed he was one of them. Thus, when Bryan came to Dayton for the Scopes Trial the KKK burned a huge cross in his honor.

NOTES

1. Quoted in Louis W. Koenig, *Bryan: A Political Biography of William Jennings Bryan* (New York: G.P. Putnam's Sons, 1971), pp. 593–94.

2. Paolo E. Coletta, *William Jennings Bryan*, vol. 3, *Political Puritan, 1915–1925* (Lincoln: University of Nebraska Press, 1969), p. 124.

3. Lawrence W. Levine, *Defender of the Faith: William Jennings Bryan: The Last Decade, 1915–1925* (New York: Oxford University Press, 1965), p. 166.

4. Quoted in Koenig, *Bryan*, p. 590.

5. George Rothwell Brown, "Bryan's Final Plea to Be Spectacular," *Washington Post*, July 1, 1920.

6. William Allen White, *Masks in a Pageant* (New York: The Macmillan Company, 1930), pp. 271–72.

7. Mark Sullivan, *Our Times: The United States, 1900–1925*, vol. 6, *The Twenties* (New York: Charles Scribner's Sons), p. 128.

8. Charles Morrow Wilson, *The Commoner: William Jennings Bryan* (Garden City, NY: Doubleday and Company, 1970), p. 407.

9. Elmer Davis, "New York Becomes Best 'Small Town,'" *New York Times*, June 2, 1924.

10. Quoted in Koenig, pp. 623–24.

11. Quoted in Coletta, *William Jennings Bryan*, vol. 3, p. 181.

12. Quoted in Koenig, p. 624.

13. Quoted in Coletta, p. 192.

14. William Allen White, *Politics: The Citizen's Business* (New York: 1924), p. 79.

15. *New York Times*, July 1, 1924.

16. Edgar Lee Masters, "The Christian Statesman," *American Mercury* 3 (December 1924): 387.

17. Quoted in Willard H. Smith, "William Jennings Bryan and Racism," *Journal of Negro History* 54 (April 1969): 129.

18. Quoted in ibid.

19. Quoted in ibid., pp. 129–30.

20. Quoted in Levine, *Defender of the Faith*, p. 258.

21. Quoted in ibid.

22. Smith, p. 147.

23. Ibid., p. 139.

24. Ibid., p. 142.

8

THE WAR ON SCIENCE

I want the world to know that this man who does not believe
in God is trying to slur the Bible.

Bryan's response to Darrow's
cross-examination in the Scopes trial

When the scientific world was preparing to observe the fiftieth anniversary of the publication of Charles Darwin's *Origin of Species* in 1909, Bryan was inveighing against anything other than a literal interpretation of the Bible. He thereby established a self-induced paradox, namely, pursuing new directions in political leadership while keeping heart and mind planted in biblical rigidities, which, in due course, eroded his influence with most Americans. The majority of people, even if they did not swallow Darwin's evolutionary theory whole, were prepared to accept parts of it or even not think about it at all. "During the first quarter of the twentieth century, scientists in western Europe and the United States accumulated an increasingly persuasive body of evidence supporting a Darwinian view of human origins, and the American people began to notice."[1] Thus was the stage set for the great 1920s debate over the teaching of evolution in the public schools. In the most visible of the battles between evolutionists and religious fundamentalist, the Scopes trial of 1925, Bryan was humiliated as a witness and died shortly thereafter, leaving posterity to sort out for itself Bryan's role in American life.

As one who had fought all his political life against the excesses of capitalism, Bryan was vexed by his understanding of the principles of natural selection and survival of the fittest. In his mind, these ideas gave succor to those who favored laissez-faire economics and rapacious competitive capitalism.

Darwinian principles, as applied to social and economic conditions, dubbed "Social Darwinism," seemed to support those who insisted that the poor deserved their poverty inasmuch as in the process of natural selection they were unable to adapt to changing social and economic conditions. Since Darwinian principles seemed to endorse the concept that it was right for the robber barons to squeeze out the weak and ill prepared, the unintelligent and unadaptable, the improvident and the physically and mentally handicapped, Bryan was appalled by Darwinian philosophy. Moreover, Darwinian concepts, in Bryan's view, likewise encouraged military buildup and imperialist hegemony over less developed peoples.

The late Stephen Jay Gould, in an article written on the occasion of the hundredth anniversary of Bryan's 1896 campaign, asserts that Bryan erred in characterizing evolution as a "doctrine of battle and destruction of the weak, a dogma that undermined any decent morality and deserved banishment from the classroom"[2] Bryan stood at the schoolhouse door and was not about to allow "Darwin's dreadful law of hate [to replace] the Bible's divine law of love as the origin of humanity."[3]

ANTI-EVOLUTION COMES TO THE
SCHOOLS OF TENNESSEE

Shortly after the 1925 session of the Tennessee General Assembly opened, Senator John A. Shelton introduced an anti-evolution bill. The Shelton bill, however, did not find support in the judiciary committee, where it died. In the Tennessee House of Representatives, John Washington Butler, an obscure member of the legislature, introduced legislation prohibiting the teaching of evolution in the public schools of Tennessee. Butler, a member of the Primitive Baptist Church, had been elected on the basis of his opposition to teaching evolution and in favor of a literal interpretation of the Bible. He was determined that Tennessee would join those other states, approximately seven of them, who were moving in the direction of banning the teaching of evolution. The Butler bill made it unlawful for any public school teacher "to teach any theory that denies the story of the divine creation of man as taught in the Bible, and to teach instead that man has descended from a lower order of animals." His bill was warmly received in the House and eventually was supported by Senator Shelton as well.

Bryan was not in complete accord with the views expressed in the proposed Butler legislation and did not participate in any way in shaping the bill as it made its way, with little opposition, through the Tennessee legisla-

ture. While Bryan opposed teaching evolution in the public schools, he opposed also the inclusion in the bill of a penalty for doing so. As he explained
in a letter to Shelton, "The special thing that I want to suggest is that it is
better not to have a penalty. I suggest this for two reasons; in the first place
our opponents . . . are always trying to find something that will divert attention and the penalty furnishes an excuse. . . . The second reason is that
we are dealing with an educated class that is supposed to respect the law."[4]

In opposing a legislatively imposed penalty, Bryan indicated that he
would have been content if the teaching of evolution in tax-supported
schools was condemned but that those who presumed to confront the law
and the policy of the school system would be shunned rather than penal-
ized. To his credit Bryan sought to refrain from zealotry and intolerance,
but during the course of the trial he seemed not strong enough to remain
faithful to this position.

In the Tennessee House of Representatives, the anti-evolution measure was adopted overwhelmingly by a vote of seventy-one to five, and in
the state senate by a vote of twenty-four to six. Austin Peay, the governor,
reluctantly signed the bill. He did so not out of religious zealotry or a conviction that the law was a good one, but because he could not find any formal protests from Tennessee's leading citizens or from the academic community at the University of Tennessee; moreover, the Tennessee State
Department of Education seemed to acquiesce in the measure largely by its
silence. Apparently, to oppose the bill was to risk one's political life.

When the governor signed the bill, Bryan exulted, "The Christian
parents of the state owe you a debt of gratitude for saving their children
from the poisonous influence of an unproven hypothesis. . . . The South is
now leading the Nation in the defense of Bible Christianity. Other states
North and South will follow the example of Tennessee."[5]

But not so fast.

In Tennessee the passage of the bill was received with little fanfare.
There was no widespread attempt to review the texts students were then using and no attempt to censor what was in them, and teachers continued to
teach biology, including evolution, from the accustomed texts and students
to study from them in the accustomed manner. "The sole attempt to en-
force the Tennessee 'monkey-bill' was due not to the actions of its friends
but of its foes."[6]

If the passage of the anti-evolution bill evoked little reaction in Tennessee, it was "big time" news in the executive offices of the American
Civil Liberties Union. The ACLU's chief, Roger Baldwin, saw the passage
as a unique opportunity to thwart anti-evolution measures, an issue he had

Figure 8.1.   William Jennings Bryan and Clarence Darrow in the courtroom during the Scopes trial in Dayton, Tennessee, 1925. Library of Congress. RN: LCUSZ62-114986.

been apprehensively watching grow for several years. The ACLU challenge to the Tennessee anti-evolution statute appeared in the *Chattanooga Times*, which had opposed enactment of the restrictive legislation. Baldwin later wrote, "When the governor signed the bill we at once proffered a press release for Tennessee newspapers, offering to defend any teacher prosecuted under it. That was the origin of probably the most widely reported trial on a public issue ever to have taken place in the United States."[7]

The American Civil Liberties Union was determined to challenge the Tennessee measure and stop the anti-evolution momentum. But at first it seemed few would step up to the challenge. While the larger cities, such as Knoxville and Chattanooga, denied they were teaching evolution, entrepreneurial spirits in Dayton saw the potential of a trial that would focus all eyes on their community; attract tourists, academics, and journalists from all over the country; and so bring prosperity to their town. Thus, the town of Dayton rose to the bait. Thirty-one-year-old mining engineer and thorough evolutionist George Rappelyea, once a resident of New York City, took the leadership in marshalling community leaders to take advantage of the ACLU offer. But who would offer himself for trial?

John Thomas Scopes, a twenty-four-year-old teacher in Dayton High School, popular with students, unmarried, "modest, tall, freckled, stoop shouldered," seemed ideal for the assignment. Born in Salem, Illinois, also the birthplace of William Jennings Bryan, Scopes, after a year of study at the University of Illinois, was the science teacher and athletic coach at Dayton High School. "The professor," as he was popularly but inaccurately known around Dayton, earned $150 dollars a month and needed a bit of convincing to serve as the lightning rod to challenge anti-evolutionary zealots.

Sixty-five-year-old William Jennings Bryan, thrice a candidate for the United States presidency, was invited to assist the prosecution of Scopes. Sixty-eight-year-old Clarence Darrow, the "Old Lion," an attorney with a fearsome reputation, and his distinguished associate, Dudley Field Malone, volunteered their services to the ACLU for Scopes's defense. They wrote, "We are willing, without fees or expenses, to help in defense of Professor Scopes."[8] Not one to shy away from publicity, Darrow seized the opportunity to score a victory for evolution. Thus Bryan, a Christian fundamentalist, and Darrow, an atheist, made it certain that there would be legal fireworks. Also on Darrow's legal team was Arthur Garfield Hays, perhaps the lawyer with the best mind. In addition, there was John Randolph Neal, a Tennessee law school dean, an eccentric who wore a long and shabby coat with hair to match.

Bryan was aided by an able but less well-known group of attorneys including Herbert Hicks and his brother Sue Hicks who had, in the first instance, invited Bryan to undertake the case for the prosecution. Chief of the prosecution team was the attorney general for the Eighteenth Judicial District, A. T. Stewart, a fine orator and, in his mid-thirties, energetic and committed. Included on the Bryan team was his son William Jr., now a thirty-six-year-old lawyer, proud to be serving with his father and, like his father, an avowed Christian fundamentalist. Thus, there would be legal pyrotechnics, but would there be enlightenment as well?

THE SCOPES TRIAL: A DUEL UNTO DEATH

Ordinarily the *Royal Palm* train would not stop in the hill towns of Tennessee but would chug along at full speed, making stops only at major destinations. But the one that left Miami, Florida, on July 6, 1925, with William Jennings Bryan on board deposited its famous passenger at 1:30 p.m. at Dayton, Tennessee, a town of but five hundred families. Perhaps never before had such a celebrity made Dayton his destination, and the locals made him feel welcome. Three hundred people cheered him as he left the train, and an automobile procession carried him down the main street. After the formal greetings Bryan, dressed in a pith helmet to protect him from the sun, walked about to get to know the town and its people.

The Bryan that stepped down from the train was not a well man. He was sixty-five years old and looked it, overweight and suffering from diabetes. William Jennings Bryan Jr., at the request of his father, joined the lawyers who would prosecute Scopes. Junior was both inexperienced and, unlike his father, a poor speaker, but he joined the team of prosecutors in recognition of his father's failing health. Many of Bryan's family and friends thought he should not undertake such a demanding assignment. They noted with alarm that he was neither eating well nor sleeping soundly and that he had become forgetful. In addition, he seemed unable to endure the blistering Tennessee heat. Mary Bryan, despite crippling and painful arthritis, insisted on joining her husband and son as they made their foray into Dayton.

If Bryan in 1925 was not at his physical and mental best, the village of Dayton had, likewise, seen better days. Dayton, situated midway between Knoxville and Chattanooga on the Tennessee River, was mainly a post–Civil War city whose roots were in the New South. It had prospered by the extension of the railroads, coal and iron mines, and the building of a blast furnace. For a time, it attracted Scottish immigrants and had flourished enough to become the county seat for Rhea County. There had been a spacious downtown square and a once handsome three-story courthouse with a clock in the tower, but by 1925 it could no longer keep time.

Also by the time of the trial, the blast furnace had closed down, and while a hosiery industry had developed, unemployment and underemployment were chronic. The town's population had dwindled from a peak of about three thousand to fewer than eighteen hundred. Little wonder, then, that town leaders and boosters sought opportunities to restore prosperity as best they could. They recognized that the trial of John Thomas Scopes, with a battery of distinguished lawyers on each side, would be at least a short-term shot in the arm. The town leaders would try to make the most of the "Monkey Trial."

Townspeople spread banners across their main streets. Merchants sold monkey dolls, some of which were stuffed with cotton candy, and watch fobs shaped like monkeys. Dayton would try to make the most of a rare opportunity and perhaps even turn the fortunes of the town around.

Most of the people of Dayton had their roots in farming and were saturated with religion. They could worship at any one of nine evangelical churches. There were Methodists, Baptists, Disciples of Christ, Presbyterians, Seventh Day Adventists, Holy Rollers, and Holy Jumpers. Their fundamentalist ministers "preached medieval dogma with the fervor of the Inquisition, and the little community shielded itself behind the Bible to avoid the contamination of modern ideas and foreign influences."[9] Dayton was a "dry" town and had but two hundred obsequious African Americans, who were not at all troublesome. There were no gamblers. Women did not smoke cigarettes or wear cosmetics or bob their hair. No woman had ever served on a jury or strayed anywhere near politics.[10]

In Tennessee, the "Volunteer State," to volunteer for military service was a fine example of patriotism, which, next to religion, was a dominating value among the men and women of Dayton. Its local hero was Alvin York, an uneducated mountain man who had been cited for his heroism in dismantling a German machine gun battalion almost single-handedly. Cordell Hull, later President Franklin Roosevelt's secretary of state, had been a member of the House of Representatives from the district, only to lose the election because of his support for the League of Nations and the Versailles Treaty. Rhea County, however, had a poll tax, with the result that eligible voters were declining in number. In the 1888 presidential election, 90 percent of adult males had voted. But after the poll tax, 70 percent voted in 1892, 58 percent in 1904, 46 percent in 1920, and only 34 percent in 1928.[11]

Bryan never fully shared the extremist views of religious zealots, and his anti-evolution views had developed slowly. In his popular 1904 chautauqua "Prince of Peace" speech, his most widely known speech next to "Cross of Gold," Bryan declared: "I do not carry the doctrine of evolution as far as some do. I am not yet convinced that man is a lineal descendant of the lower animals. I do not mean to find fault with you if you want to accept the theory. . . . While I do not accept the Darwinian theory I shall not quarrel with you about it."[12] Because more youth were attending high school than ever before, the subjects taught in school, the teachers who taught in them, the textbooks that were used became matters of widespread interest. Evolution and the parallel issue of religion in the classroom became lightning rods for diverse expressions of public views. Bryan's anti-evolution views were largely confined to the issue of teaching evolution in public school classrooms. By 1920, however, he was saying, in an address to the Constitutional Convention in Nebraska: "The greatest menace to the public schools system is its Godlessness. . . . We cannot afford to have the faith of our children undermined."[13]

As Bryan's power in American politics waned, his influence in American religion waxed. As his political influence diminished, his role in American Protestantism grew. While few Americans still looked to him for his political views, many regarded him as a religious prophet who would push back the tidal waves of modernity with which they were uncomfortable and that some found unacceptable. Only Christian love, Bryan insisted, made reform of social ills possible, and to the extent that evolution eroded faith in the power of Christian love, to that extent it must be repudiated. "Bryan joined the anti-evolutionists not in order to retreat from politics but in order to combat a force which he held responsible for sapping American politics of its idealism and progressive spirit."[14]

Bryan brought all his political skills to bear on the anti-evolution movement. According to the distinguished paleontologist Stephen Jay Gould, "Without Bryan there never would have been anti-evolution laws, never a Scopes trial, never a resurgence in our day, never a decade of frustration . . . never a Supreme Court decision to end it all. Every one of Bryan's progressive triumphs would have occurred without him. . . . But the legislative attempt to curb evolution was his baby, and he pursued it with all his legendary demoniac fury."[15] In an evening speech to the Dayton Progressive Club Bryan, in his customary Manichean way, put the issue in the forthcoming trial thus: "The contest between evolution and Christianity is a duel to the death."[16]

On July 8, 1925, Bryan and his entourage drove six miles into the mountains at Walden's Ridge to speak at the rather rustic, down at the heels, Morgan Springs Hotel. From the veranda overlooking the Tennessee Valley, he spoke to two hundred rural people from the neighboring areas, some of whom sat on railings and on steps, but most stood attentive and admiring. An old man in a wheelchair looked adoringly up "with the rapt countenance of one who listens to someone inspired." A tall mountaineer stood next to him and held a glass of water. "As he [Bryan] stood in the darkness, his figure silhouetted by thin ray of light from the hotel door, the occasional flash of lightning and rumble of thunder made the scene seem almost contrived. Bryan spoke softly and predicted the coming of a great religious revival that would begin in the South and sweep across the nation. His final words, vibrating with feeling, were met with a reverential hush. As one reporter put it, Bryan "is more than a great politician, more than a lawyer in a trial, more even than one of our greatest orators, he is a symbol of their simple religious faith."[17] People sought to touch Bryan's clothes, hold his hand, pat his back, and were sure that, like the prophets of old, he would perform miracles. As H. L. Mencken put it, "Bryan is no longer thought of as a mere politician . . . but has become converted into a great sacerdotal figure, half man and half archangel—in brief, a sort of fundamentalist pope."[18]

The trial opened on Friday, July 10, 1925, in the Rhea County Courthouse with Judge John Tate Raulston of Gizzard's Cove, Tennessee, presiding. After jury selection the court adjourned until the following Monday. Chosen for jury service were ten farmers, one fruit grower, and one merchant.[19] One juror was illiterate, the others "hard-shell Baptists and Southern Methodists, farmers of middle age, who have extremely hazy ideas about evolution but very firm beliefs as to the validity of the Bible in all things."[20] Such a jury was clearly stacked against Scopes. But what were the issues with which these men were to grapple?

Mrs. Bryan had developed the tradition of writing weekly letters to her children and other family members, in which she reported items she thought would be interesting or amusing to them. From a house loaned to the Bryan's by the local druggist, as the famous trial was about to open, Mary Bryan wrote to her family from Dayton on July 11, 1925 and observed with a certain distain:

> The mountain people have come down in great numbers to witness the opening of the trial. They are to me a new phase of American life; tall, gaunt, thin, underfed, sad; they are both interesting and pathetic. They do not shave every day and proper costume is a blue shirt, generally worn open at the neck, and a pair of blue overalls, a high-crown felt hat with a wide brim.[21]

Monday, July 13: The trial begins. An unsophisticated audience was intrigued by the setting up of microphones to broadcast the proceedings over radio and loudspeaker systems to let the proceedings be heard in town. Clarence Darrow tried, unsuccessfully, to quash the indictment. The audience, and the jury, were astonished at Darrow's outbursts. Looking at Bryan and pointing a pencil directly at him, he exclaimed: "And who is responsible for this foolish, mischievous, and wicked act who comes from Florida! . . . This is as brazen and bold an attempt to destroy liberty as was ever seen in the Middle Ages." In his closing remarks, Darrow declared:

> If you can take a thing like evolution and make it a crime to teach it in the public schools, tomorrow you can make it a crime to teach it in the private schools, and the next day you can make it a crime to teach it in

the hustings or in the churches. At the next session you can ban it in books and newspapers. Soon you may set Catholic against Protestant and Protestant against Protestant, and try to foist your own religion upon the minds of men.[22]

In Darrow's eyes, Bryan looked anything but the dignified fundamentalist lawyer-preacher who had come to save Dayton, and through Dayton, all of Tennessee, and through Tennessee perhaps the whole world from the blasphemous cadences of Darwin's *Origin of Species* and the theory of evolution. As Darrow described in his autobiography, "at the long table near the judge's bench, sat William Jennings Bryan, wearing as few clothes as possible. So few, indeed, that had he seen some girl so arrayed he would have considered her a bad sort, and straightaway turned his head the other way. His shirt sleeves were rolled up as high they would go, and his soft collar and shirt front were turned away from his neck and breast about as far as any one less modest would venture; not for the fray, but because of the weather. In his hand was the largest palm-leaf fan that could be found, apparently, with which he fought off the heat waves—and flies."[23]

Tuesday, July 14: Darrow, "the infidel," as he was now widely called in Dayton, objected when Judge Raulston announced that the day's proceedings would be opened with a prayer. The judge and spectators were dismayed at this challenge to God. But Judge Raulston overruled Darrow and asserted that inasmuch as he had always sought divine guidance he would do so again in this instance. Bryan held his tongue and a courtroom overwhelmingly supportive of the Great Commoner sat disappointed. Perhaps he held his thunder for a better opportunity?

Wednesday, July 15: Dudley Field Malone and Clarence Darrow began their defense. Malone declared that the state must prove that Scopes's teachings denied the theory of divine creation as posed in the Bible and that he taught instead that man was descended from an order of lower animals. Malone also asserted that he would demonstrate that millions of people find no incompatibility between evolution and the biblical account of the creation.

Thursday, July 16: The day was especially hot and some in the bored crowd looked for more interesting things to do. But there was an important issue to be decided: whether the defense should be allowed to call as witnesses men of science and scholarship who might show that their interpretation of the biblical version of creation was not in conflict with evolution but that the Bible in many ways was in conflict with science. Darrow was prepared to call fifteen such expert witnesses to testify in behalf of the defense. As Darrow began to examine Dr. Maynard M. Metcalf, a zoologist, Attorney General Stewart and former Attorney General McKenzie objected to the introduction of expert witnesses. Bryan, suffering from a cold, in a voice that could scarcely be heard, likewise objected on the grounds that the testimony of expert witnesses is precisely what a jury is called upon to decide. Rumor had it that after lunch Bryan would at long last be heard. The almost uniformly friendly crowd was confident that Bryan would skewer the opposition. There was an explosion of interest, but the courtroom audience would be disappointed.

Holding his huge palm-leaf fan in one hand and in his other a copy of Hunter's *Civic Biology*, from which Scopes taught, Bryan rose but trembled, to the dismay of his wife and son. However, his voice was clear as he reviewed the prosecution's objections. "We do not need any expert to tell us what the law means." Proceeding to ridicule a diagram on page 194 of Hunter's *Civic Biology* that showed a chart classifying all the animal species, including man, Bryan exclaimed, "teaching that man was a mammal and so indistinguishable among the mammals that they leave him there with 3,499 other mammals including elephants!" Gratifying applause and laughter followed from the audience—this is what they came to hear.

Bryan then picked up a copy of Darwin's *Descent of Man*, deplored the use of long words, and complained that Darwin had asserted that man descended from monkeys. "Not even from American monkeys but from Old World monkeys." Bryan urged that the case go forward and denied the need for expert witnesses. His speech was well-received and applause was abundant. But the oratory fell short of the crowd's expectations.

Moreover, Bryan was upstaged by the oratory of Dudley Field Malone, his erstwhile underling when Bryan was secretary of state. In what would later be described as the best speech of the trial, Malone cried out: "Mr. Bryan is not the only one who has spoken for the Bible. . . . There are other people in this room who have given their whole lives to God." And, Malone concluded with a flourish, "The truth always wins. . . . The truth does not need the forces of Government. The truth does not need Mr. Bryan. . . . We feel we stand with progress. . . . We feel we stand with fundamental freedom in America. We are not afraid. Where is the fear?" Perhaps in an echo of Bryan's own "Cross of Gold" speech in 1896, Malone exclaimed, "We defy it!"[24]

Fundamentalists and modernists were moved by Malone's remarks, and the ovation was genuine and prolonged. As H. L. Mencken reported, "these rustics delight in speechifying, and know when it is good. The devil's logic cannot fetch them, but they are not above taking a voluptuous pleasure in his lascivious phrases."[25] Even Bryan congratulated Malone, "Dudley, that was the greatest speech I ever heard."

"Thank you, Mr. Bryan," Malone replied, gathering up his papers, "I am terribly sorry that I was the one who had to do it."[26]

On July 20, 1925, Mary Bryan wrote her children again. If she looked down upon the denizens of Appalachia, she could hardly conceal her dislike of Jews.

> [Hays] is a Jew is as forward and self-assertive as the New York Jew can be. . . .
>
> At the end of the line is the Jew, Hayes, who reeks of East End impertinence.[27]

Friday, July 17: Judge Raulston ruled in favor of the prosecution and denied the defense the opportunity to call expert witnesses. The court adjourned until Monday, but tempers on both sides appeared frayed. Debate continued in the court of public opinion.

With the trial speeding to an early conclusion, Arthur Garfield Hays proposed to Darrow that they could score a coup by calling Bryan to the stand. If they could not call expert witnesses, why not call the Great Commoner himself? Darrow already had a list of fifty questions he had put to Bryan in the form of an open letter to the *Chicago Tribune* and a list of inconsistencies and biblical errors developed by a modernist clergyman. So as to leave as little to chance as possible, Darrow and Hays rehearsed questions and possible answers with Dr. Kirtley F. Mather, a Harvard geologist and expert witness. For two intensive hours the lawyers and the expert practiced. But Mather had a question of his own: "How in blazes do you expect to get Bryan on the witness stand."

"That's our job," came the smiling reply, "and we think we will succeed in doing it. Just leave that part of it to us."[28]

Monday, July 20: There was some feeling that this would be a momentous day, and as the crowds grew, the very floors in the courtroom began to buckle and creak. Judge Raulston wisely took precautionary action and ordered the remainder of the trial held out of doors on the courthouse lawn. As a result, the atmosphere at the trial seemed more comparable to that of a baseball game than a legal proceeding. Lured by the prospects of earning a few pennies, youngsters sold sweets and soda pop to the crowd in "the bleachers." Like popcorn at the movies, the spectators munched and drank as they watched a pitchers duel in the form of a direct confrontation between Darrow and Bryan. In anticipation of verbal pyrotechnics, they settled in for the afternoon.

Judge Raulston had excluded the admissibility of experts in science and religion, but he allowed the scholars to read their testimony into the record without a jury present. The defense, feeling disadvantaged in not having a jury hear what their experts had to say, engaged in bitter and technical recrimination with both the prosecution and the judge.

Although it had been well-rehearsed, it appeared spontaneous when, without warning and in deliberately muffled tones, Arthur Garfield Hays rose to say, "The defense desires to call Mr. Bryan as a witness."

"Judge Raulston's eyes goggled and the Commoner's palm leaf froze in his hand."[29] Over the objections of his colleagues in the prosecution and to the surprise of the judge, Bryan agreed to be cross-examined by the nation's most distinguished cross-examiner. But this was a terrible mistake. Bryan could have refused to testify, but he had not yet scored an oratorical "home run," which he wanted very much to do. He seemed confident that he would do so now.

Bryan sat in a wooden office swivel chair and faced Darrow, dressed in a blue shirt and blue suspenders. Darrow began amicably enough.

Figure 8.2. William Jennings Bryan yawning in the courtroom at the Scopes trial, 1925. Library of Congress. RN: LCUSZ62-119784.

Darrow: "You have given considerable study to the Bible, haven't you, Mr. Bryan?"

Bryan: (politely) "Yes, sir, I have tried to."

Darrow: "Do you claim that everything in the Bible should be literally interpreted?"

Bryan: "I believe everything in the Bible should be accepted as it is given there; some of the Bible is given illustratively. For instance; 'Ye are the salt of the earth.' I would not insist that man was actually salt, or that he had flesh of salt, but it is used in the sense of salt as saving God's people."

Darrow (with his thumbs in his suspenders): "But when you read that Jonah swallowed the whale—or that the whale swallowed Jonah—excuse me please—how do you literally interpret that?"

Bryan: "When I read that a big fish swallowed Jonah—it does not say whale."

Darrow: "Doesn't it? Are you sure?"

Bryan: "That is my recollection of it. A big fish, and I believe it, and I believe in a God who can make a whale and can make a man and make both do what he pleases."

Darrow: "Now, you say, the big fish swallowed Jonah, and he there remained how long—three days—then he spewed him upon the land. You believe that the big fish was made to swallow Jonah?"

Bryan: "I am not prepared to say that; the Bible merely says it was done."

Darrow. "You don't know whether it was the ordinary run of fish, or made for that purpose."

Bryan: "You may guess; you evolutionists guess."

Darrow: "But when we do guess, we have a sense to guess right . . . you are not prepared to say whether that fish was made especially to swallow a man or not? . . . But do you believe He made them—that He made such a fish and that it was big enough to swallow Jonah?"

Bryan: "Yes, sir. Let me add: One miracle is just as easy to believe as another . . . just as easy to believe of Jonah or any other miracle in the Bible."

Darrow (sarcastic): "It is for me."

Bryan (angry): "It is for me."

Darrow (smiling): "Just as hard."

Bryan: "It is hard to believe for you, but easy for me. A miracle is a thing performed beyond what man can do, you get within the realm of miracles, and it is just as easy to believe the miracle of Jonah as any other miracle of the Bible." (applause)

Darrow: "Perfectly easy to believe that Jonah swallowed the whale?"

Bryan: "If the Bible said so; the Bible doesn't make as extreme statements as evolutionists do."

Darrow: "Do you consider the story of Jonah and the whale a miracle?"

Bryan: "I think it is."

The politeness and courtesy with which the lawyerly pair began rapidly wore off. Bryan became edgy, then belligerent, as Darrow bore down on Bryan on various points of the Bible. Did Bryan know when the flood took place? How old the world was? Where did Cain obtain his wife?

Darrow: "Do you think the earth was made in six days?"

Bryan: "Not in six days of twenty-four hours." (Audience is startled.)

Darrow: "Doesn't the Bible say so?"

After further objections by the counsels for the prosecution and rebuttals from the defense:

Darrow: "All right. Does the statement, 'The morning and the evening were the first day,' and 'The morning and the evening were the second day,' mean anything to you?'"

Bryan: "I do not think it necessarily means a twenty-four hour day."

Darrow: "What do you consider it to be?"

Bryan: "I have not attempted to explain it."

Darrow: "Do you think those are literal days?"

Bryan: "I do not think they were twenty-four-hour days. . . . But I think it would be just as easy for the kind of God we believe in to make the earth in six days as in six years or in six million or in six hundred million years. I do not think it is important whether we believe it or not."

Darrow: "Do you think those were literal days?"

Bryan: "My impression is they were periods."

Darrow: "Have you any idea of the length of the periods?

Bryan: "No I don't."

Darrow: "Do you think the sun was made on the fourth day?"

Bryan: "Yes."

Darrow: "And they had evening and morning without sun?"

Bryan: "I am simply saying it was a period."

Darrow: "They had evening and morning for four periods without the sun, do you think?"

Bryan: "I believe in creation as there told, and if I am unable to explain it I will accept it. Then you can explain it to suit yourself."

Darrow: "The creation might have been going on for a very long time?"

Bryan: "It might have continued for millions of years"

Darrow: "Yes. All right. Do you believe the story of the temptation of Eve and the serpent?"

Bryan: "I do."

Darrow: "The Bible says Joshua commanded the sun to stand still for the purpose of lengthening the day, doesn't it? And you believe it?"

Bryan: "I do."

Darrow: "Do you believe that the entire sun went around the earth?"

Bryan: "No, I believe that the earth goes around the sun."

Darrow: "And you believe that is the reason that God made the serpent to go on its belly after he tempted Eve. . . . Do you believe that is why the serpent is compelled to crawl on its belly?"

Bryan: "I believe that."

Darrow: "Have you any idea how the snake went before that time?"

Bryan: "No sir."

Darrow: "Do you know whether he walked on his tail or not?"

Bryan: "No, sir. I have no way to know."

Bryan rose to his feet, his shoulder dropping with exhaustion, the fan shaking violently in his hand, his face heavy with sweat, and in a trembling voice he said to Raulston:

"Your honor, I think I can shorten this testimony. The only purpose Mr. Darrow has is to slur at the Bible. But I will shorten his question. I will answer it all at once, and I have no objection in the world. Facing the crowd, his arms raised above his head, he cried, "I want the world to know that this man who does not believe in God is trying to slur the Bible and is using a court in Tennessee—"

Darrow: "I object to that!"

Bryan (continuing) "To slur it, and while it will require time, I am willing to take it!"

Darrow (yelling and shaking his fist): "I object to your statement. I am examining you on your fool ideas; ideas that no intelligent Christian on earth believes."

As a riot in the court threatened, Judge Raulston adjourned the court. Bryan's ninety-minute ordeal was mercifully over. "He sank into his swivel chair, muttering, "Slurring the Bible . . . slurring the Bible."[30]

Under relentless questioning Darrow had elicited that Bryan believed the Great Flood took place, that the world's languages dated from the tower of Babel, and that Adam and Eve were the first human beings. Bryan admitted that he had read little of other religions or their spiritual leaders such as Buddha, Confucius, or Zoroaster. He had not studied other ancient civilizations, and he was unaware that in the sacred literature of other faiths the myth of a flood had often been incorporated. Thus Darrow demonstrated, as he intended, that Bryan was not a biblical scholar after all.

In her last letter from Dayton, dated July 25, 1925, Mary Bryan stood loyally by her man even though her husband had made a very bad showing under Darrow's cross-examination:

> This is the afternoon when Papa was called as a witness by Darrow and questioned by him in a very abusive manner. Papa stood by his guns very manfully. . . .[31]

Bryan had hoped to put Darrow on the stand the next day, but Judge Raulston would not allow it. When the court reconvened, the judge ordered Bryan's previous testimony deleted from the records and ordered that final arguments be presented. But the defense, by declining to sum up their views, deprived Bryan also of an opportunity to make the final speech of the trial, a speech to which he had devoted hours in preparation.

Since Scopes had admitted that he taught evolution, the jury took only a few minutes to make up its mind that Scopes was guilty as charged. Judge Raulston imposed a fine of one hundred dollars.

It was Darrow, not Bryan, who emerged a hero in the Scopes trial. The largely fundamentalist crowd admired the atheist's lawyerly skills and praised him for them. Bryan, on the other hand, was in the unaccustomed position of standing in second place. He had not convinced the modernists that he was one of them, while he had demonstrated to the die-hard fundamentalists he was not one of them in that he did not really take a literal reading of the Bible.

The trial ended on a celebratory note in that the reporters who had enjoyed the hospitality of Daytonians threw a party for them. "The town came. Darrow danced with the high-school girls and smoked cigarettes with their boyfriends. He waltzed with the wife of Dudley Field Malone while the entire crowd applauded them. Malone pointed to Darrow's purple suspenders and quipped: 'Not only were they the sole support of Mr. Darrow's trousers, but at times they were the principal support of our case.'"[32]

Neither Dayton nor Bryan were enhanced by the trial. The village enjoyed some notoriety for a time but no lasting prosperity. Bryan took the stage one last time, but it was one time too many, and what was left of his reputation as a political and spiritual leader died in Dayton. Scopes was offered his old job back, but he turned it down. He also rejected offers to exploit the trial by writing a book, although he did so years later. Instead, he earned a doctoral degree at the University of Chicago and became a petroleum engineer. Dudley Field Malone returned to New York. While attending a performance of the Ziegfeld Follies, he was summoned to the stage by Will Rogers, where he declared the trial to be a "victorious defeat."

Bryan, optimist that he remained, was determined that the carefully prepared remarks he was unable to deliver as a summation to the jury at Dayton would be heard, and he continued to revise them for publication in the *Chattanooga News*. It is worthwhile to remember that Bryan had prepared his summation well before the trial had begun, so what he proposed to say would be scarcely a summary of the trial but more a call to arms against evolutionists. And it was.

On Saturday, July 25, 1925, Bryan went to Winchester for a speaking engagement. Along the way he rehearsed his jury speech before a large crowd at Jasper and gave his full speech that night at Winchester. He returned to Dayton and in the evening continued to polish the cadences of his remarks. He had counted on the revised version of his intended summation to the jury to restore him in the good graces and leadership of the Christian fundamentalists, who were offended by Bryan's equivocations. But it was not to be. The following day (Sunday), Bryan died, shorn of his political standing, shorn of his prominence in the community of fundamentalists.

Neither Mencken the iconoclast nor Darrow the infidel were gracious in their comments. When the former heard of Bryan's death, he declared, scathingly, "we killed the son-of-a bitch." To those who insisted that Bryan died of a broken heart, Darrow, in a stage whisper was heard to remark, "Broken heart nothing; he died of a busted belly."

In Dayton, the brick courthouse where the trial was held still stands, and many in Dayton continue to be creationists rather than evolutionists. Yet in 2002, after fifty-one years, a federal judge ruled that in Rhea County, weekly Bible classes could no longer be held in its elementary schools. Scopes's conviction was eventually overturned, and the law under which he was indicted was repealed by Tennessee legislators in 1967.

NOTES

1. Edward J. Larson, *Summer for the Gods: The Scopes Trial and America's Continuing Debate Over Science and Religion* (New York: Basic Books, 1997), p. 14.

2. Stephen Jay Gould, "William Bryan's Last Campaign," *Nebraska History* 77 (Fall/Winter 1996): 182.

3. Larson, *The Scopes Trial*, p. 29.

4. William Jennings Bryan and Mary Baird Bryan, *The Memoirs of William Jennings Bryan* (Chicago: The John C. Winston Company, 1925), p. 484.

5. Quoted in Lawrence W. Levine, *Defender of the Faith: William Jennings Bryan: The Last Decade, 1915–1925* (New York: Oxford University Press, 1965), p. 327.

6. Ibid., p. 328.

7. Quoted in Larson, p. 82.

8. Quoted in ibid., p. 101.

9. Andre Siegfried, *America Comes of Age: A French Analysis* (New York: 1927), pp. 58–59.

10. Ray Ginger, *Six Days or Forever? Tennessee v. John Thomas Scopes* (Boston: Beacon Press, 1958), p. 71.

11. Ibid., pp. 72–73.

12. Quoted in Stephen Jay Gould, "William Jennings Bryan's Last Campaign," *Nebraska History.* (Fall/Winter 1996): 178.

13. Quoted in Levine, pp. 263–64.

14. Ibid., p. 270.

15. Gould, "William Jennings Bryan's Last Campaign," p. 177.

16. Quoted in Koenig, p. 639.

17. Quoted in and based on Levine, p. 340, and *New York Times*, July 10, 1925.

18. H. L. Mencken, "The Monkey Trial: A Reporter's Account," in *D-Days at Dayton: Reflections on the Scopes Trial*, ed. Jerry R. Tompkins (Baton Rouge: Louisiana State University Press, 1965), p. 45.

19. *New York Times*, July 10, 1925.

20. Ibid.

21. Quoted in Coletta, pp. 245–46.

22. Quoted in Mencken, "The Monkey Trial," p. 41.

23. Clarence Darrow, *The Story of My Life* (New York: Charles Scribner's Sons, 1932), p. 256.

24. Quoted in Koenig, pp. 645–46.

25. *Baltimore Evening Sun*, July 17, 1925.

26. Ibid.

27. Quoted in Coletta, pp. 255–56.

28. Quoted in Koenig, pp. 647–48.

29. Quoted in ibid., p. 648.

30. Quoted in ibid., p. 650. See also: Leslie H. Allen, ed., *Bryan and Darrow at Dayton: The Record and Documents of the Bible-Evolution Trial* (New York: Russell and Russell, 1925), pp. 133–56.

31. Quoted in Coletta, pp. 270–71.

32. Ginger, Six Days or Forever, p. 181.

9

BRYAN: JOSHUA OF
AMERICAN FUNDAMENTALISM

This is probably the last convention of my party to which I shall be a delegate. (Scattered applause) Don't applaud, I may change my mind.

William Jennings Bryan at the
1924 Democratic National Convention[1]

Although Bryan and Darrow were adversaries in the Scopes trial, Darrow had campaigned and voted for Bryan and had a bemused admiration for him. Yet, if you see Bryan through Darrow's eyes, here's how he looked to him a few days before his death. Darrow wrote:

I see him now as he sat in Dayton in that country courtroom in those blazing July days. Where was the pleasing smile of his youth which had so often lighted his face and his path? The merry twinkle had vanished from his eyes, his head was entirely bald save for two tufts of bristles back of the ears, his thin lips set in a long straight line across his face, his huge jaw pushed forward, stern and cruel and forbidding, immobile and unyielding as an iron vise. His speculations had ripened into unchangeable convictions. He did not think. He knew. His eyes plainly revealed mental disintegration. He had always been inordinately conceited and self confident but he had not been cruel or malignant. But his whole makeup had evidently changed and now he was a wild animal at bay.[2]

French President Charles de Gaulle declared that a statesman who "does not understand the character of his time . . . will fail."[3] Offered the chance to lead the nation as its president, William Jennings Bryan failed because he did not understand the character of his time. Bryan was not a deep, original, or profound thinker, and he could not afford the luxury of political pundits and pollsters common to leading politicos of our own day. Yet how many men of deep thought have we elected to the presidency and how many have been successful?

Franklin Pierce and James Buchanan were failures as president because they did not understand the anachronism of slavery in a democracy, nor did they understand the character of the secession movement. They had little passion for "saving the union," and they failed to take statesmanlike measures to avoid civil war. Herbert Hoover failed as president because he did not understand the nature of the depression over which it was his lot to preside.

Bryan electrified the Democratic Convention of 1896 and in the momentum from his "Cross of Gold" speech snatched the Democratic nomination from the grasp of "Silver Dick" Bland who had a more realistic chance of defeating William McKinley, the Republican nominee. Had Bland won the election of 1896 the early years of the twentieth century would have been under the rule of the Democrats. As it turned out, the Democrats, hypnotized by the "Boy Orator of the Platte," continued to give him their love, loyalty, and votes, but under the spell of this charismatic loser, remained out of power until 1912.

Had he been elected president in 1896, Bryan might have succeeded in persuading Congress to adopt bimetallism as a monetary standard, and there is reason to believe that he might have succeeded and might have reduced the hardship of the depression. Had he been elected president, America might not have provoked an ill-conceived war with Spain nor would it have embarked on a policy of imperialism, and it is highly unlikely that America would have occupied the Philippines. Successful presidents, Franklin D. Roosevelt said, were "moral leaders . . . who used the Presidency as their pulpit."[4] But from the presidential pulpit what moral message would Bryan choose to defend?

In his political prime, perhaps even without intending to do so, Bryan was the harbinger of today's Democratic Party. Anticipating President Franklin D. Roosevelt's New Deal, he recognized that unless the democracy weighed in on the side of the common people, Americans were destined to exploitation by malefactors of great wealth. In urging that government put its finger on the scale in behalf of the underdog, "Bryan, the pioneer, cut down the trees of the political forest, pulled up the stumps, plowed the soil, and planted the seed. . . . Bryan himself lost, but his causes prevailed."[5] Between 1896 and 1924, he was an influential mover and shaker of the national presidential conventions of the Democratic Party.

Not only was he the nation's best orator, but he was also a master politician who helped make Woodrow Wilson president.

Bryan was still somewhat naive about the idiosyncrasies of humankind. As journalist William Allen White asserted, Bryan never did hard, physical labor for any length of time, he never worked with other men in office or factory, and he never acted as a director of a business enterprise. Despite his advocacy of noble causes, he never organized or administered one, no bank bothered to make him its fiscal officer. Mary Bryan acknowledged that her husband was a "poor organizer."[6] And so, embattled though he would be until he died in 1925, Bryan's "knowledge of the actual strength and weakness, quirks and foibles of human nature was a blank page."[7]

Perhaps due to his ethereal nature, Bryan never organized his supporters among the Christian fundamentalists in a voting bloc of sufficient clout to influence local or national elections. While he remained a Democrat, his tendency was to solicit support among third parties such as the Populists, Greenbacks, and Progressives, and so he failed to alter the electoral outcome of the major parties in his favor.

During Bryan's years of scaling the political mountaintop, he chose rural rather than urban values, agrarian rather than industrial bases of power, and southern rather than northern attitudes. In each case he chose wrong. Bryan never could organize Christian fundamentalists into a disciplined voting machine that could win national elections or even a reasonable share of local elections. That political chore latter-day Christian fundamentalists have embraced with glee, even as they keep William Jennings Bryan at arm's length. Perhaps with better organizational skills he could have altered the course of history.

He supported direct election of United States senators, the graduated income tax, votes for women, prohibition of the sale of alcoholic drinks. Yet he came to these positions late and, with the exception of his leadership role for a constitutional amendment on prohibition, was never the leading organizer or the dominant force to make progressive amendments to the United States Constitution possible. According to Stephen Jay Gould, "Everyone of Bryan's progressive triumphs would have occurred without him. He fought mightily and helped powerfully, but women would be voting today and we would be paying income tax if he had never been born."[8]

Bryan preferred public speaking to public campaigning. He measured success by converts he made rather than by votes he won. Edgar Lee Masters, who came to know Bryan well, asserted that "by much talking and little thinking his mentality ran dry."[9] On the speaker's platform he went unchallenged. His audience came from afar to listen, to be enthralled, entertained, and ennobled by what they heard. They did not come to question or to debate. Thus, by the time he was challenged by Clarence Darrow at the Scopes trial, his skills as a debater, sharply honed in his youth, had atrophied and made him an easy target for a cunning trial lawyer.

Perhaps more than any other political figure on the national stage, William Jennings Bryan readily acknowledged that religion was the controlling influence in his life. But as we have seen, under cross-examination by Darrow Bryan revealed that his intellectual grasp of theological concepts was meager. To fellow evangelicals, faith was more important than knowledge, zealotry more important than rationalism, traditional beliefs far more important than modernism, and holding steadfast to a literal interpretation of the Bible more important than metaphorical exegesis of text. When Bryan compromised under withering questioning by Darrow, saying that perhaps the world was not made in a twenty-four-hour day (see p. 153), his followers lost faith in him both politically and religiously. While they came in countless numbers to mourn, he died bereft of the vast public support he had once enjoyed.

It is startling that Bryan could be a traditionalist in religion and a modernist in politics. Bryan held fast to the "old time religion" while holding the view that in alleviating the burdens of the underprivileged, reform could be achieved through the political process. Bryan was heralded by Christians of the Social Gospel movement as the "Joshua of American Fundamentalism."[10] And as a latter-day Joshua, he blew the horn for the conviction that Christians must speak out on social issues, weigh in on the side of the oppressed, and not limit their concern to personal salvation. At his best Bryan demonstrated that old-fashioned fundamentalism and populist democracy could subsist side by side. But Bryan did not go far enough, inasmuch as he failed to blend the two in an overarching theory of social responsibility.

Perhaps one way to explain Bryan's mental compartmentalization between religious orthodoxy and secular modernism was that he was intellectually lazy. He scoffed at higher criticism of the Bible and its attempt to square biblical teachings with emerging scientific developments. For example, Bryan opposed the teaching of evolution not only because it seemed to him to deny the biblical creation of the universe but also because he misunderstood it.

Stephen Jay Gould summarizes Bryan's misconception of evolution as follows:

1. He made the common mistake of confusing the fact of evolution with the Darwinian explanation of its mechanism.

2. He misinterpreted natural selection as a martial theory of survival by battle and destruction of enemies.
3. He erred in arguing that Darwinism implied that there was moral virtuousness in such a struggle to the death.[11]

Bryan failed to understand that science offers no moral guidance. But he believed elements of Darwinism, such as natural selection and survival of the fittest, were being used to justify domestic exploitation of the strong over the weak, the rich over the poor, and the warlike over the peace-loving. Bryan saw in the "survival of the fittest" justification of selfishness by elites and encouragement for the eugenic practice of killing the genetically defective. Thus, in Bryan's mind, Darwin became a political as well as a religious enemy. Among good Christians, if God was love, and Darwinian theory random and callous, then the latter must surely be the Devil.

Moreover, Bryan erred in believing that even science must be subject to majority rule. In his view, majoritarianism and science were on a collision course. Whatever its unlikely merits, if the majority of the people opposed evolution, then it must be wrong. That is, what a majority of the people want must be right and must be achieved for them. But scientific principles are not decided by majority vote. Scientific theory may be right or wrong, popular with the people or unpopular with them. But if a theory is wrong, that must be proved or disproved by scientific means not by popular votes.

The narrowness and often maliciousness of Bryan's thinking may likewise be seen in a speech he gave during the winter of 1923 at the Moody Tabernacle. The subject was evolution and he was speaking to an audience of forty-eight hundred including a hundred members of the clergy who were honored by being seated on the stage. "This audience went into roars of applause when he advocated the starvation of teachers who taught evolution. Separate them from their salaries and they won't be so smart!"[12]

How much autonomy a teacher should have in his or her classroom is an age-old debate in public education, and one that has not yet been resolved. What public school teachers can teach about war, terror, free enterprise, birth control, same-sex marriage, genetic engineering, stem cell research, or evolution are issues that are still with us. In Bryan's day, ever larger numbers of adolescents were attending high school, where discussion of contemporary controversial issues would form an important part of the curriculum. Politicians and their constituencies were increasingly concerned about such issues as what should be taught, who should teach, and what textbooks ought to be used. These were as much issues in Bryan's day as in our own. William Jennings Bryan saw these issues largely through the lens of evolution versus fundamentalist religion and believed that in public schools teachers must teach what the community wants them to teach, "The hand that writes the paycheck," he wrote, "rules the school, and a teacher has no right to teach that which his employers object to."[13]

One of the ironies of American history is that when progressivism and populism were flourishing, race relations between whites, African Americans, Asians, Filipinos, and Native Americans were at their nadir. At the Democratic National Convention of 1924 Bryan failed to denounce the Ku Klux Klan when he had the opportunity to do so.

The KKK in that year was at the zenith of its power. Even as it pretended to fight for such moral virtues as family and prohibition and against gambling, saloons, and prostitution, other Klansmen, in white robes, burned crosses, raged against blacks, scorned Catholics, and threatened Jews. But for those who chose not to see, some with presidential aspirations courted these hateful and hurtful bigots. Instead of denouncing the Ku Klux Klan as decency required, William Jennings Bryan urged that the Convention adopt a resolution in favor of religious liberty but not mention the Klan itself. "Christians, stop fighting," he intoned.[14]

When Bryan died, robed Klansmen held a service at Dayton, Tennessee, during which a large cross was lighted bearing the inscription, "In memory of William Jennings Bryan, the greatest Klansman of our time, this cross is burned; he stood at Armageddon and battled for the Lord."[15] But if Bryan was never a Klan member, he and the Klan were comrades in arms on the matter of white supremacy, racial segregation, and the lynching of African Americans. He could not see how the South would fare without white supremacy, and he could not believe that whites would keep their superior position without resort to occasional lynchings. In an article for the *Commoner*, Bryan wrote: "Too many cry out against the lawless punishment without saying anything about the horrible crime which arouses the anger of the people."[16] When an antilynching bill was before Congress in 1922, Bryan let it be known that he thought such a measure to be a grave mistake. He opposed extending the franchise to African Americans because to do so, he believed, would threaten white supremacy.

As we have seen (see p. 134), Bryan seemed to speak favorably of Catholics and Jews and seemed to oppose the anti-Semitism of Henry Ford's raising, once again, the specter of Jewish malevolence with the forgery known as *The Protocols of the Elders of Zion*. Yet, one cannot help but wonder if his attitude toward the Jews was very dissimilar from that of his wife, Mary, who characterized Arthur Garfield Hays as "an aggressive Jew" from New York (see p. 150).

While Bryan was secretary of state, Leo Frank, a Jew, who managed a pencil factory in Atlanta, Georgia, was indicted for the killing of Mary Phagan, a thirteen-year-old employee. A gang-threatened Atlanta jury came back with a guilty verdict. When the Supreme Court of the United States refused to hear the case, two million people signed petitions and a hundred thousand letters were sent to John Slaton, the progressive governor of the state, urging him to commute Frank's death penalty to life imprisonment. The Populist Tom Watson and Bryan's Populist vice presidential running mate in 1896 weighed in on the side of bigotry by inveighing against "the typical young libertine Jew." The governor of Georgia, however, did commute the sentence from death to imprisonment. Bryan wrote to the governor: "My approval of your action in commuting the sentence of imprisonment is based entirely upon the conviction that government can not afford to violate the sacredness of human life as a punishment for a crime already committed."[17]

Nowhere in this letter is there expressed any concern that Frank might have been unjustly accused and convicted because he was a Jew, and nowhere does one find a parallel letter condemning the mob that broke into the Georgia penitentiary and lynched him. No one in the lynching party was ever apprehended, and the success of the lynching brought about a renaissance for the KKK.[18] In 1913, Jews needed an outspoken advocate because anti-Semitism had become virulent. The Jews organized the Anti-Defamation League to fight in their behalf. Although William Jennings Bryan had spoken in support of individual Jews, when their need was great, as in the Leo Frank case, Bryan was silent.

Were these the actions of a "cowardly lion?"

NOTES

1. William Jennings Bryan and Mary Baird Bryan, *The Memoirs of Williams Jennings Bryan* (Chicago, The John C. Winston Company, 1925), p. 478.

2. Clarence Darrow, *The Story of My Life* (New York: Charles Scribner's Sons, 1932), pp. 276–77.

3. Quoted in Arthur Schlesinger Jr., "The Ultimate Approval Rating," *New York Times Magazine*, December 15, 1996, p. 50.

4. Ibid.

5. Louis W. Koenig, *Bryan: A Political Biography of William Jennings Bryan* (New York: G.P. Putnam's Sons, 1971), p. 11.

6. Quoted in Paolo E. Coletta, *William Jennings Bryan*, vol. 2, *Progressive Politician and Moral Statesman, 1909–1915* (Lincoln: University of Nebraska Press, 1969), p. 4.

7. William Allen White, *Masks in a Pageant* (New York: The Macmillan Company, 1930), p. 244.

8. Stephen Jay Gould, "William Jennings Bryan's Last Campaign," *Nebraska History* 77 (Fall/Winter 1996): 177.

9. Quoted in Robert W. Cherny, *A Righteous Cause: The Life of William Jennings Bryan* (Boston: Little, Brown and Company, 1985), p. 189.

10. See Sydney A. Ahlstrom, *Theology in America: The Major Protestant Voices from Puritanism to New-Orthodoxy* (New York: The Bobbs-Merrill Company, Inc. 1967), p. 74.

11. Gould, "William Jennings Bryan's Last Campaign," p. 179.

12. Edgar Lee Masters, "The Christian Statesman," *American Mercury* 3 (December 1924).

13. Quoted in Gould, p. 180.

14. Ray Ginger, ed., *William Jennings Bryan: Selections*, "Freedom of Religion and the Ku Klux Klan," (New York: The Bobbs-Merrill Company, Inc.), p. 224.

15. Quoted in Willard H. Smith, "William Jennings Bryan and Racism," *Journal of Negro History* 54 (April 1969): 134.

16. Ray Ginger, ed., "The Race Problem," *Commoner* 3 (August 21, 1903): 90.

17. Ginger, *Selections*, "Capital Punishment and the Frank Case," p. 190.

18. See Steve Oney, *And the Dead Shall Rise: The Murder of Mary Phagan and the Lynching of Leo Frank* (New York: Pantheon Books, 2003).

EPILOGUE

BRYAN AS ALLEGORY:
THE WONDERFUL WIZARD OF OZ

The Wonderful Wizard of Oz, written by Lyman Frank Baum, became the best-selling book for children in 1900, and in due course gave birth to plays, musical comedies, and movies. But did Baum write merely a children's book, or was he grappling with something deeper? Some historians have viewed *The Wonderful Wizard of Oz* as an allegory of William Jennings Bryan and his fight for the free and unlimited coinage of silver at a ratio of sixteen to one.[1]

Baum, who was born in 1856 to a wealthy family from Chittenango, New York, married Maude Gage, the daughter of a prominent suffragette, in 1882. In 1887, they moved to the prairie town of Aberdeen, South Dakota, where he edited a local weekly newspaper. While in his early twenties he had written some successful plays, some of which were produced on Broadway, but he was not a success as a newspaper editor, and the paper failed in 1891.

In 1890, Frank Baum and his wife moved to Chicago, where, at the Chicago Press Club, he learned a great deal about the battle for free silver. Baum was not a political activist and almost surely did not intend to write an allegory based on the debate over the free and unlimited coinage of silver. But in the harsh environment of the American prairie, he was inspired to write his hugely popular story for children, which, sixty-four years later, Henry M. Littlefield interpreted as an allegory on populism.[2] Other historians have elaborated and refined the Littlefield thesis.

Baum was moved by Bryan's rhetoric at the 1896 National Democratic Convention, and in the campaign that followed he was active in political rallies in behalf of the youthful Bryan. In particular, he supported Bryan's contention that farmers would be helped out of the depression by a bimetallic monetary standard of sixteen ounces of silver to one of gold. In November 1900 Bryan lost the presidency once again, but Baum, at long last, found a small publisher who agreed to publish *The Wonderful Wizard of Oz.* The fairy tale begins in unremarkable fashion: "Dorothy lived in the midst of the great Kansas prairies, with Uncle Henry, who was a farmer, and Aunt Em, who was the farmer's wife."[3] Like the story's opening line, everything about Dorothy's house is unadorned. Uncle Henry, Aunt Em, and Dorothy, an orphan probably five or six years old, live in a drab one-room house on the grim prairie. Their lifestyle reflects the austere conditions of life in the Midwest, especially under conditions of drought.

But before the tale ends, Baum's story becomes rather complex with allegorical references to the current scene "sufficiently numerous to make looking for them rewarding and informative."[4] A violent cyclone, perhaps a metaphor for the free silver movement, sweeps Dorothy, her dog Toto, and her home to the land of "Oz," whose letters may stand for ounces of gold or silver, where she lands on the Wicked Witch of the East (representing eastern money barons), kills the witch, and inherits the witch's magical silver slippers. Dorothy learns that the answer to the problems of Kansan and western farmers generally may be found in the Emerald City (Washington, D.C.) where she may meet the Wizard of Oz (the president of the United States, perhaps McKinley.)

Dorothy represents the good people of the prairie who are hurt by an unyielding gold standard. As Dorothy makes her way to the Emerald City to meet the Wizard, she follows the "yellow brick road," which stands for the gold standard, but she does so in "silver slippers," which implies a bimetallic standard. The Tin Woodman she encounters on her way is the exploited industrial worker who fears he has lost his humanity, has become heartless, and is rusting in the great depression years that ended in 1897. The Scarecrow Dorothy meets is the frightened farmer who feels he has no brain because he doesn't really understand why he is economically hurting. Dorothy, with the help of her magical silver slippers, returns to Kansas but has to contend with the Wicked Witch of the West, who represents the harsh environment of the prairie. She kills the Wicked Witch of the West with a bucket of water, symbolizing what the West could accomplish if it could overcome chronic drought. Most important, however, is that on her travels she meets the Cowardly Lion, who assures Dorothy, "I learned that if I roared very loudly every living thing was frightened and got out of the way." Bryan could magnetize an audience with his powerful oratorical roar but could not command political power. When in the presidential campaign of 1900 Bryan, America's leading avatar of silver, appeared to abandon the quest for bimetallism in favor of combating imperialism, some Populists believed that caving in on silver was a "cowardly" thing to do. It is difficult to believe that the storm that was created over silver in the 1896 campaign passed over the nation with little impact. By 1900, the Gold Standard Act, passed by Congress and signed by the president, formally committed the United States to a gold standard.

While there are differences among intellectual historians in interpreting *The Wizard of Oz* as an allegory for the debate over bimetallism, there is a general consensus among them that L. Frank Baum did not write "solely to pleasure children of today."[5] The tale works, nevertheless, whether intended or not, "as a Populist allegory."[6] Thus, perhaps it is useful in this reexamination of the life of a prominent American to raise the question, even with tongue in cheek: Was the "Cowardly Lion" none other than William Jennings Bryan?

BRYAN AS PARODY: *INHERIT THE WIND*

While Baum insisted that *The Wonderful Wizard of Oz* was written solely to give pleasure to children, Jerome Lawrence and Robert E. Lee, the authors of the 1955 play *Inherit the Wind*, insist that their play, based on the Scopes trial, "is not history." They continue, "Only a handful of phrases have been taken from the actual transcript of the famous Scopes Trial. . . . It is theatre. It is not 1925. The stage directions set the time as 'Not too long ago.' It might have been yesterday. It could be tomorrow."[7]

Although the playwrights may assert that the play is theater not history, nevertheless, the authors also credit Arthur Garfield Hays, an attorney for Scopes, with sharing the "vividness of the Dayton adventure from his own memory and experience."[8] The play has, likewise, been influential in shaping the image of Bryan as a buffoon, a politico out of touch with reality, one who failed to respond to the political and scientific challenges of an emerging world order, and as a woefully ill-informed fundamentalist Christian who sought to fight the onset of modernism in America.

The play burst upon the American public during the relatively placid 1950s. World War II had ended, and while Senator Joe McCarthy was smoking out alleged Communists and the world was traumatized by a Cold War essentially between the United States and the Soviet Union, *Inherit the Wind* seemed to serve as a warning about American smugness and American dominance.

The title of the play comes from a line in the Book of Proverbs: "He that troubleth his own house/Shall inherit the wind." The play was a warning that behind the complacency of the 1950s there were tensions lying just below the surface, including McCarthyism; racial segregation, especially at school and at church; crime; and poverty, to say nothing of the bare beginning of a feminist "revolution." In 1955, as in 1925, the traditional competed with the innovative, the old way with the modern way. Should women be encouraged to enter the workplace or should they continue to stay home in their time-honored role of nurturing the family as wife and mother?

The play was first shown on Broadway in 1955 and was released as a United Artists movie directed by Stanley Kramer and starring Spencer Tracy and Frederick March in 1960. In 1965, Hallmark Hall of Fame produced a television version of the play, and in 1995 Tony Randall's National Actors Theater staged a revival. The movie is widely available in video rental stores, and on college campuses and among amateur theater groups *Inherit the Wind* is a popularly performed theater classic.

While the play is full of historical inaccuracies, it is from the play and its various incarnations on film, stage, and television that the most widely held perceptions of the views and character of William Jennings Bryan are shaped. If Bryan is indeed Baum's "cowardly lion," is he also H. L. Mencken's "tinpot pope in the coca-cola belt?"[9] Do either of these descriptions do justice to the life of William Jennings Bryan?

Bryan grew to maturity in an age of the McGuffy *Reader* and Horatio Alger's stories of the rise to success of poor boys. He died in an age of Darwin and evolution. During the course of his career in politics and in religion, he allowed himself to be whipsawed between these two disparate worlds—the former, in which he felt comfortable, and the latter, in which he remained an alien. He exemplified Margaret Mead's prescient words that no man will live all his life in the world in which he was born, and no man will die in the world in which he grew in his maturity.

If we look back at his career, it is interesting, but perhaps futile, to conjecture what his place in history might have been had he not taken part in the Scopes trial, had not become a leader of the anti-evolution forces, and had not taken a leadership position in the fight for prohibition. His career was launched in his defeat for the presidency in 1896 and floundered after prosecuting Scopes in the famous trial of 1925. What would have happened to his historical reputation had he died at the zenith of his career in 1896, instead of at its nadir in 1925?

In the 1955 play, the distinguished actor Paul Muni was lured out of a six-year retirement to take the role of Clarence Darrow, and the equally talented Ed Begley took the role of William Jennings Bryan, while Tony Randall played the part of H. L. Mencken. Ed Begley may have come closer to the truth than he realized when in an interview during which he reflected on the roles he had taken, which often had to do with frustrated, unsuccessful, and unfulfilled men, "I guess you might call me the most successful failure in town."[10] Certainly Bryan, likewise, may be viewed as one of many successful politicians who failed.

William Jennings Bryan was honored more in death than in life. He was buried among heroes at Arlington National Cemetery. Admirers named a museum, a library, a park, a college, and a hospital in his honor. The Nebraska State Historical Society administers Fairview, the Bryans' home in Lincoln. In 1934, President Franklin Roosevelt spoke at the dedication of a Bryan statue in the nation's capitol.

In life he was denied tranquility as he stumped the country in political campaigns and paid lectures on the chautauqua circuit in pursuit of peace, economic opportunity, political equality, majority rule, and Christian morality. In death, likewise, tranquility eludes him. Sometimes it appears that he is still stumping the country, still haranguing, still acting as a kind of gadfly or, less kindly, a cranky grandfather who will give our conscience little rest. One biographer describes William Jennings Bryan as "America's Don Quixote," but in tilting at the challenges he faced, the judgment of history is that for the most part he failed.[11] But did he?

Like Marley's ghost in Dickens's *Christmas Carol*, Bryan appears destined to haunt the corridors of American history as he seeks a niche in the national psyche. William Jennings Bryan never stopped talking, and he took to his coffin his posthumous "last message," a speech he was denied the opportunity to give as his summary in the Scopes trial. One still has the feeling that because of the historical limbo to which history has consigned him, this intrepid optimist is asking for one more chance. He would still love to give that speech.

NOTES

1. See Mark Evan Swartz, *Before the Rainbow: L. Frank Baum's The Wonderful Wizard of Oz* (PhD diss., 1996), pp. 29–32.

2. Henry M. Littlefield, "The Wizard of Oz: Parable on Populism," *American Quarterly* 16 (Spring 1964): 47–58.

3. L. Frank Baum, *The New Wizard of Oz* (New York: The Bobbs-Merrill Company, 1903), p. 1.

4. See Hugh Rockoff, "The Wizard of Oz as a Monetary Allegory," *Journal of Political Economy* 98 (1990): 745.

5. Ranjit S. Dighe, "L. Frank Baum's The Wonderful Wizard of Oz, with Annotations," in *The Historian's Wizard of Oz*, ed. Ranjit S. Dighe (Westport, CT: Praeger, 2002), p. 42.

6. Ibid., p. 8.

7. Jerome Lawrence and Robert E. Lee, *Inherit the Wind* (New York: Random House, 1955), p. ix.

8. Ibid.

9. Quoted in Carol Iannone, "The Truth About Inherit the Wind," *First Things* 70 (February 1997): 28–33.

10. Quoted in "Inherit the Wind Makes a Broadway Entrance," http://xroads .virginia.edu/~UG97/inherit/1955home.html.

11. LeRoy Ashby, *William Jennings Bryan: Champion of Democracy* (Boston: Twayne Publishers, 1987), p. 175.

SUGGESTIONS FOR
FURTHER READING

Allen, Leslie. H. *Bryan and Darrow at Dayton: The Record and Documents of the Trial.* New York: Russell and Russell, 1967.

Anderson, David D. *William Jennings Bryan.* Boston: Twayne Publishers, 1981.

Bryan, William Jennings, and Mary Baird Bryan. *The Memoirs of William Jennings Bryan.* Chicago: The John C. Winston Company, 1925.

Buckley, Lawrence, G. *William Jennings Bryan in American Memory.* PhD dissertation, 1998.

Cherny, Robert. *A Righteous Cause: The Life of William Jennings Bryan.* Boston: Little, Brown and Company, 1985.

Clements, Kendrick Allen. *William Jennings Bryan and Democratic Foreign Policy, 1896–1915.* PhD dissertation, 1970.

Coletta, Paolo E. *William Jennings Bryan: Political Evangelist.* 3 Vols. Lincoln: University of Nebraska Press, 1964.

Curti, Merle Eugene. *Bryan and World Peace.* New York: Garland Publishing, Inc., 1971.

Dighe, Ranjit S. *The Historians and the Wizard of Oz.* Westport, CT: Praeger, 2002.

Epp, Kenneth. *The Impact of the Theological Views of William Jennings Bryan upon His Educational Ideas.* PhD dissertation, 1995.

Gardner, Martin, and Russell B. Nye. *The Wizard of Oz and Who He Was.* East Lansing: Michigan State University Press, 1994.

Ginger, Ray. *Six Days or Forever? Tennessee v. John Thomas Scopes.* Boston: Beacon Press, 1958.

Glad, Paul W. *McKinley, Bryan and the People.* Philadelphia and New York: J. B. Lippincott, 1964.

———. *The Trumpet Soundeth: William Jennings Bryan and His Democracy, 1896–1912.* Lincoln: University of Nebraska Press, 1960.

——— (ed.). *William Jennings Bryan: A Profile.* New York: Hill and Wang, 1968.

Hibben, Paxton. *The Peerless Leader: William Jennings Bryan.* New York: Farrar and Rinehardt, 1929.

Kaplan, Edward S. *U.S. Imperialism in Latin America: Bryan's Challenges and Contributions, 1900–1920*. Westport, CT: Greenwood Press, 1998.

Koenig, Louis W. *Bryan: A Political Biography of William Jennings Bryan*. New York: G.P. Putnam's Sons, 1971.

Larson, Edward J. *Summer for the Gods: The Scopes Trial and America's Continuing Debate over Science and Religion*. New York: Basic Books, 1997.

Larson, Julie Marie. *A Narrative Analysis of the Scopes Trial*. PhD dissertation, 1995.

Levine, Lawrence C. *Defender of the Faith. William Jennings Bryan: The Last Decade*. New York: Oxford University Press, 1965.

Scopes, John T., and James Presley. *Center of the Storm: Memoirs of John T. Scopes*. New York: Holt, Rinehart and Winston, 1967.

Swartz, Mark Evan. *Before the Rainbow: L. Frank Baum's The Wonderful Wizard of Oz on Stage and Screen to 1939*. PhD dissertation, 1996.

Tompkins, Jerry R. *D-Days at Dayton: Reflections on the Scopes Trial*. Baton Rouge: Louisiana State University Press, 1965.

Williams, Wayne C. *William Jennings Bryan*. New York: G.P. Putnam's Sons, 1936.

Wilson, Charles Morrow. *The Commoner: William Jennings Bryan*. Garden City, NY: Doubleday and Company, 1970.

INDEX

Addams, Jane, *10*
Alcott, Bronson, 8
Aldrich, Chester, 123
Altgeld, John Peter, 45, 48, 50–51, 54, 56, 66
American Civil Liberties Union, 141–42. *See also* Scopes trial
American Federation of Labor. *See* Gompers, Samuel
Andrews, E. Benjamin, 66
Ashurst, Henry, 132
Atwood, John, 48

Baird, Francis (Fannie), xix
Baird, John, 18
Baird, Mary. *See* Bryan, Mary (nee Baird)
Baldwin, Roger, 141–42. *See also* American Civil Liberties Union
Balfour, Arthur, 84
Baruch, Bernard, 135
Baum, Lyman Frank; *The Wonderful Wizard of Oz* by, xix, 167–69
Beecher, Edward, 8
Beecher, Henry Ward, 8
Begley, Ed, 171. *See also Inherit the Wind*
Bellamy, Edward, 27
Belmont, August, 55, 87

Beveridge, Albert J., 87
bimetallism. *See under* Bryan, William Jennings: political philosophy of; and currency issue
Blackburn, Joseph, 47, 48
Bland, Richard P. ("Silver Dick"), 47–48, 50, 56, 160
Bliss, Tasker H., 120
Boer War, 81
Boies, Horace E., 33, 47–48, 56
Boxer Rebellion, 81
Boyd, James E., 28
Brandeis, Louis, 135
Bryan, Charles, 90, 128, 131; nomination for vice president in 1920, 133
Bryan, Frances, 4
Bryan, John, 3
Bryan, Mariah (nee Jennings), 3–5; and education of William Jennings Bryan, 7
Bryan, Mary Elizabeth (nee Baird): attitudes toward Jews, 150, 164–65; in Dayton, Tennessee. *See* Dayton, Tennessee; health of, xvii, 128, 130, 144; at Jacksonville Female Academy, 17–19; legal career of, 24; life in Lincoln, Nebraska, 22–23, *92*; and Scopes trial. *See* Scopes

trial; and suffrage, 125; and William
Jennings Bryan; children with, birth
of Ruth, 21; birth of William
Jennings Bryan Jr., 24; courtship
with, 17–19; life in Washington,
D.C., 30–31, 110; and *The Memoirs
of William Jennings Bryan*, xix, 11,
13–14, 25, 30; marriage to, 21, 97;
and politics, 39, 65; travels abroad,
84–85, 87–88; and William's
funeral, xvii–xviii

Bryan, Ruth, 21, 87

Bryan, Silas, 3; death of, 6–7, 18;
influence on William Jennings
Bryan's oratory, 7; political career
of, 4–7, 26; religious attitudes of,
5

Bryan, Virginia, 3

Bryan, William Jennings; birth of, 1,
3–4; and Catholics, 94; childhood
of, 4–8; and the *Commoner*
newspaper, 83–85, 93, 102, 104,
117, 125, 128; compared to
Abraham Lincoln, 1–2; "Cross of
Gold" speech by, 7, 51–55, 57–59,
160; in Dayton, Tennessee. *See*
Dayton, Tennessee; death of,
xv–xvii, 156; education of, in
public speaking, 7; during
childhood, 7–8; at Illinois College,
8–12, 15, 17–19; at Union College
of Law, 19–21; failings of, 71,
159–165; and Franklin D.
Roosevelt, 112, 130, 171; funeral
of, xvii–xviii, 171; as Great
Commoner, 12, 61, 68n45; and
Haskell affair, 94–95; health of, xv,
76–77, 110, 115–16, 130, 159; and
Inherit the Wind, 169–71; and Irish-
Americans, 94; and Jews, 94,
134–35, 164–65; and Leo Frank
case, 165; and the Ku Klux Klan,
xvi, xviii, 133–34, 136–37, 164; law

partnership with Adolphus Talbot,
21–23; legacy of, xvii; and Leo
Tolstoy, 84–85; and Mary Elizabeth
Bryan (nee Baird); children with,
birth of Ruth, 21; birth of William
Jennings Bryan Jr., 24; courtship,
17–19; life in Washington, D.C.,
30–31, 110; marriage to, 21, 97;
travels abroad, 84–85, 87–88; urged
to leave politics by, 39. *See also*
Bryan, Mary Elizabeth (nee Baird);
memoirs of, xix, 1, 3, 10–11, 25,
30, 43, 59; life in Lincoln,
Nebraska, 22–23, *92*; name of, 4;
oratorical skills of, 41, 81; in
childhood, 7; in college years, 9–15;
lectures by, 42–43, 127; on the
chautauqua circuit, 14–15, 77, 97,
103–4, 106. *See also* "Cross of
Gold" speech by; physical
appearance of, 17–18, 51, 76–77,
116, 131, 159; political career of;
emergence as a national figure, 33;
in local and state politics
(Nebraska), 23–24; in U.S. House
of Representatives; nomination by
Democratic Party, 24–26; first
campaign in 1890, 28–30; first
term, 30–33; campaign for second
term, 33–34; second term, 35–38;
andidacy for the U.S. Senate,
38–39; presidential ambitions of,
42; and 1896 presidential campaign,
59–65; and the Democratic
National Convention, 46–57; and
The First Battle, 43, 67; reasons for
defeat, 65–67; at the Republican
National Convention, 45. *See also*
"Cross of Gold" speech by; as
Democratic Party leader, 71,
160–61; and 1900 presidential
campaign, 76–82; aftermath of the
election, 83–84; and the

Democratic National Convention, 78–79; reasons for defeat, 82–83; and 1904 presidential campaign; decision not to run, 85; and the Democratic National Convention, 71, 86–87; and 1908 presidential campaign, 89–90; and the Democratic National Convention, 89–92; electoral results, 92–93; reasons for defeat, 93–95; and 1912 presidential campaign, 97–99; as Secretary of State, 99–102, *103*, 104–12; resignation of, 109–12; and U.S.-Latin American relations, 106–7; and 1916 presidential campaign; and the Democratic National Convention, 116–18; and 1920 presidential campaign; and the Democratic National Convention, 127–30; and 1924 presidential campaign; and the Democratic National Convention, 130–34, 159; political philosophy of, 20, 25–26; and anti-imperialism, 74–76, 78–79, 81, 88–89; and currency policy, 33–34, 102; and free silver campaigns, 35–38, 42–43, 59–65, 78; and pacifism, 81, 85, 100, 105–6, 118–19; and Populist movement, 26–28, 33, 36–39, 59–60, 79; and prohibition, 28, 99, 102–3, 116, 120–24; and Seventeenth Amendment (1913), 102; and Sixteenth Amendment (1913), 102; and Spanish-American War, 72–75; and suffrage, 124–25; and Nineteenth Amendment, 125; and World War I, 107–12, 115–16, 118–19; racial attitudes of, 8, 107, 135–36, 164–65; religious attitudes of, xv–xvi, 13, 77–78, 101; during childhood, 6; evangelicalism of, 127–28, 162; opposition to

evolution, 8, 135, 139–41, 145–46, 162–63; in Salem, Illinois. *See* Salem, Illinois; and the Scopes trial. *See* Scopes trial. social attitudes of, 24, 127; wealth of, 127, 131–32; and W. E. B. DuBois, 94; and *The Wonderful Wizard of Oz*, 167–69; and Woodrow Wilson, 98–102, *103*, 117–18, 125

Bryan, William Jennings Jr., 24, 84; on Scope trial prosecution team, 143–44. *See also* Scopes trial

Bryce, James W., 102

Buchanan, James, 160

Burleson, Albert Sidney, 112

Butler, John Washington, 140

Cannon, Joseph, 92

Carnegie, Andrew, 66, 74

Carter, Jimmy, 98

Cather, Willa, 34

Catt, Carrie Chapman, 124

Chautauqua (or chautauqua lectures?), 14–15

Chicago Daily News, xvii

Civil War, 6

Clark, James B. ("Champ"), 98, 99

Clay, Henry, 12

Cleveland, Grover, 23, 33, 35, 38, 41–42, 45, 47, 86, 91

Cockrel, Francis Marion, 86

Cody, William F. ("Buffalo Bill"), 79

Commoner. See under Bryan, William Jennings

Coolidge, Calvin, xvi

Cox, James, 129

Coxey, Jacob S. ("General"), 27, 44

Coxey's Army. *See* Coxey, Jacob S.

Crisp, Charles F., 31

Croker, Richard, 55, 63, 81–82. *See also* Tammany Hall

"Cross of Gold" speech. *See under* Bryan, William Jennings

Dahlman, James C., 123
Daniel, John W., 47, 48
Daniels, Josephus, 55, 66, 86–87, 93, 105, 112
Darrow, Clarence, xvi, 54, *142*, 143, 147–55, 170; opinion of Williams Jennings Bryan, 159. *See also* Scopes trial
Darwin, Charles, 139–140. *See also* Scopes trial
Davis, John W., 132–133
Dawes, Alan, xvi
Dawes, Charles G., 92
Dayton, Tennessee, xv–xvi, 142–45, 155–56. *See also* Scopes trial
Debs, Eugene V., 43–44
Democratic National Conventions (1896, 1900, 1904, 1908, 1912). *See under* Bryan, William Jennings
Dillon, John, 84
Douglas, Stephen A., 5, 12
DuBois, W. E. B., 94
Dulles, Allan, 120
Dulles, John Foster, 120

Edison, Thomas Alva, 116
Emerson, Ralph Waldo, 8, 106

Ford, Henry, 115, 135
Frank, Leo, 165

Garrison, Lindley M., 112
George, Henry, 27
Gompers, Samuel, 91, 93–94
Gould, Stephen Jay, 140, 161, 162–63
Great War, The. *See* World War I
Gresham, Walter Q., 41

Hanna, Marcus (Mark), 45, 61, 67, 81
Harris, William T., 8
Harrison, Pat, 132
Harrity, William F., 48

Haskell, Charles N., 94–95
Hay, John, 72–73
Haymarket bombing (1886), 45
Hays, Arthur Garfield, 143, 150–51, 165, 169
Hearst, William Randolph, 72, 85–86, 94–95
Hicks, Herbert, 143
Hicks, Sue, 143
Hill, David Bennett, 48, 51
Hill, Jim, 62
Hitchcock, Gilbert M., 43
Hoar, George, 81
Holcomb, Silas A., 73
Hoover, Herbert, 160
Horner, Charles F., 14
House, Edward, 100, 108, 120
Houston, David M., 112
Howe, Julia Ward, 124
Hughes, Charles Evans, 117–18
Hull, Cordell, 145
Humphrey, Hubert H., 57

Illinois College. *See under* Bryan, William Jennings
Inherit the Wind, xix, 169–71. *See also* Scopes trial
Irish, John, 58

Jennings, Mariah. *See* Bryan, Mariah (nee Jennings)
Johnson, Andrew, 20
Johnson, Hiram, xvi–xvii
Jones, Hiram K., 8
Jones, James K., 49
Jordan, David Starr, 74

Kahn, Julius, 135
Kahn, Otto, 135
Kellogg, Frank B., xvi
Kern, John W., 90
Kramer, Stanley, 170. *See also Inherit the Wind*

Ku Klux Klan. *See under* Bryan, William Jennings

Lane, Franklin K., 112
Lansing, Robert, 108, 120
Lawrence, Jerome, 169. *See also Inherit the Wind*
Lease, Mary Ellen, 27, 33
Lee, Robert E., 169. *See also Inherit the Wind*
Lewis, Henry T., 56
Lincoln, Abraham, 5, 20, 41, 73; compared to Williams Jennings Bryan, 1–2, 12
Lippmann, Walter, 25
Literary Digest, 51
Lloyd, Henry Demarest, 60
London Times, xvii
Los Angeles Times, xvii
Louisville Courier-Journal, 111

Malone, Dudley Field, 143, 148, 149–50
March, Frederick, 170. *See also Inherit the Wind*
Martin, John, 6
Masters, Edgar Lee, 55, 161
Mather, Kirtley F., 150
Matthews, Claude, 47
McAdoo, William, xvi, 130, 132
McKinley, William, 34; and 1896 presidential campaign, 45, 54, 61–62, 65–67; and 1900 presidential campaign, 78, 81–83; assassination of, 85; and Spanish-American War, 73, 75; as the wizard in *The Wonderful Wizard of Oz*, 168. *See also* Baum, Lyman Frank
Mead, Margaret, 170
Mencken, H. L., 147, 156, 170. *See also* Scopes trial
Merriam, Charles, 24–25
Miller, George L., 23, 28
Monkey trial. *See* Scopes trial

Moore, John Bassett, 105, 108
Morgan, J. P., 108
Morgenthau, Henry, 135
Morton, J. Sterling, 23–24, 33–35, 38
Mullen, Arthur F., 122
Muni, Paul, 170–171. *See also Inherit the Wind*
Murphy, Charles F., 90, 93. *See also* Tammany Hall

Nation, Cary, 122. *See also* prohibition
National American Woman Suffrage Association, 124
Neal, John Randolph, 143
New Republic, xvii
New York Journal, 51
New York Times, 111–12, 131; coverage of 1896 Democratic National Convention, 47, 51–54
Nicholas II (Czar), 84
Norton, S. F., 61

Panic of 1893, 35, 38, 61
Parker, Alton B., 86, 91
Peay, Austin, 141
Phillips, Wendell, 8–9
Pierce, Franklin, 160
Pius X (Pope), 84
populism. *See Populist movement*
Populist movement, 26–27, 35–36, 59–60, 79. *See also under* Bryan, William Jennings
prohibition, 28, 99, 102–3, 120–24. *See also under* Bryan, William Jennings

Randall, Tony, 170–71. *See also Inherit the Wind*
Raulston, John Tate, 147–48, 150–51, 155. *See also* Scopes trial
Redmond, John, 84
Rockefeller, John D., 89
Rogers, Will, 156

Roosevelt, Franklin Delano, 44, 95, 129, 160; and William Jennings Bryan, 112, 130, 171
Roosevelt, Theodore, 72–73, 82, 89, 93–95, 136; and 1904 presidential election, 85–86
Rosenwald, Julius, 135
Russell, William E., 51

Salem, Illinois, 3, 143
San Francisco Chronicle, xvii
Schurz, Carl, 82
Scopes, John T., xv, 143, 155–56. *See also* Scopes trial
Scopes trial, xv–xvi, 139–156, 159; aftermath of, 155–56; Clarence Darrow's cross-examination of William Jennings Bryan, 151–54; Mary Bryan's letters concerning the case, 147, 150, 155; origins of, 140–42; summary of proceedings, 147–51
Sewall, Arthur, 56–57, 60
Shallenberger, Ashton C., 122
Shelton, John A., 140
Sherman Silver Purchase Act (1890), 35–37
Smith, Alfred E., xvii
Smith, Mollie, 4–5
Spanish-American War, 72
Springer, William, 31
Standard Oil Company, 94
Stevenson, Adlai, 47, 79
Stewart, A. T., 143
Storrs, Henry E., 8
Straus, Nathan, 135
Straus, Oscar, 135
Sturtevant, Julian Monson, 9
suffrage. *See under* Bryan, William Jennings

Sulzer, William, 50Taft, William Howard, 89, 92–94, 99, 111

Talbot, Adolphus, 21–23
Tammany Hall, 55, 63, 81–82, 90, 93, 99
Teller, Henry M., 59–61
Tennessee: teaching of evolution in, 140–41. *See also* Dayton, Tennessee and Scopes trial
Tilden, Samuel J., 66
Tillman, Ben ("Pitchfork Ben"), 27, 47, 50–51
Tolstoy, Leo, 84–85
Tracy, Spencer, 170. *See also Inherit the Wind*
Truman, Harry S., 2
Trumbull, Lyman, 20–21, 45

Union College of Law. *See under* Bryan, William Jennings
University of Tennessee, 141
Untermeyer, Samuel, 135

Van Wyck, Charles H., 27–28
Vifquain, Victor, 73
Vilas, William F., 51
Villard, Oswald Garrison, 13

Washington, Booker T., 136
Washington, George, 12
Washington Post, xvii, 64
Watson, Thomas, 27, 61, 165
Weaver, James B., 27, 33
Webster, Daniel
compared to William Jennings Bryan, 12
Wellman, Walter, 87
White, Henry, 120
White, Stephen, 47, 49
Whitney, William C., 47, 55
Wilson, Woodrow, 77, 95, 129, 136; and 1912 presidential election, 97–98; and 1916 presidential election, 116–18; death of, 132;

inauguration of, 101; and William Jennings Bryan, 98–102, *103*, 107, 117–18, 125; and World War I, 107–12, 115–16, 118–20

Wise, Stephen S., 134–35

Women's Christian Temperance Union, 102. *See also* prohibition

and *under* Bryan, William Jennings

The Wonderful Wizard of Oz. See under Baum, L. Frank

World War I, 107–12

York, Alvin, 145

ABOUT THE AUTHOR

Gerald Leinwand, Ph.D., is president emeritus of Western Oregon University and founding dean of the school of education at Bernard Baruch College of the City University of New York. He is the author of many books, including *1927: High Tide of the Twenties* (2001) and *Mackerels in the Moonlight: Four Corrupt American Mayors* (2004). He is currently working on a biography of former vice president Hubert H. Humphrey.